开发性金融机构
问责机制研究报告

GLASS HALF FULL

THE STATE OF ACCOUNTABILITY
IN DEVELOPMENT FINANCE

[美]克里斯汀·吉诺维斯（Kristen Genovese）

[荷兰]玛丽埃塔·凡·惠杰斯特（Mariëtte van Huijstee）

[美]萨拉·辛格（Sarah Singh）

[美]凯特琳·丹尼尔（Caitlin Daniel）

编

陈渝

译

社会科学文献出版社
SOCIAL SCIENCES ACADEMIC PRESS (CHINA)

| 目　录 |

致 谢

　　作者希望向为本报告做出不可估量的贡献的人们致以谢意。首先，我们感谢凯特·福里斯特［Kate Forrester，问责顾问（Accountability Counsel）的实习生］为建立申诉数据库做出的关键性的贡献。感谢塔伊斯·派瓦·路德维格（Taís Paiva Ludwig）和凯特琳·布坎南（Caitlin Buchanan，美国大学华盛顿法学院的学生）在全文引注方面给予的帮助。感谢埃米莉·戈德曼［Emily Goldman，国际包容性发展组织（Inclusive Development International）的实习生］的研究支持。感谢莉迪亚·德·莱妮［Lydia de Leeuw，跨国企业研究中心（SOMO）］在报告草稿审校过程中的帮助。感谢以下在报告写作过程中给予我们宝贵意见和做出贡献的人们：理查德·比斯尔（Richard Bissell，美国国家科学院）、马修·费希尔－戴利［Matthew Fischer-Daly，棉花运动（Cotton Campaign）］、戴维·亨特（David Hunter，美国大学华盛顿法学院）、格哈特·斯古伊尔［Gerhard Schuil，跨国企业研究中心（SOMO）］及丹尼尔·塔扬［Daniel Taillant，人权与环境中心（Centre for Human Rights and Environment）］。作者还要感谢为案例研究接受访问的申诉人和调查受访者，他们与我们分享了自己关于本报告评估的独立问责机制和开发性金融机构在实际运作方面的经历和体验。我们还要感谢各独立问责机制本身为报告草稿提供的建设性意见。

缩略词

ADB	亚洲开发银行
AfDB	非洲开发银行
BIC	银行信息中心
CAO	合规顾问/巡查官办公室
CM	申诉机制
CR	合规审查
CSO	民间组织
CSRC	企业社会责任顾问
DEG	德国投资与开发有限公司
DFI	开发性金融机构
EBRD	欧洲复兴开发银行
EIB	欧洲投资银行
E&S	环境与社会
Exs.	指导原则检查官
FMO	荷兰开发银行
IAM	独立问责机制
ICM	独立申诉机制
IDB	美洲开发银行
IFC	国际金融公司
ILO	国际劳工组织
IP	世界银行监察组
IRM	独立审查机制
ITF	国际运输工人联盟

ITUC	国际工会联盟
JBIC	日本国际协力银行
JICA	日本国际协力机构
MICI	独立咨询与调查机制
MIGA	多边投资担保机构
NAPE	国家职业环保人士协会
NFC	新森林公司
NJGM	非司法申诉机制
OA	问责办公室
OECD	经济发展与合作组织
OPIC	美国海外私人投资公司
PBS	基本服务保护
PCM	项目申诉机制
PS	问题解决
SEZ	经济特区
SPF	特别项目协调员
SME	中小企业
UETCL	乌干达电力传输有限公司
UNDP	联合国开发计划署
UNGP	联合国商业与人权指导原则
WB	世界银行

词汇表

申诉　向独立问责机制正式提交的书面请求，描述由开发性金融机构资助的活动导致的或将要引起的实际或者潜在损害。一些独立问责机制将其称为请求。

申诉人　签名并提出申诉的个人、群体或组织。大多数（但不是全部）独立问责机制要求申诉人为直接受到所诉活动影响的人。一些独立问责机制将申诉人称为请求人。提出人（对申诉人更为笼统的称谓）也在本报告中使用。除了那些直接受到所诉活动影响的人、他们的代表或民间组织，提出人也可以包括公司、独立问责机制或开发性金融机构的领导层。

有结论的案件　有结论的案件是那些已经结案或者尚在监测之中的案件。

开发性金融机构　也称为开发银行或国际金融机构。开发性金融机构对意在促进经济发展的活动进行投资，这些活动可能包括建设水电大坝、铁路项目，或法律和机构改革。

结果　产生了结果的申诉过程，在这一过程中，通过问题的解决，达成了解决方案及（或）独立问责机制公开了合规审查报告。不被认为是"结果"的是那些仅与实施对话的过程有关的程序性协议，或仅与解决临时性问题的小的协议有关的解决方案。解决方案的数据以独立问责机制报告中的信息为基础进行采集。由于研究者没有跟进申诉人以对他们的观点进行判定，所以值得注意的重要一点是，将某案件记录为"达成了解决方案"，并不意味着是对该解决方案的质量或可接受性的判断。

实质性阶段　申诉进程的"实质性"阶段，指的是问题的解决或合规审查。当本报告称申诉已进入了实质性阶段，衡量的是对话过程或完整的合规调查得以启动的频率有多大，而不是它们实际上得以完成的频率有多大。

　　支持组织　对申诉提供协助的民间组织。协助的内容包括进行研究、审查申诉、在独立问责机制处理申诉过程中为申诉人提供建议，及（或）在相关机构中协助提供辩护支持。支持组织通常并不在申诉中列明，或仅仅在其支持能力范围之内得以列入。

　　使用者　这一术语指的是两组人群的组合：（1）直接受开发性金融机构资助的活动影响，并向独立问责机制提出申诉的人（申诉人）；（2）支持他们的民间组织。

摘　要

　　真正的发展尊重人权，其旨在惠泽民众，并受民众的影响。然而，目前开发性金融机构（DFIs）所实践的"发展"，在很多情况下伴随着土地失权、资源丧失、生计掠夺和环境恶化的现象。本报告涉及过去 21 年间向各开发性金融机构所设 11 个独立问责机制（IAMs）提出的 758 例申诉，其中每一例都讲述着社区生活因所谓的"发展项目"而恶化的故事。这一数字恐怕还仅仅是冰山一角，因为大多数受项目影响的人群对这类独立问责机制的存在一无所知。

　　虽然本报告意在确保受发展项目损害的人们得到足够的救济，但 11 家共同撰写本报告的民间组织①的最终目标是：开发性金融机构追求以人权为基础的发展模式。②作者乐于看到更少的人受到伤害，从而对独立问责机制的需求也变得更少。作者还希望看到，将来受影响群体的诉求得到更好的处理。在那一天到来之前，开发性金融机构的问责体系为受现有发展模式所害的人群和社区提供了至关重要的同时也有些简陋的支持。

　　问责体系由两部分组成：独立问责机制和开发性金融机构，二者均有其管理层和董事会。它们都要履行使该系统运转的责任，并为受影响方提供救济。为了对各自的运作情况进行评估，本报告的撰写机构进行了定量

---

①　问责顾问（Accountability Counsel）、两端（Both ENDS）、国际环境法中心（CIEL）、中东欧银行监察网络（CEE Bank Watch）、纽约大学法学院人权与全球正义中心（CHR&GJ）、跨国企业研究中心（SOMO）、制衡组织（Counter Balance）、可持续发展政策基金会（FUNDEPS）、国际包容性发展组织（IDI）、自然正义（Natural Justice）、美国大学华盛顿法学院国际比较环境法项目等 11 家民间组织。

②　For a vision of what real development looks like, see International Accountability Project, *Back to Development: A Call for What Development Could Be* (2015), available at bit. ly/backtodevelopment [hereinafter IAP, Back to Development].

和定性的研究。他们运用其自身的专家经历，分析了独立问责机制和开发性金融机构的程序和实践。更重要的是，他们对申诉人的经历进行了分析。

作者发现，问责体系这杯水是半满还是半空，取决于观察者的视角。对于申诉人来说，问责体系无疑有胜于无，因为除此之外他们常常申诉无门。然而，对于受发展项目影响的人群和社区受到的损害，申诉机制的成果很少能提供足够的救济。他们的诉求可能被认可，他们提出的问题可能在国际层面受到关注，有的时候（虽然频率并不足够高）他们的生活可能也因申诉而改善。那究竟什么阻止了问责体系更好地服务于申诉人的利益呢？独立问责机制能够而且应当进一步改进其实践。比如，它们应当为申诉人提供案件进展状态的定期更新；应当建立程序，以更加有效地防止申诉人遭到报复及在报复发生时做出反应；应当严格遵守其设定的期限限制，对案件信息进行完整的网上公开，承认申诉人与开发性金融机构及其客户之间的权力失衡并采取措施进行应对。

然而，这些问责机制终究只能在设立和管理它们的开发性金融机构掌控的环境下运行。开发性金融机构并不要求客户向受项目影响的群体披露独立问责机制的存在，这从一开始就阻碍了独立问责机制的可及性；它们还对独立问责机制接受申诉的时间进行了限制。对于通过问题解决程序来产生解决方案，它们并没有做出贡献。对于独立问责机制发现的不合规现象，它们并不始终如一地进行回应。在制订行动计划解决违规问题时，它们也很少与申诉人进行足够的磋商。

以上种种不足导致不仅仅是申诉结果受到影响，而且越来越少的申诉能够产生任何结果。在所有 684 例有结论的申诉（结案或者进入监测阶段）中，① 仅半数以下（43%）被认为合格。仅 20% 以下有结论的申诉最终产生了成功协商的处理方案（8%）或公开披露的合规报告（11.5%）。开发性金融机构管理层仅在 7% 有结论的申诉中提出了行动计划。

无论您认为问责体系这杯水是半满还是半空，作者希望在有一点上可以达成共识，即问责机制还能够进一步完善。本报告提出了两部分的建议。第一部分通过寻找出应当被所有独立问责机制和开发性金融机构采用的最

---

① 这指的是那些已经结案或者尚在监测中的案件，占向所有独立问责机制提交案件总数（758）的 90%。

佳实践，来使现有机制趋于完美。不过，作者指出，仅仅采纳最佳实践并不足以确保申诉人已经受到的伤害得到补偿。现有体系的建立是以开发性金融机构将在该体系中承担责任这一假设为前提的。然而，在世界银行于1993年建立史上第一个独立问责机制后的20余年间，开发性金融机构已经充分显露它们要么没有意愿要么没有能力承担责任。

建立一个新的问责体系已经迫在眉睫。这一体系中，问责机制有权力做出有约束力的决定，开发性金融机构不再向各国法院主张司法豁免。只有开发性金融机构就其在全球各处资助的活动对人群和社区造成的损害被真正问责的时候，它们才会对其发展模式进行重新审视。

1 引言

1.1 背景

开发性金融机构，也称开发银行，投资于意在助力经济发展的活动。这些活动可能包括修建水电大坝、铁路项目或者法律和机构改革。尽管这些项目努力减少贫困并创造就业，但经验显示，开发性金融机构投资的项目事实上可能对其力求帮助的人们造成伤害。尽管开发性金融机构制定的政策意在防止对环境和社会的负面影响，但其资助的活动可能导致，事实上也已经导致了各种各样的损害，包括火电站造成的空气和水污染、为矿业和基础设施项目开路带来的强制搬迁、生物多样性的损失，以及其他多种损害。

独立问责机制的建立，促使开发性金融机构及其客户对开发性金融机构的政策负责，并为受开发性金融机构资助的活动影响的个体和社区提供救济渠道。这些独立问责机制在结构、功能和程序上存在差异。1993 年，世界银行监察组作为第一个此类机制得以设立。次年，第一例申诉（见词汇表）提交。① 如今，这样的机制已有十余个。十多年前，这些机制组成了一个网络，② 自此，有了数次对其中一个或多个机制进行有效性评估的

---

① 国际复兴开发银行及国际开发协会，世界银行监察组，国际复兴开发银行 93 – 10 号/国际开发协会 93 – 6 号决议（1993 年 9 月 22 日），见 http://ewebapps. worldbank. org/apps/ip/PanelMandateDocuments/Resolution1993. pdf（创立监察组）。

② While it is unclear which IAMs officially belong to the network, a non-exhaustive list of IAMs can be found here: http://www. iadb. org/en/mici/partners, 8163. html.

努力和尝试。① 2012 年，在联合国可持续发展大会 20 周年纪念大会上，这些独立问责机制发布了一份关于其共同的工作的报告。② 然而，至今仍然没有关于开发性金融机构问责体系功能的系统性比较分析，也没有从使用者（见词汇表）角度对其有效性进行的评估。本报告旨在填补这一空白。

之前的研究大多数仅关注这些机制本身的有效性。然而，独立问责机制仅仅是开发性金融机构问责体系的一半。开发性金融机构董事会和管理层（问责体系的另一半）也必须纳入评估的范围。在现有的任何一家开发性金融机构中，都是董事会对独立问责机制进行授权。通常，董事会会选择独立问责机制的组成人员，为其提供预算，对其功能设限，并最终为开发性金融机构资助的活动的结果负责。开发性金融机构的管理层同样在该体系中扮演至关重要的角色，他们对独立问责机制的调查发现进行回应、与申诉人（见词汇表）进行磋商以制订解决违规问题的行动计划，并将从案件中汲取的经验教训运用到将来的项目中去。只有上述两部分都得以运行并且都运行良好，这一体系才有可能发挥作用。

1.2 目标

本报告所呈现的研究围绕以下问题展开：独立问责机制和对其进行管理的开发性金融机构在何种程度上为申诉人受到的人权损害提供有效的救济？③ 研究从使用者［直接受开发性金融机构资助的活动影响并已经向独立问责机制提起了申诉的人群（申诉人）及支持他们的民间组织］的角度，对 11 个独立问责机制及相应的开发性金融机构的政策和实践进行了

① See Martijn Willem Scheltema, *Assessing the Effectiveness of Remedy Outcomes of Non-Judicial Grievance Mechanisms*, Dovenschmidt Q. 2014, Feb. 12, 2014, at 190–97; Mathieu Vervynckt, *An assessment of transparency and accountability mechanisms at the European Investment Bank and the International Finance Corporation* (Eurodad, Oct. 2015), http://www.eurodad.org/files/pdf/560bbcee7a3d1.pdf; see generally Maartje van Putten, Policing the Banks (2009).

② Kristen Lewis, *Citizen-driven Accountability for Sustainable Development: Giving Affected People a Greater Voice—20 Years On* (June 2012), https://www.opic.gov/sites/default/files/files/citizen-driven-accountability.pdf.

③ 不同的独立问责机制使用不同的术语来表述申诉人及收到的申诉。其他用语还有"请求"和"请求人"。本报告使用"申诉人"和"申诉"作为其他所有类似术语的笼统称谓。

评估。

研究团队使用了多样化的方法向民间组织网络和申诉人收集信息，以获得使用者的体验。报告的作者认为，衡量一个问责体系能否良好地提供救济的一个重要方法，是申诉的个人或社区成员是否相信他们已经得到了足够的救济。换言之，主观的满意是救济效率的重要标准。本研究还通过收集和分析能够公开获取的关于已提交的申诉及其结果的数据，对问责体系的功能运行进行评估。

本研究项目提出的观点旨在改善问责体系（包括开发性金融机构和独立问责机制），从而为申诉人提供足够的救济。尽管我们进行的是具有批判性的评估而且提出的建议目标宏大，但这些评估和建议均产生于建设性的精神理念。所有对本报告做出贡献的组织都努力寻求建立有效而运行良好的问责体系来为受开发活动影响的个体和社区提供救济。我们的愿景是助力于强化这些体系，确保开发性金融机构对受其资助的活动损害的人们负起责任。

1.3 研究方法

本报告试图对向所有独立问责机制提交的申诉的公开数据进行分析。[①] 因此，作为报告基础的研究仅涉及那些公开申诉信息的独立问责机制，而未公开所接收的申诉信息或至今未接收到申诉的独立问责机制不在本报告的研究范围。[②] 本报告对下列 11 个独立问责机制及其对应的开发性金融机构进行评估。

- 非洲开发银行（AfDB）的独立审查机制（IRM）
- 亚洲开发银行（ADB）的问责机制（AM）
- 加拿大采掘业办公室的企业社会责任顾问（Canadian CSR Counsellor）[③]

---

① By doing this, the report builds on Accountability Counsel's report. Accountability Counsel, *Recent Trends in Accountability: Charting the Course of Complaint Offices* (2014).

② 如巴西开发银行监察员、加拿大出口发展署合规官员、日本贸易保险机构检查官、澳大利亚出口金融和保险公司法务总监。

③ 加拿大采掘业办公室的企业社会责任顾问在这个列表中是一个特例，因为它不是一个开发性金融机构，而是一个对加拿大采掘行业具有管辖权的国家机制。报告之所以涵盖它，是因为它加入了本报告重点分析的独立问责机制网络。

- 荷兰开发银行（FMO）和德国投资与开发有限公司（DEG）的独立申诉机制（ICM）
- 欧洲复兴开发银行（EBRD）的项目申诉机制（PCM）
- 欧洲投资银行（EIB）的申诉机制（CM）
- 美洲开发银行（IDB）的独立咨询与调查机制（MICI）
- 国际金融公司（IFC）和多边投资担保机构（MIGA）的合规顾问/巡查官办公室（CAO）
- 日本国际协力机构（JICA）及日本国际协力银行（JBIC）的指导原则检查官
- 美国海外私人投资公司（OPIC）的问责办公室（OA）
- 世界银行（WB）监察组（IP）

本报告是数家民间组织合作的结果，这些组织倡导开发性金融机构负起更大责任并提高其对申诉人的救济水平。这种合作包括分享收集的信息、网上分享结果和分析、撰写报告及同行审议。

数据收集包括以下几个组成部分。

（1）运用对 11 个独立问责机制提起的全部申诉的数据库，对向独立问责机制提起的申诉及达到的阶段进行的定量分析。

（2）运用以《联合国商业与人权指导原则》（UNGP）中的关于非司法申诉机制（NJGMs）有效性标准为基础的评估框架，对独立问责机制和管理它们的开发性金融机构进行的定性过程评估。

（3）以 2014 年 7 月 1 日至 2015 年 6 月 30 日期间已经结案或者达成了结果（问题解决阶段达成的解决方案或者公开的合规审查报告，见词汇表）的申诉为基础，对独立问责机制和管理它们的开发性金融机构进行的定性结果评估。

（4）由各机制和专家进行的审议。

在本报告写作的准备过程中，我们并未考虑使用者无法获取的信息（如独立问责机制或开发性金融机构的内部信息）。我们仅从写作时公开的信息和机制使用者直接提供的信息中获取数据。独立问责机制在报告审阅阶段提供给我们的信息，我们都在报告中明确标明信息来源。对独立问责机制及相应开发性金融机构的定性评估，以《联合国商业与人权指导原则》

中的"原则 31"中描述的有效性标准为基础进行。[①] 该有效性标准适用于所有国家和非国家申诉机制，也适用于裁判性的（如合规审查）和以对话为基础的机制（如问题解决）。尽管该标准的本意是在商业与人权领域使用，但本报告作者认为，这些标准与更广泛的领域相关，并且总的来说与民间组织在《联合国商业与人权指导原则》制定之前就已经使用的标准一致。[②]

《联合国商业与人权指导原则》
（UNGP）原则 31
《非司法申诉机制的有效性标准》

为确保其有效性，国家或非国家非司法申诉机制应具有如下所示特征。

A. 合法性：

以得到其所面对的利益相关者集团的信任，并对申诉过程的公正负责。

B. 可及性*：

得到其所面对的所有利益相关者群体的了解，并向可能面临特殊壁垒者提供足够的援助。

C. 可预测性：

提供清晰和公开的程序，附带每一阶段的指示性时间框架、明确诉讼类型、可能结果以及监测执行情况的手段。

D. 公平性**：

努力确保申诉方有合理的途径获得信息、咨询意见和专门知识，以便在公正、知情和受尊重的条件下参与申诉进程。

E. 透明度：

随时向申诉各方通报进展情况，提供充分信息来反映该机制的表现，以建立对其有效性的信任并符合任何有关的公共利益。

F. 权利兼容：

确保结果和补救与国际公认的人权相一致。

---

① 《工商企业与人权：实施联合国"保护、尊重和补救"框架指导原则》"原则 31"中的有效性标准见下文方框。

② "原则 31"包括第八项标准。不过，该标准只适用于业务层面的申诉机制，因此与开发性金融机构的问责体系无关。

G. 有持续的学习来源：

利用有关措施，找出有助改进该机制的经验教训。

*该指导原则中文版称为"可获得性"。

**该指导原则中文版称为"平等性"。

资料来源：联合国人权事务高级专员办事处，《商业与人权指导原则：贯彻执行联合国"保护、尊重与救济"框架指导原则》，2011，见 http://www.ohchr.org/Documents/Publications/GuidingPrinci-plesBusinessHR EN.pdf。

本报告的定性分析部分整合了申诉人和机制使用者的看法，报告作者也是其中之一。这一定性分析方法的内在特征，决定了本报告展现的机制使用者的经历和看法仅为他们自己的立场，并不代表所有独立问责机制使用者的观点。同样，由于并不是所有的独立问责机制或开发性金融机构都在本研究撰写期间有达成了结果的申诉，且本报告的作者无法与每一位申诉人取得联系，以获知所有有结论的申诉的情况，因此第4章中的案例分析并不旨在比较各个独立问责机制或开发性金融机构为申诉人提供救济的情况。在本报告的附件1中（请见以下链接 www.glass-half-full.org），我们提供了关于研究方法（包括研究局限）的更多细节。

1.4 阅读指南

本报告章节结构如下。

第2章对向独立问责机制提交的申诉进行定量分析。

第3章对照《联合国商业与人权指导原则》中《非司法申诉机制的有效性标准》，对独立问责机制及开发性金融机构的程序方面进行评估。

第4章对上一年度已经结案的案件结果进行评估。

第5章在两个层面对独立问责机制及开发性金融机构提出建议：

（1）将最佳实践融入现有问责体系的改革；（2）对问责体系进行更根本的改变，以提高为受害方提供足够救济的可能性。

另外，如有兴趣了解对每个独立问责机制或开发性金融机构单独进行的评估及本报告所使用的研究方法，可以浏览 www.glass-half-full.org 阅读以下附件。

附件 1：方法论详解

附件 2：以《联合国商业与人权指导原则》中《非司法申诉机制的有效性标准》为基础的评估模板

附件 3：对机制使用者的调查问卷

附件 4：案例分析的访谈问题

附件 5：非洲开发银行的独立审查机制

附件 6：亚洲开发银行的问责机制

附件 7：加拿大采掘业办公室的企业社会责任顾问

附件 8：欧洲复兴开发银行的项目申诉机制

附件 9：欧洲投资银行的申诉机制

附件 10：荷兰开发银行和德国投资与开发有限公司的独立申诉机制

附件 11：美洲开发银行独立咨询与调查机制

附件 12：国际金融公司和多边投资担保机构的合规顾问/巡查官办公室

附件 13：日本国际协力机构及日本国际协力银行的指导原则检查官

附件 14：美国海外私人投资公司问责办公室

附件 15：世界银行监察组

2　独立问责机制功能的事实和数据

2.1　引言与主要发现

本章对所有独立问责机制自其成立起至 2015 年 6 月 30 日接收的所有申诉进行全面的定量分析。下面的 2.2 节将对所使用的方法进行解释说明，附件 1（方法论详解，见 www. glass-half-full. org ）及报告全文脚注中有更多的详细介绍。这里的定量分析的重点是独立问责机制处理申诉的过程，尤其是案件是否在申诉过程的实质性阶段达成结果。"实质性"阶段是问题解决阶段或合规审查阶段（见词汇表）。

主要发现总结如下。

（1）过半数申诉涉及基础设施项目，最普遍提到的诉求与磋商不够充分、信息公开不完全、尽职义务履行不够以及项目的后续环境影响有关。

①在已披露的申诉中，57% 的申诉涉及基础设施项目。（见图 5）

②在对针对的问题内容进行了公开的申诉中，42% 的申诉针对磋商与信息公开，42% 的申诉针对尽职义务，44% 的申诉针对特定的环境问题，如污染和生物多样化方面的问题。（见图 6，值得注意的是一项申诉可能针对若干个问题）

（2）在申诉处理过程的每一个阶段都能发现申诉数量的急剧减少，这意味着许多符合要求的申诉在能够达成结果之前就结案。在 684 件有结论的案件（见词汇表）中，申诉处理进展如下。（见图 11）

①近 43% 的有结论的申诉（结案或处于监测之中）符合要求。

②28% 的申诉进入了实质性阶段。

③仅 20% 以下的申诉产生了结果。这些申诉又分以下几种情况：8% 的

有结论的案件中当事各方成功对处理方案进行了协商谈判，略少于12%的有结论的案件形成了公开披露的合规报告。

④开发性金融机构管理层在7%的有结论的案件中制订了行动计划。

（3）许多符合要求的申诉实际上从未进入问题解决或合规审查阶段。这多是独立问责机制裁决的结果。

①291个符合要求并有结论的案件中，仅66%进入了实质性阶段。[①]

②78个有结论的案件符合进入问题解决阶段的要求（同时符合申诉人的意愿），而其中59%未能进入该阶段，这是因为独立问责机制裁决认为不必要或不恰当。

③符合进入合规处理阶段的有结论的案件中，73.5%未能进入该阶段，原因是独立问责机制裁决认为不必要或不恰当（见图9）。

④291例符合要求并有结论的申诉中，略少于一半（44%）有了结果。[②] 在192例进入实质性阶段的有结论的申诉中，67%达成了结果。

⑤76例被发现违规的案件中，管理层制订了行动计划的占64.5%。

（4）在使用独立问责机制过程中没有民间组织支持的社区和个人提出的申诉无疾而终的概率大于有民间组织参与的案件。民间组织参与案件对案件结果似乎有强有力的正面影响（见图13.1和13.2）。

①总的来说，在没有任何民间组织支持的有结论的案件中，被认定符合要求的占62%，进入实质性阶段的占38.5%，达成结果的仅占19%。与之相反，有国际民间组织参与的有结论的案件中，被认定符合要求的占87%，进入实质性阶段的占70%，达成结果的占63.5%。

②与个人或社区在没有任何民间组织支持的情况下提起的符合要求的申诉相比，如果有一个本国民间组织参与，符合要求的申诉达成结果的概率增加近40%。如果一个国际民间组织参与到符合要求的申诉中（要么单独参与要么与一个本国民间组织共同参与），这一概率提高近175%。

---

① 这里所衡量的只是对话过程或完整的合规调查发起的频率，而不是它们实际完成的频率。

② 任何一个案件，只要通过问题解决达成了解决方案及/或公开披露了合规审查报告，即为产生了"结果"。

2.2 关于方法论的附加说明

以下定量分析以作者编制的数据库为基础进行，该数据库包括独立问责机制自成立起至 2015 年 6 月 30 日公开的所有案件。[①] 案件信息来自这些独立问责机制的网站和年度报告或类似出版物。下面就方法论作几点强调。

第一，本报告并不对所有 758 个案件进行数据分析，而仅对 684 个 "有结论" 的案件进行案例分析。这些案件或者已经结案或者处于监测之中。对分析范围进行这样的限制是为了在简洁性、明确性和完整性之中求得平衡。将案例分析限制在以上案件，避免了将那些尚未有机会进入申诉处理的一定阶段的未结案件纳入研究范围带来的不准确性。另外，将处于监测之中的案件纳入研究范畴，而不是仅限于分析已结案的案件，确保了研究涵盖独立问责机制的最成功案例：那些已经产生了结果而需要接受监测的案件。如果报告对除上述两类案件之外的其他 "子案件" 进行研究，分析案件的总数将在行文或脚注中注明。

第二，分析常常提到进入 "实质性的阶段" 的案件，这指的是问题解决阶段或合规审查阶段。申诉 "达到了实质性的阶段"，指的是对话或完整的合规调查被提上日程，与对话或合规调查是否实际上完成无关。如果申诉被独立问责机制认为已经进入问题解决或合规审查阶段，但进程在对话或完整的调查被提上日程之前就已结束，则这些申诉并不能算作进入了实质性的阶段。比如，申诉处理在合规审查评估阶段终结，则不能视为已经进入了合规审查。

第三，报告的分析中，任何一个案件通过问题解决达成了解决方案和/或合规审查报告得以公开披露则被认为产生了 "结果"。可能的情况下，我们试图在分析中仅对那些就申诉提出的问题达成了实质性合意的解决方案进行报告。报告不包括那些解决方案，它们仅涉及对话过程的、程序性的协议或关于临时性问题的小协议。解决方案的数据是以独立问责机制自身公

---

① 作者于 2015 年 10 月 8 日最后一次查看各个机制的案件登记和公布的年度报告。此日期后，如果关于具体案件有新的信息予以公开披露，我们仅基于机制对案件的反馈将案件额外信息添加到数据库中。

布的信息为基础的。由于研究者并未对申诉人进行跟进从而判定他们的观点和看法，所以要特别指出，本报告将一个案件视为达成了解决方案并不牵涉作者对该解决方案的质量或者可接受性的评价。

2.3　事实与数据

本节展示一系列关于独立问责机制申诉主要特征的描述性数据，如：申诉递交的年份，独立问责机制接收的申诉数量，申诉产生的地区，申诉的现状，谁提起了申诉，申诉涉及的项目类型以及申诉提出了何种问题。

2.3.1　历年申诉状况

自 1994 年第一例申诉递交世界银行监察组（在其成立一年后）的 21 年间，独立问责机制大范围增加，且可见度和案件数量均大幅增加。截至 2015 年 6 月 30 日，各独立问责机制共收到 758 例申诉。

图 1 是每年向独立问责机制提起的案件数量的图形概况。总的来说，向独立问责机制提起的申诉的数量在过去 20 年间有了实质性的增长，仅 2013 年就有 130 例申诉被提起。案件年均增长的高峰出现在 2008 年至 2013 年间，年均案件数从 23 件猛增至 130 件。这一急剧增长的部分原因是那几年大量新的独立问责机制建立，如美洲开发银行（IDB）的独立咨询与调查机制（MICI）及欧洲复兴开发银行的项目申诉机制（PCM）。

图 1 所显示的发展趋势总的来说振奋人心。截至 2013 年，每年申诉案件的稳定增长反映的，不仅是受国际开发项目负面影响的人们寻求救济的途径有数量上的增加，还有现有机制可见度和可及性的增强。虽然申诉数量在 2014 年有所回落，我们并不清楚这种回落反映的是案件数量在不寻常高峰之后回到了平稳状态还是下降趋势的开始。2014 年案件提交的数量为 82 件，接近 2012 年 95 件的水平。2013 年案件数量达至顶峰似乎源于合规顾问/巡查官办公室（CAO）和亚洲开发银行（ADB）的问责机制（AM）的受案数量升至历史最高点。而独立咨询与调查机制（MICI）申诉数量的下降加剧了 2014 年总案件数量的回落，该机制在 2011 年至 2013 年间年均申诉均超过 20 件，而在 2014 年仅 8 个案件。世界银行监察组是唯一一在 2013 年和 2014 年没有经历案件数量下降的机制，每年均接收 8 个申诉。

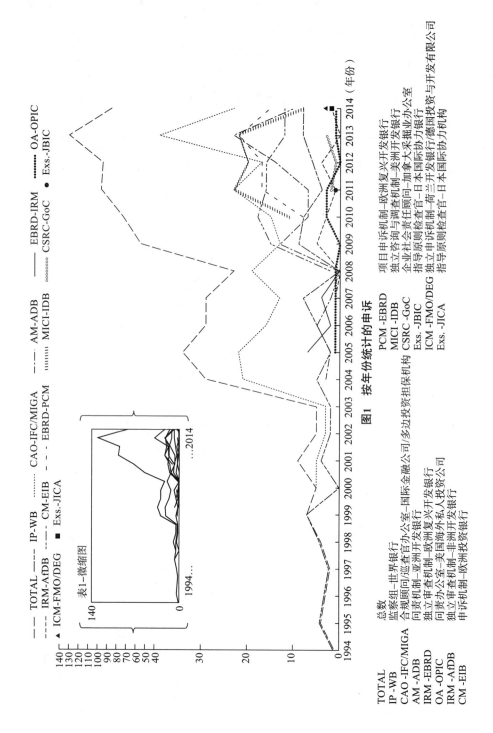

图1 按年份统计的申诉

TOTAL	总数	PCM -EBRD	项目申诉机制-欧洲复兴开发银行
IP-WB	监察组-世界银行	MICI-IDB	独立调查机制-美洲开发银行
CAO -IFC/MIGA	合规顾问/巡查官办公室-国际金融公司/多边投资担保机构	CSRC -GoC	企业社会责任顾问-加拿大禾掘业办公室
AM -ADB	同责机制-亚洲开发银行	Exs. -JBIC	指导原则检查官-日本国际协力银行
IRM -EBRD	独立审查机制-欧洲复兴开发银行	ICM -FMO/DEG	独立申诉机制-荷兰开发银行/德国投资与开发有限公司
OA -OPIC	同责办公室-美国海外私人投资银行	Exs. -JICA	指导原则检查官-日本国际协力机构
IRM -AfDB	独立审查机制-非洲开发银行		
CM -EIB	申诉机制-欧洲投资银行		

　　2015 年的案件数可能显示了独立问责机制作为一个体系整体是否正在面对案件数量下降的趋势。根据 2015 年 10 月 8 日能够公开获取的信息，2015 年 1 月 1 日至 6 月 30 日收案数仅为 35 件。如果下半年收案数同样不多，2015 年全年申诉将降至与 2010 年相近的数量。

2.3.2　申诉在哪里提起？

　　图 2* 显示了各个独立问责机制接收的申诉的分布。迄今为止，合规顾

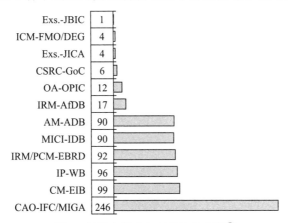

图 2　按独立问责机制统计的申诉①

---

*	Exs. -JBIC	指导原则检查官 – 日本国际协力银行
	ICM-FMO/DEG	独立申诉机制 – 荷兰开发银行/德国投资与开发有限公司
	Exs. -JICA	指导原则检查官 – 日本国际协力机构
	CSRC-GoC	企业社会责任顾问 – 加拿大采掘业办公室
	OA-OPIC	问责办公室 – 美国海外私人投资公司
	IRM-AfDB	独立审查机制 – 非洲开发银行
	AM-ADB	问责机制 – 亚洲开发银行
	MICI-IDB	独立咨询与调查机制 – 美洲开发银行
	IRM/PCM-EBRD	独立审查机制/项目申诉机制 – 欧洲复兴开发银行
	IP-WB	监察组 – 世界银行
	CM-EIB	申诉机制 – 欧洲投资银行
	CAO-IFC/MIGA	合规顾问/巡查官办公室 – 国际金融公司/多边投资担保机构

① 关于欧洲投资银行（EIB）的申诉机制（CM）的说明：尽管欧洲投资银行总共收到了超过 300 个申诉，但多数都没有包含在我们的分析中。欧洲投资银行的申诉机制的权限要比其他独立问责机制的权限大得多。除了项目对社区影响的案件外，它还接受银行客户提出的有关采购和其他问题的案件。考虑到本报告研究的目的，许多案件被排除在外，以使欧洲投资银行的申诉机制与其他机制更具有可比性。因此，只有与社会或环境议题有关的案件，以及作为一个子类的与信息披露相关的案件，才包含在我们的数据集中。而与治理、采购、人力资源、客户与投资者关系有关的申诉都未包含，总的来讲，这些案件与银行项目对当地社区的影响无关。

问/巡查官办公室是最常用到的独立问责机制：自 2000 年接收案件开始，国际金融公司（IFC）和多边投资担保机构（MIGA）的合规顾问/巡查官办公室（CAO）已经处理了 246 个案件，它们接收的案件总数占所有独立问责机制申诉的 32%。

尽管合规顾问/巡查官办公室在接收总数方面占主导地位，其他独立问责机制有时会在某一年处理不相上下数量的案件。某些区域性开发银行的独立问责机制（主要是美洲开发银行的独立咨询与调查机制、亚洲开发银行的问责机制及欧洲复兴开发银行的项目申诉机制）在某些年份的案件数量与合规顾问/巡查官办公室基本持平。比如，2012 年合规顾问/巡查官办公室接收 17 例申诉，独立咨询与调查机制接收 20 例，问责机制接收 14 例，项目申诉机制接收 17 例。在其他年份，向合规顾问/巡查官办公室提起的申诉明显高于其他任何一个独立问责机制的案件量。以 2014 年为例，合规顾问/巡查官办公室接收申诉 23 例，而项目申诉机制接收 15 例，问责机制接收 10 例，独立咨询与调查机制仅接收 8 例。

在对这些数据进行解读时，应当着重说明，那就是独立问责机制信息公开的程度各有不同。有些机制（如独立咨询与调查机制及亚洲开发银行的问责机制）对所有案件进行报告，甚至包括没有予以登记的案件，而其他独立问责机制（如非洲开发银行的独立审查机制和日本国际协力机构的指导原则检查官）仅报告符合其登记标准的案件。

2.3.3　申诉来自哪里？

来自欧洲和中亚的案件数量最多，占地区信息公开的 679 个案件的 28%。拉丁美洲和加勒比地区紧随其后，所占比例仅略低于 28%。仅有一小部分申诉来自中东及北非，低于案件总数的 4%。

2.3.4　提起的申诉处于何种状态？

图 3 按照案件在 2015 年 6 月 30 日所处状态对所有申诉进行了划分。在状态已知的 757 例申诉中，[①] 约 87% 已经结案，仅约 13% 依然处于未结状态

---

① 企业社会责任顾问有一个案件的状态未知。

或者处于监测之中。总的来说，约 17%^* 的案件通过独立问责机制达成了结果。[1] 如果仅考虑有结论的案件，这个数字则升至 19%^*。

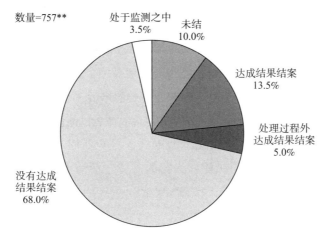

图 3　按状态统计的申诉

** 状态已知的案件的总数。

　　有趣的是，独立问责机制将 5% 的申诉记录为已经"以过程外达成结果的方式结案"。那些案件大多数是向世界银行监察组提起的，而监察组有两个引起争议的做法，鼓励在机制的典型申诉处理过程外达成申诉处理方案：试点计划（Pilot Program）和脚注 7（Footnote 7）。[2] 两个属于这一类别的案件是通过监察组的试点计划来处理的，而其他大多数则通过监察组脚注 7（或其前身）来处理。后者为世界银行管理层提供了机会，在监察组进行正式调查之前对申诉提出的问题进行处理。

　　除监察组以外的独立问责机制中被标以"以过程外达成结果的方式结案"的案件通常是申诉人和项目公司或相关政府部门成功在机制外进行了谈判。

---

* 原文如此。——译者注
[1] 这幅图包括结案案件和仍在监测中的案件，但所有的案件都是有结果的。
[2] 脚注 7 指的是《监察组操作程序》脚注 7 设立的程序。虽然脚注 7 以及试点计划都是规定在《监察组操作程序》中，但是通过这两种程序取得的结果被认为是在监察组的处理过程之外达成的，因为这两种程序搁置了监察组的正常程序，以便为银行管理层提供自行解决问题的机会。关于试点计划和脚注 7 的更多信息请参照第 4.1.2 节。

2.3.5 谁提起了申诉?①

图 4 按照申诉人的类型对申诉人信息已知的 456 例申诉进行分类。由于每个案件都可能会有多种类型的申诉人，图 4 展示了每一种类型的申诉人所提出的案件所占的百分比。

个人是最常见的申诉人，他们在 56% 的案件中单独或者联合提出申诉。民间组织在数量上位居第二，单独或者联合提出的申诉占总数的 48%。非常重要的是，民间组织通常与社区成员一道作为申诉人或者以他们的名义进行申诉。

国际民间组织参与了很大比例的申诉，尽管他们通常对申诉提供支持而不是直接申诉。② 民间组织能够进行的支持性活动比作为申诉人更加非正

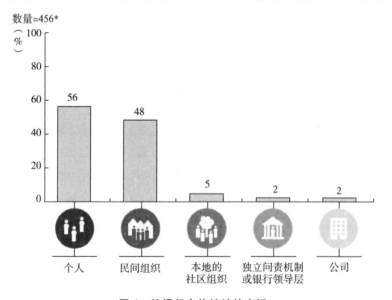

图 4 按提起主体统计的申诉

* 已知文件中记录的案件总数。

① 这部分包含的数据与提起或支持申诉的组织和个人的类型有关。为此目的，申诉提起人是指，正式签署申诉或者作为申诉代表在申诉中得到正式确认的一方。独立问责机制通常也是这样来认定申诉发起人。支持申诉的组织通常不会出现在申诉中，或者只在其支持能力范围内出现。然而，有些支持机构的信息是可以公开获取的，但大部分都无法知。因此，关于支持机构的数据收集主要依赖于民间组织自我报告。这是定量分析中唯一没有全部依赖公开获取的信息的部分。

② 附录 1 "方法论详解"（www.glass-half-full.org）的方法论详细解释了申诉提出人和支持者的区别，以及收集支持机构相关信息的方法。

式，这些活动可能包括：协助进行研究、审阅申诉书、在申诉进行中为申诉人提供意见，或在一些机构中协助申诉人进行辩护。总的来看，国际民间组织以申诉人或者支持机构（见词汇表）的身份参与了 26% 的案件。

独立问责机制自身或者银行领导层成员提出了 2% 的申诉。[①] 几乎所有这样的申诉（十例中的九例）是合规顾问/巡查官办公室的案件。其中，国际金融公司执行副主席提出了 1 例申诉，世界银行集团主席提出了 1 例，合规顾问/巡查官办公室的副主席提出了 7 例。剩下的最后一例申诉是欧洲投资银行的申诉机制的案件，由该银行行长提出。

2.3.6　何种类型项目招致申诉？

图 5 根据 502 个相关信息公开的案件展示了申诉涉及的行业。许多申诉涉及一个以上的行业。如，一个输油管道建设的申诉可能被记录为同时涉及采掘业和基础设施行业。图 5 显示了案件涉及行业的比例。

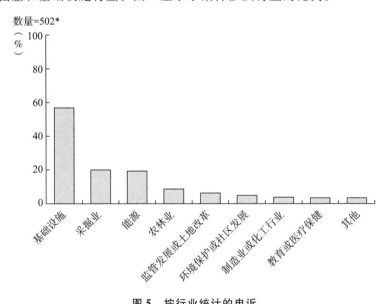

图 5　按行业统计的申诉

＊行业已知的案件的总数。

---

① 有些独立问责机制的程序规则不允许问责机制本身或者银行领导层提出申诉，而其他问责机制允许这种做法，不过这种情况从来没有出现过。

三个行业比较突出：基础设施、采掘业和能源。其中，基础设施是至今收到申诉最多的行业，该领域的申诉占总数的 57%。能源和采掘业各占 20% 左右。

不出所料，这些行业通常都与申诉常涉及的问题有关，如拆迁和污染。不过，申诉也来自很大范围的其他行业，包括那些明确地产生直接社会或环境效益的项目，比如教育或医疗保健项目（它们通常都被视为切合社会需求的行业）是 4% 的申诉所针对的主体。同样，6% 的申诉涉及的项目的设计初衷是促进环境保护及可持续社区发展。

2.3.7　申诉提出何种类型的问题？

图 6 以 480 例信息已知的申诉展示了关于申诉提出的问题的数据，这些问题大多与人权有关。大多数申诉提到了多个问题，有的甚至多到 10 个。因此，与前两个图一样，图 6 展示了每一个问题涉及的申诉比例。

最大的问题类别（磋商与信息公开、尽职义务和环境问题）中，每个问题都在超过 40% 的申诉中被提到。图中的"环境"是一个复合类别，包括了污染、生物多样性和其他如植被破坏等的环境问题。

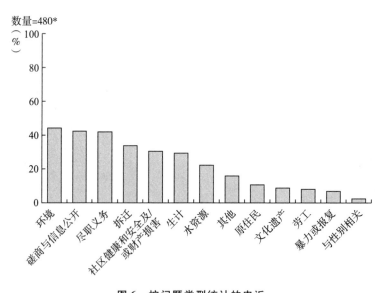

图 6　按问题类型统计的申诉

* 提出的问题已知的案件的总数。

其他几个问题也值得强调。暴力和其他报复行为是 7% 的案件中涉及的问题，这包括暴力（近 4% 的案件）及其他报复问题（4% 的案件）。与性别相关的问题（包括与性别有关的暴力、歧视和其他问题）仅在 2.5% 的案件里被提到。

图中的"其他"包括非常宽泛的一系列问题。有些被归类为"其他"的问题（如腐败和采购）在独立问责机制的职权范围之外，而其他申诉涉及多种难以归类的问题，如项目执行错误、关闭学校和能源价格问题等。

2.4 申诉在各机制中的进展

这一节对独立问责机制中案件的进展进行追踪，尤其展示了案件在这样的程序中进展到何种程度以及在多大频率上达成了结果。这里分析的案件通常限于有结论的案件，它们要么已经结案要么正在监测之中。在这一数据集中，684 例申诉有了结论，占向独立问责机制提出的所有案件的 90%。

由于并非所有机制都有一个正式的登记期间，所以一般来说，本报告所讨论的处理阶段包括资格审查、问题解决和合规审查。如前所述，问题解决和合规审查阶段被共同视为"实质性"阶段。本节衡量案件结果的重要指标是有结论的案件中达成处理结果的案件的比例。上文已经提到，如果问题解决阶段达成解决方案和/或合规报告予以公布，案件则记录为已经达成结果。

2.4.1 资格审查

图 7 显示了 684 例有结论的申诉中独立问责机制认为合格的案件的比例。过半数有结论的申诉要么未予登记要么被认为不合格，仅 42.5% 的申诉最终被认为合格。

本报告在所有申诉中收集的数据并不对申诉未予登记或被认为不合格的理由进行追踪。因此，难以评估为何仅低于半数的申诉被认为合格。所有相关数据能够被获取的独立问责机制都制定了程序性的规则来对案件登记和资格审查决定进行管理，有些规则能够直接运用，而有些可能需要独立问责机制进行判断。

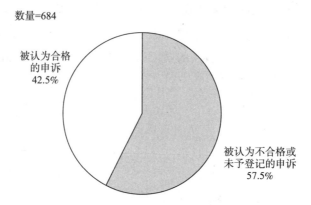

数量=684

被认为合格
的申诉
42.5%

被认为不合格或
未予登记的申诉
57.5%

图 7 被认为合格的申诉 VS 被认为不合格的申诉

我们推测，一部分未予登记及不合格的案件之所以不合格，毫无疑问是基于这些规则（如向不受理采购或腐败申诉的独立问责机制提出此类申诉）。然而，其他不合格或不予登记的案件可能是因为问责机制对相关决定存在不同意见。4.1 就 2014 年 7 月 1 日至 2015 年 6 月 30 日未进入或未完成实质性处理阶段而结案的申诉进行了一个单独的分析，对决定背后的理由提出了有价值的见解，并对一些围绕资格和登记决定出现的争议进行了讨论。

2.4.2 申诉处理进展：损耗

申诉经过了资格审查阶段，仍然远不能确定是否能够进入独立问责机制处理过程的实质性阶段。总的来说，291 个合格并已有结论的案件中，33% 的案件未能进入实质性处理阶段。资格审查和实质性阶段之间超过30% 的损耗率提出了独立问责机制是否有能力提供有效救济的问题，这需要进一步探讨。

合格的申诉可能因各种原因进入不了实质性处理阶段。图 8 和图 9 以101 个合格且有结论，而且应该能够进入问题解决阶段但未能进入的案件，和 128 个合格且有结论，并应该能够进入合规审查阶段但未能进入的案件为基础，用图的形式展示了这些原因。合格的申诉未能进入实质性处理阶段的最普遍原因包括：独立问责机制独立决定申诉没有必要或不适合进入问题解决或合规审查阶段，申诉人选择不进入问题解决或合规审查阶段，实施项目的公司或政府拒绝参与问题解决，或者开发性金融机构董事会拒绝授权批准进行合规调查。

　　大部分未进入实质性处理阶段的合格案件，涉及独立问责机制和银行领导层。就问题解决阶段而言，78 个合格且有结论却未如申诉人所愿进入问题解决的案件中，59% 的案件缘于独立问责机制认为不必要或不合适。更重要的是，合格且有结论但未能进入合规审查阶段的申诉中，接近 74% 的申诉未能进入的原因是独立问责机制认为不必要或不合适。另外 5.5% 的这类案件未能进入合规审查阶段的原因是开发性金融机构董事会拒绝授权进行调查。这样的情况仅发生在两个金融机构中：美洲开发银行，其董事会在过去五年中拒绝对三例独立咨询与调查机制申诉进行合规调查授权；世界银行，其董事会在监察组开始运作的头几年四次拒绝授权监察组进行调查。[①]

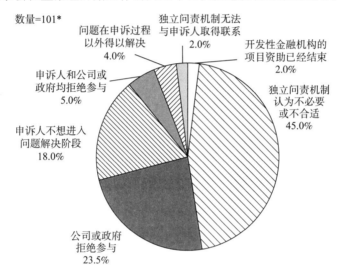

数量=101*

问题在申诉过程
以外得以解决
4.0%

独立问责机制无法
与申诉人取得联系
2.0%

开发性金融机构的
项目资助已经结束
2.0%

申诉人和公司或
政府均拒绝参与
5.0%

独立问责机制
认为不必要
或不合适
45.0%

申诉人不想进入
问题解决阶段
18.0%

公司或政府
拒绝参与
23.5%

图8　为何合格的申诉未能进入问题解决阶段

　　＊本应能够进入问题解决阶段但是未能进入，合格及有结论的案件的总数（它们被提供问题解决的机制认为合格）。

　　关于图 9，还有一点需要进一步解释。因为"申诉未重新提交"而未能进入合规审查阶段的申诉仅包括那些在亚洲开发银行的问责机制开始运作的头几年，其程序规定尚未修改之前提起的申诉。旧的程序规定中，问题解决和合规审查被视为单独的申诉处理过程，经过了问题解决阶段或被认为没有资格进入问题解决阶段之后，申诉人必须明确地重新申请进入合规

---

　　① 1998 年以来，世界银行董事会没有阻止过监察组的任何调查。

审查。不过，这已不再是问题，2012 年通过的新程序规定，已经不再要求
重新提出申请。

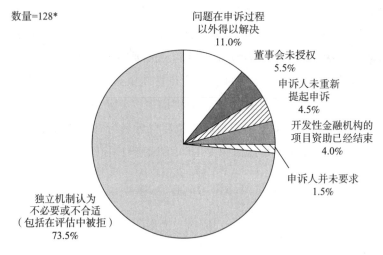

图 9　为何合格的申诉未能进入合规审查阶段

　　* 本应能够进入合规审查阶段但未进入，合格及有结论的案件的总数（它们被提供合
规审查的机制认为合格）。

　　图 10 对 291 个进入了问题解决和合规审查阶段或二者之一的合格且有
结论的案件情况以百分比的形式进行了总结归纳。① 相对来说，申诉既进入
问题解决阶段又进入合规审查阶段的情况并不常见：34% 的进入问题解决
阶段，36.5% 的进入合规审查阶段，而仅 6.5% 的进入了两个阶段。如前所
述，很大一部分申诉（33% 的合格且有结论的申诉）从未进入两个实质性
处理阶段的任何一个。4.1 节将对申诉在达成结果之前终结申诉处理进程可

---

　　① 对仅进入问题解决阶段、仅进入合规审查阶段，以及同时进入问题解决和合规审查阶段这
三种情况的案件比例统计，因每个申诉可使用的功能不同而进行了控制，如何控制取决于
向哪个独立问责机制提交案件，以及通过何种方式提交案件。例如，仅进入问题解决阶段
的案件百分比的统计排除了监察组案件（因为监察组没有问题解决功能）；仅进入合规审
查阶段的案件比例的统计又排除了企业社会责任顾问受理的案件（因为企业社会责任顾问
不提供合规审查的功能）；而同时进入问题解决和合规审查阶段的案件比例的统计又将监
察组案件和企业社会责任顾问案件同时排除在外。还有一些因为申诉提交方式的原因而被
排除在外，尤其是由银行或独立问责机制领导层向合规顾问/巡查官办公室提起的申诉和由
不代表直接受影响社区的民间组织向项目申诉机制（PCM）提交的申诉仅有资格进行合规
审查，因此这些案件被排除在"仅进入问题解决阶段"和"既进入问题解决阶段又进入合规
审查阶段"的比例统计之外。由于这些控制因素的影响，所有的百分比相加会超过 100%。

能的原因进行进一步阐述。

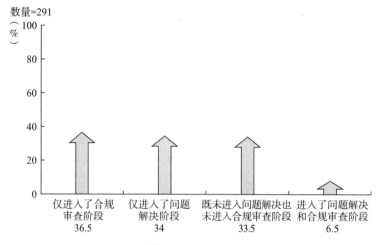

图 10　合格及有结论的申诉的进展

2.4.3　申诉处理进展：步骤和结果

图 11 根据申诉到达了何种独立问责机制的处理阶段和达成了何种结果对有结论的案件进行分析。在每一个阶段都有明显的损耗。684 例有结论的申诉分别进入了申诉处理的下列阶段：近 43% 的申诉被认定合格，28% 的申诉进入实质阶段，低于 20% 的申诉产生了结果。这 20% 产生了结果且有结论的申诉又可做如下分类：8% 的案件中当事各方成功进行谈判并达成了处理方案，略低于 12% 的案件的合规报告得以公开。另外，开发性金融机构管理层在 7% 的有结论的案件中制订了行动计划。这在 76 个最终发现存在违规现象的案件中占 64.5%。[①]

图 11 应当被解读为一个描述性而不是评价性的图，因为并不是所有的申诉都有资格达成结果。如，并不是所有的申诉都符合资格审查的标准。因此，图 11 中所展示的案件在不同阶段终结处理进程这一情况本身并不意味着系统失效，但这种情况的确需要进一步分析。

当注意力集中到 291 例合格及有结论的申诉时，能够观察到近半数（44%）达成了结果。但重要的是，将案件归类为达成了"结果"并不考虑

---

① 这个数字包含了独立问责机制发现的所有违规的案件，不管合规报告是否公开。

合规报告的结论、处理方案或行动计划的执行，或申诉人对处理结果的满意度，因为这些信息通常不在能收集的数据范围之内。如果本研究能够追踪所有有结论的案件的这类信息并将其纳入"结果"的定义之中，可能被归为达成结果的案件将会少一些。第 4 章就申诉人对 2014 年 7 月 1 日至 2015 年 6 月 30 日的几个案件达成的结果的满意度进行了观察分析。

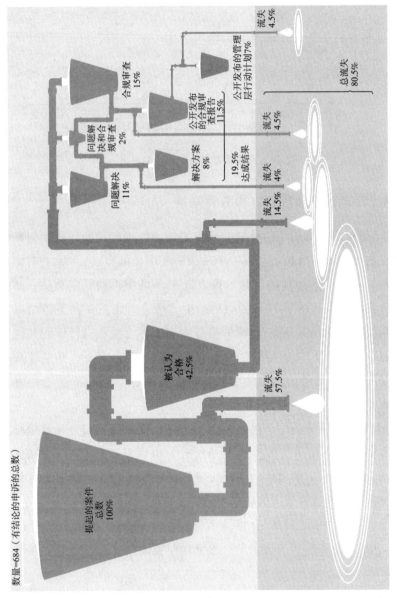

图11 申诉进展及损耗

2.4.4　各独立问责机制的申诉处理进展

图 12 对主要独立问责机制中有结论案件的发展进程进行了比较。[①] 不同机制之间差异巨大，这种差异不仅体现在申诉进入各个处理阶段的比例上，也体现在案件的最终结果上。总的来说，世界银行集团的独立问责机制（合规顾问/巡查官办公室和监察组）的案件在申诉处理进程中的损耗率较区域性开发银行的独立问责机制低。然而，合格及申诉取得处理结果的比例是个例外，这一比例在前者的案件中高于后者的案件。

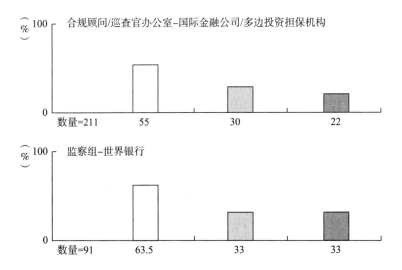

---

① 尽管非洲开发银行也被认为是一个重要的区域性开发银行，但是该图中没有包含该银行，因为该银行的独立审查机制只收到了 17 个申诉（其中只有 10 个进行了登记），样本太少可能会使结果存在偏差。同样，欧洲投资银行的申诉机制也没有包含在该图中，因为关于其案件的信息披露非常有限。欧洲投资银行的申诉机制的很多案件只披露了简短几句话，介绍申诉及其经过的过程。有些案件虽然提供了更详细的概要，但通常这些信息与案件页其他部分的信息不一致。而这些相互矛盾的信息往往与申诉机制处理过程中申诉进展的阶段有关，因此我们很难获得图 12 所需的信息类型。此外，尽管申诉机制 2013 年的政策表明，合规审查终结时的报告应该发布在其网页上，而事实上，欧洲投资银行的申诉机制极少公布申诉处理过程的相关报告。本报告出版之时，欧洲投资银行的申诉机制才刚开始在其在线案件登记系统中披露更多的信息，包括报告以及与案件相关的其他文件。申诉机制表示还将披露更多的信息，相信在不久的将来，我们就可以对申诉机制的申诉处理过程进行更好审视。

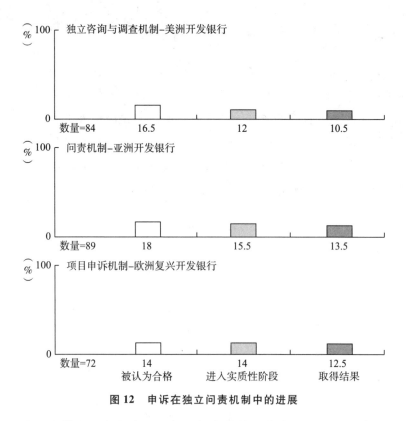

图 12 申诉在独立问责机制中的进展

监察组有结论的案件中，63.5%的案件被认定合格，33%的案件进入了实质性处理阶段。值得注意的是，所有进入实质性阶段的案件都取得了处理结果。这个高比例部分反映出监察组的程序不包括问题解决阶段，因此将许多通过问题解决达成结果时出现的不被控制的变量从申诉过程中去除。在监察组被认为合格且有结论的案件中，51.5%取得了处理结果。

世界银行集团的两个独立问责机制中，合规顾问/巡查官办公室的损耗率比较高，该机制有结论的案件中55%被认定为合格，30%进入了实质性处理阶段，22%取得了处理结果。在合规顾问/巡查官办公室合格且有结论的案件中，40%取得了处理结果。在区域性开发银行所属的独立问责机制中，亚洲开发银行的问责机制案件损耗率最低，18%的有结论的案件被认定为合格，15.5%进入了实质性处理阶段，13.5%取得了处理结果。问责机制合格且有结论的案件中，75%取得了处理结果。对于问责机制和其他区域性开发银行的独立问责机制而言，对这一数据进行解读应当考虑到被认为合格的有结论的申诉的总数相对较小，在 10 到 16 之间。

项目申诉机制有结论的案件中仅 14% 被认为合格，但所有被认为合格的申诉都进入了实质性处理阶段且其中的 12.5% 取得了处理结果。图 12 显示的 5 个独立问责机制中，项目申诉机制是唯一一个在资格审查和进入实质性阶段之间不存在任何案件损耗的机制。其中至少有一部分原因是在项目申诉机制的程序规定之中，没有那些在其他机制中通常导致损耗的步骤，如评估过程或进入实质性处理阶段之前须经董事会审批的要求。（见图 8 和图 9，这两个图反映了申诉为什么没有进入实质性处理阶段）项目申诉机制合格且有结论的案件中，90% 取得了处理结果。

在独立咨询与调查机制中，稍高比例（16.5%）的有结论的案件被认定为合格，但仅 12% 的案件进入了实质性处理阶段，10.5% 的案件达成了处理结果。独立咨询与调查机制合格且有结论的案件中，64.5%* 取得了处理结果。

2.4.5　申诉处理进展：有与没有民间组织参与

图 13.1 及图 13.2 根据国际或本国民间组织是否参与申诉对有结论案件的处理进程和结果进行了展示。① 如果民间组织提起了申诉（单独提起或与以社区为基础的申诉人共同提起）或者为申诉人提供支持，则该组织被认为参与了案件。

总的来说，在独立问责机制处理进程中，个人或社区组织在没有民间组织支持的情况下提起的申诉没有本国民间组织提起或支持的申诉走得那么远，或者前者达成处理结果的情况不如后者常见。而相对于有本国民间组织参与的申诉而言，国际民间组织参与（通常但并不总是，与以社区为基础的申诉人和/或本国民间组织一起）的案件在独立问责机制处理进程中走得甚至更远，而取得处理结果的情况也更常见。

---

*　原文如此。——译者注
①　有些机制不同时提供问题解决和合规审查功能或者受提起人类型所限仅提供合规审查功能，图 13.1 和图 13.2 对进入问题解决或合规审查阶段或达成结果（只有首先进入了一个实质性阶段才可能产生的结果）的案件比例的统计顾及向这类机制提起的案件而进行了控制调整。例如，监察组仅提供合规审查功能而企业社会责任顾问仅提供问题解决功能。此外，有些不代表直接受影响社区的民间组织向欧洲复兴开发银行项目申诉机制提起的案件仅具有合规审查的资格。

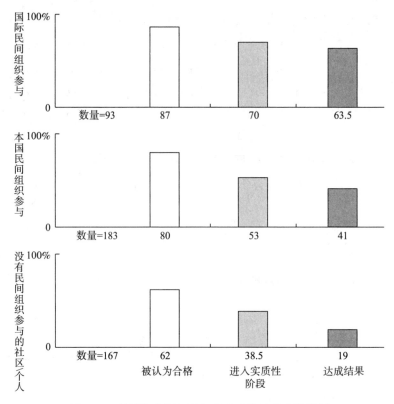

图 13.1 按照民间组织参与的情况统计的申诉进展

社区或个人在没有民间组织支持的情况下单独提起的申诉中，62%被认定为合格，38.5%进入了实质性处理阶段，19%达成了处理结果。与之形成对比的是，80%有本国民间组织参与的申诉被认定为合格，53%进入了实质性处理阶段，41%取得了处理结果。有国际民间组织参与的申诉表现甚至更好：87%被认定为合格，70%进入了实质性处理阶段，63.5%取得了处理结果。

图 13.2 呈现的其他一些结果反映的是每一种类型的申诉进入问题解决和合规审查阶段的比例，以及达成解决方案、合规报告公开披露或管理层行动计划公开披露的比例。总的来说，没有民间组织参与的申诉进入问题解决阶段的比例远高于进入合规审查阶段的比例（28%进入了问题解决阶段，而16%进入了合规审查阶段）。与之形成对比的是，有国际民间组织参与（同样，通常是与本地社区或本国民间组织一起）的申诉进入合规审查阶段的比例远高于进入问题解决阶段的比例（55%进入合规审查阶段，而

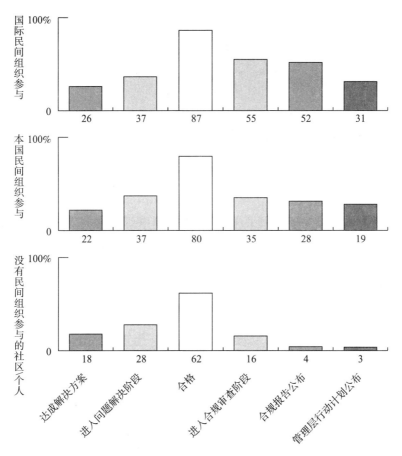

图 13.2　按照民间组织参与的情况统计的详细申诉进展

37%进入问题解决阶段）。有本国民间组织参与（通常与当地社区一起或代表当地社区）的申诉进入问题解决阶段的比例与进入合规审查阶段的比例基本相同（37%进入问题解决阶段，而 35%进入合规审查阶段）。

换言之，申诉进入问题解决阶段的比例的差异小于进入合规审查阶段的比例的差异。案件是否有民间组织参与，进入合规审查阶段的比例差异巨大：仅 16%的在没有民间组织支持下提起的申诉进入了合规审查阶段，而55%的有国际民间组织支持的申诉进入了这一阶段。

我们运用回归分析法，测试了民间组织的参与对合格的申诉最终取得处理结果的概率的影响，结果证实了缺乏民间组织支持的个人和社区在申诉进程中面临的困难。附件 1（方法论详解，见 http://www.grievancemecha-nisms.org/resources/brochures/glass-half-full）对这一回归分析的结果进行了详细说明，并对方法论进行了注解。这一回归分析仅考虑了有结论的合格申诉，并根据申诉至独立问责机制的数据进行了控制。

仅由个人或社区组织提起而缺乏任何民间组织支持的申诉在独立问责机制进程中的表现次于有其他组织支持提起的申诉。与由个人或社区组织在没有任何民间组织支持下提起的合格申诉相比，有本国民间组织参与的合格申诉能达成处理结果的概率上升了近40%。当国际民间组织参与一个合格的申诉，不管是单独参与还是与本国民间组织一同参与，这些概率上升了近175%。

2.4.6 申诉处理进展：独立问责机制申诉处理进程耗时多少？

图14展示了申诉进程到结束时或到更大的独立问责机制开始监测之前所花的平均时间。其他的数据（包括问题解决和合规审查阶段持续的时间）见表1。①

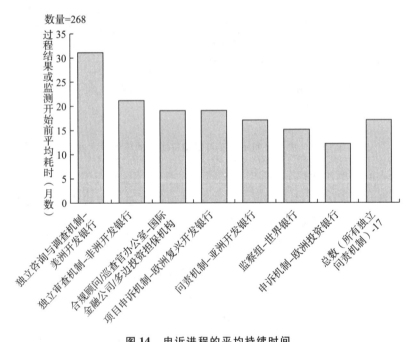

图14 申诉进程的平均持续时间

---

① 由于大量申诉未予登记或在提交后很快被认定不合格，为了防止某些独立问责机制的耗时数据被人为缩短，这里显示的耗时仅使用合格申诉的数据进行计算。

表1　额外的按月计的持续时长数据（仅合格案件）

独立审查机制	处理进程的平均时间*	问题解决阶段的平均时间	合规审查阶段的平均时间
总数	17（268）**	12（63）	12（92）
合规顾问/巡查官办公室 – 国际金融公司/多边投资担保机构	19（103）	14（31）	16（12）
监察组 – 世界银行	15（57）	不适用	17（30）
独立咨询与调查机制 – 美洲开发银行	31（11）	13（9）	23（2）
问责机制 – 亚洲开发银行	17（14）	10（12）	13（7）
独立审查机制/项目申诉机制 – 欧洲复兴开发银行	19（10）	2（3）	12（9）
申诉机制 – 欧洲投资银行	12（51）	不适用***	2（24）
独立审查机制 – 非洲开发银行	21（5）	12（5）	20（2）

* 这里衡量的处理进程是申诉进程结束之前或进入监督程序之前的时间。
** 组成每个数据的案件数量列在括号内。
*** 没有关于申诉机制 – 欧洲投资银行问题解决持续时长的可用数据。

　　总的来说，一个合格的申诉退出独立问责机制处理进程或进入监测之前的平均时间为17个月。问题解决和合规审查阶段的平均时间相同：12个月。

　　不同机制之间持续时间的差异很有限——单个独立问责机制的平均持续时间通常在5个月*之内。这一总趋势的一个显著例外是独立咨询与调查机制。合格的独立咨询与调查机制案件处理过程到结束时或到进入监测之前，平均持续时间是31个月，是总平均耗时的1.8倍以上。同样引人注目的是独立咨询与调查机制案件合规审查阶段的平均时长——23个月。然而，仅两个案件完成了合规审查。[1]

2.5　讨论

　　过去二十年里，独立问责机制遍地开花，为受开发项目损害的居民和

---

* 原文如此。——译者注
[1] 尽管独立咨询与调查机制最近正在进行重组，但似乎还没有影响到我们对于案件处理耗时的统计。该机制设立后案件处理耗时相对稳定。然而，由于重组工作将一直持续到2015年6月30日，仍有几个案件的处理因为机制重组而被推迟。一旦这些案件结案，独立咨询与调查机制的案件处理平均耗时可能会增加。

社区寻求救济提供了一个必要的平台。这些机制的大量增加和近年来接收申诉的数量的不断增长是一个鼓舞人心的信号,这很好地反映在它们的可见度和可及性上。然而,独立问责机制可能将经历一个申诉数量下行的趋势。应当密切关注 2015 年申诉总量的数据,如果下行趋势的确出现,需要时应当找出原因并加以纠正。

而且,尽管独立问责机制及其接收申诉的数量的增长很好地鼓舞了人心,其处理进程每一个阶段出现的损耗却令人担忧。过半数的申诉没有通过登记和资格审查阶段,大量被认为合格的案件未能进入实质性处理阶段。合格且有结论的申诉中 44% 达成了处理结果,尽管这个比例是一个正面的指标,独立问责机制仍应当继续努力提升能力,为申诉人带来有用的处理结果。另外,应当公布更多案件在登记或资格审查阶段终结的比例如此之高的原因。[①]

同样,独立问责机制应当注重使流程更容易为没有民间组织支持的社区和个人所使用并提高其使用价值。没有民间组织支持的个人和社区所面临的困境令人担忧,因为这种情况占有结论的申诉的比例至少为 24%。而且,单独提起申诉的个人和社区可能比有民间组织支持的更加脆弱和孤立,因此独立问责机制为这类申诉人的权益而良好运作显得更加迫切。为了成为能够为受开发性金融机构项目损害的人们提供救济的有效申诉机制,独立问责机制及开发性金融机构必须做出更多的努力来确保它们的申诉处理进程能为所有的申诉人平等获得,无论他们对该体系的认知和进行复杂和详细的申诉的能力如何。

在为受开发项目影响的人们持续提供有效的程序方面,必须取得重大进展,以确保他们得到救济。总之,本报告分析的数据显示,独立问责机制应当朝着这个目标努力。

---

① 参见第 4 章机制问责处理过程各个阶段案件损耗的讨论。

3 程序性鸿沟：对政策
和实践的定性研究

研究团队对照《联合国商业与人权指导原则》中《非司法申诉机制的有效性标准》对独立问责机制及其所属的开发性金融机构的政策和实践进行了评估。附件 5 – 15（www.glass-half-full.org）对每一个独立问责机制和开发性金融机构进行了评估分析。下文是对这些分析发现的综合汇总。本研究展示了最佳实践的几个例子，但这些实践看起来并未在所有独立问责机制和开发性金融机构中得到广泛复制或采纳。相反，正如接下来将详细描述的那样，开发性金融机构董事会在最近的独立问责机制审议中进行的改革在很多方面降低了其效用。似乎许多独立问责机制和开发性金融机构并没有争相在建立最稳健和公平的问责进程方面做得更好，相反，它们都在采纳那些满足其自身及客户利益的政策和做法，而不是为了满足问责程序要帮助的人群的利益。

3.1 合法性

在取得民间组织和受项目影响的社区的信任方面，独立问责机制面临一场艰苦的战役。毕竟，这些机制恰恰建立在那些对被认为造成了损害的项目进行资助的金融机构内部。机制的工作人员常常是申诉人能够见到的开发性金融机构唯一的工作人员。建立信任并由此加强独立问责机制合法性的方法之一是设立一个有民间组织和其他外部利益相关者参与的选拔过程，从而显示开发性金融机构独立问责机制工作人员的独立性。在本报告评估的独立问责机制中，国际金融公司和多边投资担保机构的合规顾问/巡查官办公室做出了最好的榜样。合规顾问/巡查官办公室建立了一个有民间组织、学术机构和私营部门代表参加的提名委员会，该委员会向世界银行集团主席推荐一位合规顾问/巡查官办公室副主席（VP）的候选人。另外一个例子是欧洲复兴开发银行的项目申诉机制，该机制官员和专家的选拔过程中有外部利益相关者（虽然不一定是民间组织）的参与。

选拔过程中多样化的视角会带来独立问责机制员工更大的多样性。有些独立问责机制，如世界银行监察组，力求确保员工地理上的多样化，而员工专业背景可能会很相似。在环境、劳工和人权民间组织的工作经历会在独立问责机制有很大的用武之地，因为这些机制需要经常与当地、所在国和国际的民间组织打交道。然而，很少有独立问责机制员工来自公民社会。由于没有渠道真正进入招聘程序，所以我们不可能判定其原因是缺乏民间组织申请者还是民间组织候选人没能入选。

独立问责机制收集民间组织及其他外部利益相关者意见的另一条道路，是建立一个提供指导和反馈的顾问团队。如，合规顾问/巡查官办公室有一个7人战略顾问团队，它由来自私人部门、学术机构的代表组成。由于没有成员牵扯进向合规顾问/巡查官办公室提出的申诉中，利益冲突得到了避免。

3.2 可及性

第一个独立问责机制建立之后二十多年来，确保这些机制有效的最大挑战之一仍然是最根本的那一个：受项目影响的人没有意识到这些机制的存在。这些机制的使用者甚至机制本身也确认了这种意识的普遍缺乏。[1]一份近期的报告调查了8个国家800位受开发活动[2]影响的民众，发现83%的

---

[1] Compliance Advisor/Ombudsman, *Review of IFC's Policy and Performance Standards on Social and Environmental Sustainability and Policy on Disclosure of Information* (May 2010), http://www.cao-ombudsman.org/documents/CAOAdvisoryNoteforIFCPolicyReview_May2010.pdf; Edward S. Ayensu, "Second Review of the Independent Review Mechanism (IRM) of the African Development Bank Group," *Report of the Consultant* (Sept. 2014), http://www.afdb.org/fileadmin/uploads/afdb/Documents/Compliance-Review/2nd_IRM_Review_-Consultant_s_Report_-_ENG.pdf.

[2] For a vision of what real development looks like, see International Accountability Project, *Back to Development: A Call for What Development Could Be* (2015), available at bit.ly/backtodevelopment [hereinafter IAP, Back to Development].

民众从未听说过世界银行监察组。虽然独立问责机制通过举办民间组织工作坊及参加公众活动在提高公众意识方面进行了很大的努力,[①] 它们仍然能够并且应当进行更多的尝试来改善对外联络,包括以多语种提供信息并对网站进行改进。然而,开发性金融机构确保独立问责机制可及性的最重要措施是要求其客户在与受项目影响的民众进行磋商的过程中向民众公开这些机制的存在和可用性。

开发性金融机构越来越多地要求其客户建立项目层面的申诉机制。尽管这些机制可能在处理个别的问题时有所帮助,但受影响的民众可能并不相信一个项目层面的机制足以完全解决他们的问题,因为这些机制常常正是由可能已经造成了损害的主体来设计和运行的。[②] 因此,项目层面的申诉机制也应告知其使用者当其对该机制处理结果不满意或者社区对使用这些机制缺乏信心的时候,他们可以使用独立问责机制。如果未能主动提供这样的信息,则为申诉人设立了一个事实上的资格要求,即申诉人必须有充分的资源和能力自行发现该机制。

独立问责机制为服务于受项目影响的社区而设,但开发性金融机构目前仅靠偶然性来确保需要它们的人最终能够找到它们。亚洲开发银行在这些银行中独树一帜地要求员工和客户共同公开其问责机制的信息。虽然这一要求并未明确在贷款协议中引用,一般认为亚洲开发银行的信息公开和安保政策要求客户披露这类信息。[③]

世界银行最近在一份网上公布的项目文件中提到了监察组。不过,这份文件是否进行了翻译并主动提供给了受项目影响的民众则并不清楚。而且,文件也提到了世界银行的申诉服务及项目层面的申诉机制。这两个程序分别由银行管理层及其客户运营,因此并不能算是独立的申诉机制。在

---

① Inspection Panel, IAMs – CSO Outreach Workshop in Turkey (May 2015), http://ewebapps. worldbank. org/apps/ip/Lists/NewsFromThePanel/NewsFromThePanelDisp. aspx? ID = 211&source = http://ewebapps. worldbank. org/apps/ip/Pages/News-from-the-panel. aspx; Inspection Panel, CSO Outreach Workshop in Zagreb, Croatia (July 2015), http://ewebapps. worldbank. org/apps/ip/Lists/NewsFromThePanel/NewsFromThePanelDisp. aspx? ID = 217&source = http://ewebapps. worldbank. org/apps/ip/Pages/News-from-the-panel. aspx.

② Centre for Research on Multinational Corporations (SOMO), *The Patchwork of Non-Judicial Grievance Mechanisms* (Dec. 2014), http://grievancemechanisms. org/resources/brochures/non-judicial-grievance-mechanisms-apatchwork-1/at_ download/file.

③ 以 2015 年 10 月 19 日收到的亚开行问责机制提供的审阅意见为基础。

项目文件中提到这样的机制可能会给受项目影响的社区造成困惑，并将他们从监察组转移开。

一旦申诉人找到了合适的机制，他们在提起申诉的过程中可能遇到障碍。美洲开发银行的独立咨询与调查机制和欧洲复兴开发银行的项目申诉机制最近都对程序进行了更改，新的程序不允许申诉人就已经被考虑进行投资但尚未获最后批准的项目要求进入问题解决或合规审查。项目审批之前对客户有大量的要求，包括环境与社会尽职调查和与受项目影响民众的磋商，对此开发性金融机构能够并且应该负责。总的来说，人们越早提出对一个项目关注的问题，越能更早通过修改项目设计或改进消减措施来对这些问题进行容纳消化，而这两个方面都能通过合规审查或问题解决来实现。这种早期申诉机会使独立问责机制能够防止负面影响的出现而不是在损害已成定局之后才去解决问题。

有几个独立问责机制仅接受在贷款支付后一定时间内提出的申诉。然而，只要贷款未偿还，贷款协议中的环境与社会要求就是适用的，开发性金融机构应当对这些要求的执行情况进行监督。如果它们未能确保环境与社会要求的执行，申诉人应当有机会向其问责。或者，申诉人可能希望参与到问题解决中去。申诉人和开发性金融机构的客户是否想要参与对话很少取决于贷款发放的状态，而取决于双方能否都从冲突解决中受益。如果潜在的申诉人由于有关贷款发放的信息未予公开而没有途径了解其申诉是否符合资格，这些程序上进行的限制就尤其有问题。比如，欧洲复兴开发银行项目申诉机制不接受在最后一次贷款发放后超过12个月以上提起的要求进行问题解决的申诉。然而，由于有关贷款状态信息未予公开，申诉人必须冒着投入了时间和资源进行申诉最后却因为提出太晚而申诉被拒的风险。不过同时，项目申诉机制也有正面的例子，它在贷款已经偿还且项目已经结束之后仍然接受要求进行合规审查的申诉。在项目结束后仍然接收申诉确保了开发性金融机构吸取教训并在将来的项目中对实践进行改进，虽然受已经结束的项目影响的民众很少从中得到直接的益处。

这些申诉提出时间的限制造成的可及性欠缺，要么是由于独立问责机制自身关于其议事规则的决定，要么是这些机制所附属的开发性金融机构董事会加诸的要求。赋予这些机制采用和修改其议事规则的权力非常必要，同时给予所有利益相关者提出意见的机会，这将强化其独立性并因此提高其合法性。

可及性方面的另一个限制出现在申诉过程当中：独立问责机制的实践太过经常地将不那么老练的申诉人置于劣势地位。他们没有能力提起复杂的申诉，无法在申诉中对当事方的开发性金融机构的政策进行确定并分析其如何被违背。虽然大多数独立问责机制并不正式要求最初的申诉具备这些要素，但实践中独立问责机制似乎偏爱更加老练的申诉人。有几个独立问责机制（国际金融公司和多边投资担保机构的合规顾问/巡查官办公室、欧洲投资银行的申诉机制、欧洲复兴开发银行的项目申诉机制、加拿大采掘业办公室的企业社会责任顾问以及美国海外私人投资公司的问责办公室）仅要求一人即可提起申诉。如第2章的数据显示，相对于没有民间组织支持的个人或社区提起的申诉而言，有民间组织支持提起的申诉被认为合格的概率高很多，而且这类申诉达成结果的概率也高很多。考虑到许多独立问责机制都声称将重视提供当地社区能够用来解决问题的申诉程序，这一趋势尤其令人沮丧。当地社区可以独立向某机制提起申诉而不需要寻求法律咨询或外界其他协助，这常常被强调为独立问责机制优胜于传统司法救济渠道的地方。但为了有效地发挥这种优势，独立问责机制和开发性金融机构必须做出更多努力来确保申诉程序对所有的申诉人具有平等的可及性，而不管他们对于这一体制的了解如何或提起复杂详细的申诉的能力如何。

3.3 可预测性

机制使用者经常提到的一个问题是申诉处理的拖延和机制无法遵守其程序规定的期限。这一问题的结果是进程的不可预测性。拖延可能有以下原因：机制无力应付繁重的工作量、开发性金融机构在对独立问责机制进行回应时未能遵守其期限限制以及简单的管理不当。当然，独立问责机制可能仅在最后一个问题上有控制力。其他两个方面是属于开发性金融机构的责任。机制的预算是由开发性金融机构审批的，因此如果独立问责机制需要更多的人手来处理收到的申诉，它只能在开发性金融机构批准提高预算的情况下才能如愿。在后一章的案例分析中将会看到，无论是何种原因造成的拖延都会使申诉人相信独立的处理进程已经受到了干扰。当机制未就申诉处理状态与申诉人进行足够的沟通时（这在实践中很普遍），这种情况尤甚。

与申诉人缺乏沟通这个问题不仅仅在申诉人遭遇申诉处理拖延时出现。机制的使用者希望机制在为申诉人提供申诉状态更新方面更加主动，即使只是说明申诉正在按照计划进行处理。频繁的交流有助于申诉人知道自己可以从申诉处理中期待什么。机制与申诉人进行交流沟通的程度，似乎不仅在不同的机制之间有差别，而且不同案件中也存在差异。

赋予独立问责机制对其调查和纠纷解决结果进行监测的职权，提高了纠纷解决进程的可预测性。因为这种赋权有助于确保承诺得以践行及银行采取措施来应对已经出现的违规问题。然而，不是所有的独立问责机制都有这种监测权限，多数机制仅有有限的权威。比如，以合规审查为例，许多独立问责机制仅限于对开发性金融机构为应对其调查发现的违规问题制订的管理层行动计划的执行进行监督。但是，如果管理层行动计划不足以应对机制发现的问题，即使计划完全落实，也可能仍然不能解决违规的问题，因而申诉人提出的问题也得不到回应。

3.4 公平性

公平的申诉处理过程会给予申诉人与开发性金融机构及其客户同样的参与权，但很少有独立问责机制做到这一点。许多独立问责机制的议事规则允许开发性金融机构对报告草稿进行审阅和评议，同样的机会却并没有给予申诉人。比如，合规顾问/巡查官办公室把调查报告的草稿分享给国际金融公司来征求意见，却不给予申诉人同样的机会。处理过程终结时，独立问责机制和开发性金融机构就报告和如何做出恰当的回应与开发性金融机构董事会进行讨论时，申诉人从未能参与，而且他们很少有机会通过书面方式表达观点。项目申诉机制和问责机制在这方面做得很好，它们的程序规定最终报告提交相关董事会时应当加入申诉人的意见。

同样的问题是，开发性金融机构常常未能对独立问责机制调查报告中发现的违规情况给予足够的回应。在下一章详细的案例分析和用户调查（见附件3）中，这个问题反复被提及。总的来说，申诉人对开发性金融机构及其客户对他们关注的问题进行回应所采取的步骤并不满意，这些问题涉及的或者是过程或者是内容。申诉人称，开发性金融机构在制订意在应对独立问责机制发现的问题的管理层行动计划时并未与他们磋商。要进行有意义的磋商，申诉人首先必须能够知晓独立问责机制的调查发现。在 8 个开发性金融机构中，申诉人在开发性金融机构人员就管理层行动计划与其进行磋商之前无法接触到独立问责机制的调查报告。这意味着，申诉人在被开发性金融机构人员问到应该在管理层行动计划中包括什么样的措施来纠正违规时实际上不了解独立问责机制是否或在何种程度上发现了违规情况。国际金融公司甚至完全不被要求与申诉人进行任何磋商。相反，合规顾问/巡查官办公室的调查报告和国际金融公司提出的行动计划都发送给世界银行集团主席，由其进行审阅和批准。申诉人第一次看到这两种文件中的任何一种都是在主席批准之后。这样的磋商失败是申诉人对开发性金融机构及其客户提出的应对其关心的问题的措施不满意的部分原因。

大多数时候，当独立问责机制发现开发性金融机构未能遵守其自身政策或程序并给个人或社区带来损害时，开发性金融机构的回应考虑的不是与违规行为成正比的行动，也未能解决开发性金融机构试图造福的民众所关注的问题。如在下一章将会看到的那样，对那些要求进行或只能要求进行合规审查的申诉人来说，投入了资源和数年时间到申诉处理过程之后，由于开发性金融机构未能对申诉人提出的问题给予有意义的回应，他们可能看不到（通常也没有看到）具体的益处或者境遇的改变。

开发性金融机构回应不足的问题由于上诉程序的缺乏而加剧了严重性。申诉人必须接受批准开展争议所涉项目的机构（即董事会）做出的决定。申诉人如果对处理结果不满意，没有一个真正独立的机构供其上诉。一个引人注目的例外是欧洲投资银行的申诉机制。如果申诉人对处理过程或者该银行的回应不满意，他们可以向欧盟监察员（European Union Ombudsman）上诉，监察员能决定是否存在管理失当，而监察员对管理失当的解释包括不遵守法律和不尊重人权。① 然而，通过了上诉程序的案件太少，以至于无法据此判断上诉程序是否增加了申诉人取得成功结果的机会（更多信息见附件 9）。其他的开发性金融机构如果建立类似上诉程序，将不得不将权力委托给外部机构或将案件提交给外部机构处理。

---

① At your service, European Ombudsman, http://www.ombudsman.europa.eu/atyourservice/could-hehelpyou.faces (last visited Nov. 12, 2015).

3.5 透明度

独立问责机制必须透明运作以对利益相关者负责，建立其有效性的信心，尊重受到威胁的公共利益。报告作者的分析显示，独立问责机制对接收申诉的信息公开在种类和数量上差异都很大。一种极端情况是，有些独立问责机制不公开过往或正在处理的申诉的内容、已结案件处理结果或单个申诉处理决定的理由等方面的任何信息。[①] 另一个极端的情况是，一些独立问责机制公布所有过往和正在处理的申诉名单并附有每一个申诉所处状态、申诉人提交的文件资料的链接、开发性金融机构对申诉指控的回应、其他申诉处理进程的文件资料及一份对独立问责机制申诉处理决定进行的详略得当的分析报告。[②] 但即使这样的机制也并不对所有不合格的申诉进行公布。大约半数的独立问责机制处于这两个极端中间。比如，欧洲投资银行的申诉机制仅在今年上网公布了其接收的申诉的完整案件登记。然而，根据欧盟隐私法，该行还必须提供这些案件的大多数文件或信息。[③] 其他独立

---

① 例如，以下独立问责机制没有在其网页上披露任何过去的或现有的申诉，因此不包括在本报告范围之内：巴西开发银行巡查官，http://www.bndes.gov.br/SiteBNDES/bndes/bndes en/Navegacao Suplementar/Ouvidoria；加拿大出口开发公司合规官员，http://www.edc.ca/EN/About-Us/Management-and-Governance/Compliance-Officer/Pages/default.aspx；株式会社日本贸易保险检查官，http://www.nexi.go.jp/en/environment/objection.html；澳大利亚出口融资与保险公司，http://www.efic.gov.au/about-efic/our-organisation/complaints-mechanism/。

② 非洲开发银行的独立审查机制，http://www.afdb.org/en/independent-review-mechanism/managementof-complaints/。世界银行监察组，http://ewebapps.worldbank.org/apps/ip/Pages/All-PanelCases.aspx。国际金融公司和多边投资担保机构的合规顾问/巡查官办公室，http://www.cao-ombudsman.org/cases/。美国海外私人投资公司的问责办公室，http://www.opic.gov/who-we-are/office-of-accountability/public-registry-cases。荷兰开发银行和德国投资与开发有限公司的独立申诉机制，http://www.fmo.nl/project-related-complaints，http://bit.ly/2MB7VEo。以上提供了每个案件的大部分信息，包括申诉内容、管理层回应以及各独立问责机制的分析。

③ 欧洲投资银行的申诉机制的网页上有一个索引，列举了收到的申诉的标题及诉称问题性质方面有限的信息。参见欧洲投资银行的申诉机制案件，http://www.eib.org/about/accountability/complaints/cases/index.htm。然而，除了最近的少数情况外（如，关于塞尔维亚贝尔格莱德支路项目的申诉案件，http://bit.ly/2MB7VEo），该索引通常不提供相关文件的副本，并且许多案件都缺乏申诉机制对案件的分析。申诉机制每年公布《申诉机制年度行动报告》，提供 1）案件数据，包括接收到的、认定为不可接纳的、已结案的，或者登记的案件数量；2）对某些结案的和未决案件的描述；3）一份附件，其中完整列举收 （转下页注）

问责机制公布了申诉文本并公开其所作的分析及案件状态信息，但详略程度参差不齐。①

一个申诉程序要良好运行，申诉人需要的不仅仅是关于独立问责机制的信息和来自独立问责机制的信息，首要的是，他们需要渠道获取关于开发性金融机构资助的活动的信息。关于可用信息的数量及他们可使用的获取信息的方式，不同的开发性金融机构甚至不同的项目活动都会有所不同。比如，非洲开发银行公布项目文件但并不是所有文件都在同一个地方公布，这要求潜在的申诉人搜遍开发性金融机构的数据库来找到所有有关的信息。荷兰开发银行仅在最近才开始公开其资助的一些活动。然而，即使是具有最高的环境与社会风险的项目，相关信息都极度有限。对每一个公开的项目，荷兰开发银行公布三段文字分别定位项目客户、目标和荷兰开发银行对该项目的管辖权，没有提供环境与社会影响评价的链接。

开发性金融机构不仅支持那些将资金投入到一个特定活动或项目的传统的项目融资，目前也使用许多不同类型的融资媒介，这些媒介的使用使受影响民众更加难以发现资金来源。例子之一是通过其他"金融中介机构"进行融资，如私募基金或商业银行。对金融中介机构进行资助的开发性金融机构（如国际金融公司）会确定其直接客户而不是资金最终接收者的身份。换言之，它们很少披露客户的身份，其客户支持的子项目的地点和目的

（接上页注③）到的所有申诉及其大概主题、在申诉过程中所处的状态及（如果有关的话）结果。参见，欧洲投资银行《申诉机制年度行动报告》（2014 年 11 月），http://www.eib.org/infocentre/publications/all/complaints-mechanism-annual-report-2014.htm。

① 例如，美洲开发银行的独立咨询与调查机制（http://idblegacy.iadb.org/en/mici/by-country,7631.html）以及欧洲复兴开发银行的项目申诉机制（http://www.ebrd.com/work-with-us/project-finance/projectcomplaint-mechanism/pcm-register.html），都提供申诉信息以及对申诉处理决定非常详细的分析，但有时也没有将开发性金融机构管理层对于申诉问题的回应作为单独文件对外公开。日本国际协力机构《环境指南》指导原则检查官（http://www.jica.go.jp/english/our work/social environmental/objection/index.html）提供审查要求的链接，列明评估阶段，提供文件链接，阐述《环境指南》指导原则检查官的最终决定，但对于做出此决定的原因没有进行分析或只进行非常有限的分析。亚开行的项目特别协调人（http://www.adb.org/site/accountability-mechanism/problem-solving-function/complaint-registry-year）公布了收到的申诉以及对申诉的审查分析，但没有提供被拒案件的详细分析。不过，亚开行合规审查小组没有充分披露申诉处理的相关信息（http://compliance.adb.org/dir0035p.nsf/alldocs/BDAO-7XGAWN? OpenDocument）。加拿大采掘业办公室的企业社会责任顾问对其驳回的或不予受理的申诉提供有限的评估分析（http://www.international.gc.ca/csr counsel-lor-conseiller rse/Registry-webenregistrement.aspx? lang = eng）。

也很少公布。虽然受子项目影响的民众如果遭遇损害有权向有关独立问责机制提起申诉，但实践中他们几乎连开发性金融机构参与到项目中都不可能知道。[1]

3.6　权利兼容性

只有在独立问责机制对开发性金融机构的表现进行衡量的标准本身具有权利兼容性的情况下，申诉处理的结果才可能权利兼容。不幸的是，极少有开发性金融机构明确做出人权方面的承诺。那些做出此类承诺的开发性金融机构（如美国海外私人投资公司和欧洲投资银行）并没有以融入项目设计中的可行的政策和指导说明的方式使这些承诺具有操作性。联合国特别报告员已经敦促世界银行在其正在审议的环境和社会安保政策中纳入人权标准。[2]

开发性金融机构及其独立问责机制能够做出更多努力来保护每一个参与申诉过程的人员的安全，包括申诉人、顾问和民间组织。除了承诺对申诉人身份保密，独立问责机制并无其他制度防止报复或在其发生时进行回应。因为开发性金融机构经常设有国别或者区域办公室（这与设在开发性金融机构总部的独立问责机制不同），它们的员工有最佳的能力对针对申诉人遭遇的报复进行干预。然而，开发性金融机构似乎并无制度或者协议来解决那些对其资助的活动进行批评的人的安全问题。能够表达对开发性金融机构资助的活动的关注而无须惧怕自身安全受到威胁对于确保可持续发展至关重要，开发性金融机构的磋商要求得以充分贯彻落实的重要性更不言自明。不能足够确保对申诉人进行保护，遭到报复的风险可能阻挡人们向独立问责机制申诉的步伐，从而限制其获得救济的渠道。不幸的是，下一章描述的监察组受理埃塞俄比亚的案件展示了当开发性金融机构和独立

---

① Kate Geary, Oxfam Int'l, *The Suffering of Others: The Human Cost of the International Finance Corporation's Lending Through Financial Intermediaries* (Apr. 2015), https://www.oxfam.org/sites/www.oxfam.org/files/file_ attachments/ib-suffering-of-others-international-finance-corporation-020415-en. pdf [hereinafter Oxfam Int'l, The Suffering of Others].

② Letter from UN Special Mandate Holders, *to Jim Yong Kim*, World Bank Pres. (Dec. 12, 2014) (available at http://www.ohchr.org/Documents/Issues/EPoverty/WorldBank. pdf).

问责机制缺少对安全风险进行评估、防范和解决的制度时会出现什么样的结果。没有一个独立问责机制有权力采取强制性行动来防范或者终结开发性金融机构资助项目的负面人权影响。这一权力目前只有最初批准该项目的主体才具有，通常是开发性金融机构的董事会。不过，如果相信项目将造成严重的不可修复的损害，一些独立问责机制（包括项目申诉机制、独立审查机制、合规顾问和独立咨询与调查机制）可以在申诉过程的任何时候建议开发性金融机构暂停对问题项目的资助或项目进程 。然而，似乎这一权力从来未被动用过。所有其他独立问责机制都能通过这种权力从中获益，尽管这能在何种程度上确保对人权的尊重还取决于这些机制使用它的意愿的大小。

3.7　经验教训

独立问责机制在其调查中发现相同政策违规重复出现的频率反映了开发性金融机构并未从独立问责机制案件中吸取足够的系统性经验教训以改进其政策的落实。最引人注目的证据之一是世界银行最近的原住民强制安置投资组合审议（Involuntary Resettlement Portfolio Review），审议发现"银行处理安置问题的制度存在重大的潜在失败"。① 尽管监察组多年来反复发现世界银行不遵守其非自愿安置政策，这一功能失调以及随之而来的对被安置人员的损害仍持续发生着。② 独立问责机制的调查发现和经验教训若要更好地融入未来的项目设计和政策落实，可以通过建立管理追踪制度来实现。这可能类似于亚洲开发银行针对不合格申诉使用的制度，③ 该制度对开

---

① Social Development Department，World Bank，*Involuntary Resettlement Portfolio Review*：*Phase II*：*Resettlement Implementation*（June 16，2014）.

② Submission to the World Bank's Safeguard Review and Update Process from the Inspection Panel，*Lessons from Panel Cases*：*Inspection Panel Perspectives*（May 2013），http：//ewebapps. world-bank. org/apps/ip/Documents/IPN_ Inputs_ SafeguardsReview_ May2013. pdf ［hereinafter Inspection Panel Comments on World Bank's Safeguard Review］.

③ 亚洲开发银行，问责机制政策37，196（2012），http：//www. adb. org/documents/accountabili-tymechanism-policy-2012。政策规定"在处理完不合格的申诉案件后，由特别项目协调人办公室（OSPF）或合规审查小组（CRP）将案件移交给各业务部门，业务部门撰写报告简要说明申诉内容、涉及问题、为解决问题而采取的行动、利益相关方的决定或协议、结果和经验教训。"

发性金融机构处理申诉人提出的问题的应对措施及其从中吸取的、将运用到未来项目中的经验教训进行追踪记录。

许多开发性金融机构反复投资于同一客户或相同的行业，即使这些客户或活动已经屡遭申诉。开发性金融机构不应该资助那些被发现违规的客户进行的具有类似环境与社会影响的活动，除非这些客户已经对出现的问题进行了补救并显示了它们完全执行环境与社会标准及防止未来再次造成损害的决心和能力。

咨询建议职权（如合规顾问/巡查官办公室）也能有助于独立问责机制对开发性金融机构应该在哪些地方改进政策或执行政策进行解释说明。但即使是那些不具有正式咨询建议职能的独立问责机制也已经找到了富有创意的方法，在其案件中对发展方向进行界定和强调，这些方法常常包括在年度报告中的分析或（如亚开行问责机制的做法）每三年发布的一份"学习报告"（Learning Report）中。但是，无论采取何种形式，这些建议似乎常常被开发性金融机构束之高阁。比如，监察组案件中积累的经验教训很显然应当体现在世行环境与社会安保政策更新中。这些案件提供了关于政策落实面临的挑战和政策不足等方面丰富的信息资源。然而，在对安保政策审议磋商程序进行概括的最初的方法文件中，世行并未提到监察组。① 如果民间组织没有要求而监察组也没有主动提出，世界银行是否会从监察组的观点看法中获益，这一点并不清楚。②

① World Bank, *The World Bank's Safeguard Policies Proposed Review and Update: Approach Paper* (Oct. 2012), http://consultations. worldbank. org/Data/hub/files/consultation-template/review-and-update-world-banksafeguard-olicies/en/materials/safeguardsreviewapproachpaper. pdf.

② Inspection Panel Comments, *Comments on the Second Draft of the Proposed Environmental and Social Framework from the Inspection Panel* (June 17, 2015), http://ewebapps. worldbank. org/apps/ip/Style% 20Library/Documents/Inspection% 20Panel% 20Comments% 20on% 202nd% 20Draft% 20ESF% 20 - % 2017% 20June% 202015. pdf.

4 实地反思：定性结果分析

运用《联合国商业与人权指导原则》中《非司法申诉机制的有效性标准》对独立问责机制和开发性金融机构进行评价面临一个挑战，因为这些标准主要关注的是过程，而不是结果。但对一个申诉过程的效用真正的测试是诉称的问题是否得到解决，申诉人的境遇在提出申诉后是否得到了改善。本章中，作者对独立问责机制及开发性金融机构产生的结果进行评价。由于独立问责机制和开发性金融机构的有效性在不同时间有所不同，作者重点关注 2014 年 7 月 1 日至 2015 年 6 月 30 日已经有结论的案件。因此，本章对独立问责机制和开发性金融机构最近的表现进行简要描述。

如第 2 章所述，目前大多数的申诉在达成结果之前已结案。许多这样的申诉因为未能达到最低的登记标准和资格标准而结案，但也有大量案件虽然被认为符合资格仍然未能进入实质性处理阶段。本章第 1 节对所有在研究进行期间未能进入或未能完成实质性处理阶段的申诉及独立问责机制给出的理由进行介绍。

2015 年，达成第 2 章所定义的处理结果的独立问责机制申诉数量相对较少。本章第 2 节的案例分析从申诉人的视角展开，描述了他们在申诉处理过程中的体验及他们如何看待处理结果。由于这些案件并不是在各金融机构之间平均分配，不可能进行比较分析。相反，案例分析展示了申诉人最近的经历，这些经历有益于对问责机制进行改革，使其对权利者的需求进行更多回应。

案例分析中出现的主题反映了作者从更广范围的机制使用者中听到的声音：积极的一面是，总的来说，申诉人称他们受到了独立问责机制的公平对待，而且对他们关注的问题得到认真对待表示感谢。例如在哥伦比亚阿维安卡案中，合规顾问/巡查官办公室合规审查确认申诉人的申诉成立。

然而，我们并没有看到多少实地发生的真正的改变。布贾加利案件中，半数的申诉人得到了补偿的承诺，虽然这一承诺尚未兑现。不过，另一半申诉人仍在等待类似的承诺。

案例分析还确认了一个事实：申诉人说他们在申诉之后感觉到了压力并且受到了威胁。下文提到的案例中，开发性金融机构和独立问责机制似乎都没有对此进行足够的回应，这证实了它们都需要制定制度来更好地保护申诉人并在报复行为发生时做出反应。

本章案例分析和上一章的调查中反复得出的一个结论是：未能确保申诉人受到的冤屈得以纠正的原因在于，开发性金融机构没有能力及意愿承诺采取措施处理申诉人的冤屈。过于频繁出现的情况是，申诉人最后拿到独立问责机制的报告，这份言辞有力的报告详细例数开发性金融机构环境与社会标准落实中存在的重大缺陷，但申诉人未能从开发性金融机构那里得到同样强有力的回应。同样，即使在开发性金融机构的客户已经在对话过程中对申诉人做出了有意义的承诺，开发性金融机构也很少（如果曾有的话）参与救济，尽管其实是它们促使损害的发生。

4.1　末路：无果而终的案例

作者并不期待每一个申诉都能够或者应该走完整个申诉进程。比如，针对开发性金融机构并没有参与的活动而提出的申诉理应被拒。然而，如此大量的申诉在达成结果之前结案，这值得仔细考虑，从而判断是否存在能够消除或者减少的不必要障碍或负担。

2.4 概述未能满足资格要求的申诉或未能进入实质性处理阶段的申诉的比例。正如图 8 和图 9 所示，一些申诉由于独立问责机制无法控制的原因未能通过实质性处理阶段。本节重点关注由于独立问责机制做出决定而使申诉未能通过的原因。① 本报告作者对每一个独立问责机制网站上提供的 2014 年 7 月 1 日至 2015 年 6 月 30 日之间未达成结果即结案的申诉的信息进行了

---

① 这部分特别关注图 7 中不合格案件的原因：为什么独立问责机制认为对图 8 和图 9 的案件进行问题解决和合规审查是不必要或不合适的，以及为什么独立问责机制认为图 8 和图 9 的案件已在申诉之外得到了解决？

分析。根据这些信息（或这些信息的缺失），本报告做出了以下7个宽泛的分类。

1. 没有解释：机制没有对结案或驳回申诉做出任何解释。

2. 撤案：申诉被申诉人撤回。

3. 申诉不完整：申诉人没有提供申诉获得被独立问责机制考虑的资格所必需的所有信息。

4. 纠纷在独立问责机制进程外得以解决。机制认为申诉已得到解决或者正通过以下方式之一在申诉人与开发性金融机构或借款人/客户之间进行处理：1）对话、磋商、调解或者类似的纠纷解决活动；或2）其他由开发性金融机构或借款人/客户独立采取的行动。

5. 超出独立问责机制的职权范围。基于以下原因申诉处于独立问责机制的职权、管辖权或权威之外：1）作为申诉主题的活动或行为不是该开发性金融机构活动或拟议投资组合的组成部分（即活动或行为非该开发性金融机构资助，且/或未被该开发性金融机构考虑予以投资）；2）申诉所称损害不是该机制有权审查的类型；3）申诉人未能满足一个或者多个程序性的前提条件；或4）争议涉及的活动完全不在该机制的实质管辖范围之内（见方框1中的范例）。

6. 并行的处理进程：由于已经存在关于申诉主题的未决诉讼或其他正在进行的涉事金融机构以外的正式处理程序，该机制拒绝申诉进入其处理过程的实质性阶段。

7. 因果联系不足：该机制认定被质疑的行为和/或申诉主张的损害与该开发性金融机构资助的行为在空间或时间上的联系过弱，或者申诉完全未能指出有问题的行为或损害与机构融资之间有足够的因果联系。

方框1：

矿业对话技术援助，海地

开发性金融机构/独立问责机制：世界银行/监察组

开发性金融机构客户：海地政府

申诉人：海地采矿集体正义组织（Kolektif Jistis Min an Ayiti）及受影响社区

提供支持的民间组织：纽约大学人权与全球正义中心（NYU CHR & GJ）和问责顾问（Accountability Counsel）

申诉日期：2015 年 1 月 7 日

结案日期：2015 年 2 月 6 日

申诉理由：世界银行提供技术，帮助海地政府起草新的全国矿业法。申诉人提出以下担忧：1）矿业法没有对本地社区和环境给予足够保护；2）政府缺乏执行新法中任何法令的能力；3）海地人民（尤其是可能受矿业直接影响的社区）并未获得关于新法的足够信息且未就其发展被充分咨询。

结案理由：尽管发现这些担忧"重大而合法"，监察组认为对该案件进行复查超出了其职权范围，因为该项目是通过一个银行执行的信托基金进行资助的，而银行的业务政策（包括安保政策）对该信托基金不适用。

在案件尚未进入或者完成申诉过程的实质性处理阶段便结案的理由中，至少有两个值得进一步审视。第一，开发性金融机构和一些独立问责机制狭隘地定义项目范围，可能将那些想要通过申诉质疑这种定义的潜在申诉排除在外。第二，当独立问责机制寻求其自身程序以外的替代性处理过程时，狭隘的项目定义或独立问责机制的自由裁量权为合规审查造成的障碍进一步加大。

4.1.1 定义项目范围

一个开发性金融机构（及其独立问责机制）定义一个给定项目的范围的方式能够决定该机制纠正与项目有关的冤情的能力。几个独立问责机制不允许某些案件进入实质性阶段的一个共同理由是相关开发性金融机构支持的项目与所诉称的行为或损害之间的因果联系不足。独立问责机制对这种逻辑的依赖凸显了如何界定项目范围及如何理解项目影响的重要性。界定项目边界总是包含一个主观判断：项目仅包括那些开发性金融机构直接资助的活动，还是延伸到其他并非由该机构资助但对项目可行性很有必要的活动，或者那些如果开发性金融机构资助项目不存在就不会发生的活动？项目范围是否包括开发性金融机构资助的活动的后果，如果包括，项目负面影响归责有何时间或空间上的限制？如果一个开发性金融机构将预算支持泛泛地提供给全行业的改革或活动（尤其是国家层面的活动），而不一定是根据这些改革采取的行业内的特定活动，回答这些争论激烈的问题①则尤其困难。如果一个开发性金融机构资助的是项目的早期准备阶段（如矿物勘探或大范围的基础设施可行性研究）而不是生产或执行阶段（如矿物开采或水电大坝修建或其他基础设施安装），类似的问题也会出现。

某些独立问责机制似乎比其他独立问责机制更加愿意质疑开发性金融机构对自身项目的定义。在某案例中，合规顾问/巡查官办公室没有接受国际金融公司对其项目范围的狭隘定义。国际金融公司对巴布亚新几内亚特别经济区法律框架的开发提供支持，一项申诉提出了与一个受该框架约束的特别经济区有关的问题。② 国际金融公司表示，所诉称的损害与其项目并没有因果联系，因为该项目并不对单个的特别经济区进行资助。③ 虽然合规顾问/巡查官办公室最终在进行合规审查之前结束了案件，但结案并不是基于国际金融公司的项目定义，而是因为国际金融公司的建议并未被采纳进巴布亚新几内亚的法律框架。这样，合规顾问/巡查官办公室留下了一个问责的可能性，一旦国际金融公司的建议被采纳执行，它就可能为造成的后果负责。

然而，并不是所有的独立问责机制都采取这种方式。在另一个案件中，申诉人诉称，由于社会与环境影响评价不足，欧洲复兴开发银行对一家黄金开采公司（吕底亚国际）的投资可能导致阿穆尔萨金矿开采活动的环境与社会损害。④ 欧洲复兴开发银行坚持认为，该行批准的对该公司的股权投

---

① See, e. g., Alf Jerve, Chairperson, World Bank Inspection Panel, *Defining the boundaries of a project: Where does Bank accountability stop? Lessons from Panel cases and beyond*, *Presentation at World Bank Spring Meetings* (Apr. 18, 2013) (presentation available at ewebapps. worldbank. org/apps/ip/Documents/IPN_ SpringMeetingsAreaofInfluence_ session_ Apr2013. pdf).

② 在进行合规审查的评估之前，申诉进入了合规顾问/巡查官办公室的问题解决阶段，各方达成了协议。因此，根据第2章所描述的方法，案件被视为已经进入实质性阶段，但由于协议并未得以执行，故不被视为案件达成了结果。问题解决失败之后，合规顾问/巡查官办公室对是否进行合规审查作了考量，并最终否决进行合规审查。因此，随着本案确实进入了实质性阶段（争端解决），该项目提供了有关独立问责机制在合规审查之前结束案件的有用说明，因为所称损害与项目之间的因果联系不足。

③ International Finance Corporation, Compliance Advisor/Ombudsman, Papua New Guinea/PNG SEZ-01/Madang Province, http://www. cao-ombudsman. org/cases/case_ detail. aspx? id = 175.

④ European Bank for Reconstruction and Development, Project Complaint Mechanism, DIF Lydian (Amulsar Gold Mine), Request Nos. 2014/03 and 2014/3, http://www. ebrd. com/work-with-us/project-finance/projectcomplaint-mechanism/pcm-register. html.

资仅用于矿物勘探和项目准备，而非矿物开采或生产活动。项目申诉机制接受了这种对项目的狭义界定，认定申诉关注的是矿场的最终潜在影响，但欧洲复兴开发银行并没有承诺对其进行投资，因而申诉没有资格进入合规审查。[①] 这种对项目范围的解释没有考虑矿物勘探和项目准备活动的唯一目的就是为采矿打下基础，也没有考虑到这些活动如果成功将导致一系列与矿物开采有关的环境与社会影响这一事实。

对项目边界进行判定关系到申诉的实质内容，如果不对申诉指控进行应有的考虑或独立问责机制不进行彻底的评估，就无法做出这样的判定。独立问责机制不加质疑地依赖开发性金融机构对项目的描述，这破坏了其在发现开发性金融机构既违背了可行性政策或原则的字面规定，也违背了其内在精神的情况下为申诉人提供救济的能力。而且，对项目进行狭隘界定并因此将潜在收益和负面影响排除在外，开发性金融机构可能不知不觉地限制了自己的有效性。

4.1.2 平衡合规审查与问题解决

过去一年未进入或未完成一个实质性处理阶段即结案的案件的数据反映了申诉人在试图进行完整的合规审查过程中会持续遇到的障碍。正如第2章强调的那样，在128例合格且有结论但未能进入合规审查的申诉中，由于独立问责机制认为不必要或不合适而未启动合规审查的占73.5%。甚至在申诉已经被认为合格后，如果问题解决程序不可用或被证明不成功，或者如果申诉人直接要求进行合规审查，独立问责机制仍然有巨大的自由裁决权决定是否对开发性金融机构遵守其自身政策进行评估。这种自由裁决权被运用的方式有可能不清晰且不可预测。

在某些兼具问题解决和合规审查功能的机制中（如合规顾问/巡查官办公室），不同机制愿意通过各功能处理的问题的类型存在显著差异。虽然按照独立问责机制程序的规定，同一个申诉能通过问题解决或合规审查功能

---

① 参见中东欧银行监察网络（CEE Bankwatch）和跨国企业研究中心（SOMO）致欧洲复兴开发银行董事会的信（2015年2月24日），http://grievancemechanisms.org/ltronAmulsarfinal.pdf。

中的一种或两种来处理，① 但实践中常常不是这样。某些类型的申诉可能太个别或者太特殊，不能通过旨在解决系统性问题或模式的正式合规调查来处理。但分界线并不总是很清楚。② 比如，在某些案件中，问题解决失败之后，合规顾问/巡查官办公室认为虽然这些问题与国际金融公司资助项目的社会影响有关，但数量或者严重性不足，合规顾问/巡查官办公室因而认定所涉申诉类型不适合进行合规审查。③ 当促使申诉转向独立问责机制的合规功能的原因是客户对参与纠纷解决心存抵触或对合规审查更加偏好，结果就令申诉人尤其不安——只是到那时申诉才被终结而不进行完整的调查。④ 在这样的案件中，申诉人不会得到独立问责机制或开发性金融机构对所诉冤屈的任何有意义回应。在其他情形中，独立问责机制对替代性程序或其标准化程序赋予的自由裁决权的运用阻断了合规审查的发生但同时又没有

---

① See, e. g. , European Inv. Bank, *The EIB Complaints Mechanism-Principle*, *Terms of Reference and Rules of Procedures* (Oct. 2012) , http://www. eib. org/attachments/strategies/complaints_ mechanism_ policy_ en. pdf; European Bank for Reconstruction and Dev. , *Approval of New Governance Policies*, http://www. ebrd. com/whatwe-do/strategies-and-policies/approval-of-new-governance-policies. html (linking to the 2014 updates of the Environmental and Social Policy, Public Information Policy, and PCM Rules of Procedure) ; Dutch Development Bank [FMO], *Independent Complaint Mechanisms* (2013) , https://www. fmo. nl/l/en/library/download/urn: uuid: e15d0940 − 2f57 − 4dd8 − be94 − cfe11101218a/independent + complaints + mechanism + fmo. pdf? format = save_ to_ disk&ext = . pdf; German Development Bank [DEG], *Independent Complaints Mechanism* (2013) , https://www. deginvest. de/DEG-Documents-in-English/About-DEG/Responsibility/DEG_ Complaints-Mechanism_ 2014_ 05. pdf.

② It is not clear, for example, what the CAO means by "substantial concerns" or "systemic importance," in the following oft-repeated phrases: "complaints⋯indicative of substantial concerns regarding the environmental and social outcomes of the project or issues of systemic importance for IFC such that would merit a compliance investigation. " IFC Compliance Advisor/Ombudsman, *Compliance Appraisal*: *Summary of Results*, *Yanacocha*, *Complaints 04 − 07* (May 29, 2015) , http://www. cao-ombudsman. org/cases/document-links/documents/CAOAppraisalofYanacocha_ May292015_ forweb_000. pdf (emphasis added) .

③ See, e. g. , IFC Compliance Advisor/Ombudsman, *Compliance Appraisal Report*: *Appraisal of IFC investment in Harmon Hall*, *Mexico* (Apr. 8, 2015) , http://www. cao-ombudsman. org/cases/document-links/documents/CAOCompliance_ AppraisalReport_ Mexico_ HarmonHall02 − 06and08_ Apr082015. pdf.

④ See, e. g. , *CAO Cases*, *Chile: Hidromaule-01/San Clemente*, http://www. cao-ombudsman. org/cases/case_ detail. aspx? id = 226; IFC Compliance Advisor/Ombudsman, *Compliance Appraisal*: *Summary of Results*, *IFC Investment in Hidromaule*, *Chile* (June 22, 2015) , http://www. cao-ombudsman. org/cases/document-links/documents/CAOCompliance_ AppraisalReport_ Chile_ Hidromaule-01_06222015_ forweb. pdf.

足够的问题解决手段。比如，世界银行监察组运用其新的"早期解决方案"（或"试点计划"）处理了两个申诉。① 在另一件去年结案的申诉中，监察组对其标准程序进行了有争议的解释，首先，在世界银行管理层试图处理申诉人提出的问题时监察组暂缓对申诉进行考量；然后监察组在判定管理层的行动充分解决了申诉的实质问题后，做出了与其调查发现相反的建议。这些程序的使用对机制对于申诉人的可预测性造成威胁，尤其是在不清楚它们将如何应用的情况下。

申诉人有权选择问题解决作为合规审查的替代方案或者作为处理其冤屈的第一步。事实上，引导申诉进入调解或其他协商纠纷解决方式作为第一步可能被证实是有效防止或减少损害的途径。但监察组的早期解决方案中采取的方式算不上是调解或问题解决。这一试点计划缺乏程序性的保障来应对申诉人和银行管理层及其他项目方之间的权力失衡。比如，由于缺乏调解人员或其他任何调解所具有的保护和制衡功能，该计划并不算是正式的问题解决程序，它并不能很好地确保申诉人有意义地参与设计和落实解决其冤屈的措施。

独立问责机制功能的适用顺序可能会影响申诉从一个阶段进入另一阶段的能力或一个甚至两个阶段的处理结果。申诉人应被允许选择其希望首先使用的功能（问题解决或合规审查），或同时选择两个功能。对话和协商纠纷解决的效能在很大程度上取决于申诉人对其权利的了解和主张权利的能力。有时候，申诉人对独立问责机制合规审查过程中信息和分析的获取可能有助于矫正申诉人与开发性金融机构及其客户之间的力量失衡。另一些情况下，问题解决阶段的实质内容和过程（包括成功与失败）事实上可能暴露出需要通过合规审查进行审视的问题。

至少，无论申诉被审查的顺序如何，独立问责机制应当确保问题解决的结果不会比开发性金融机构环境与社会标准所要求的更加不具有保护力。

---

① World Bank Inspection Panel, *Paraguay: Sustainable Agriculture and Rural Development Project*, http://ewebapps. worldbank. org/apps/ip/Pages/ViewCase. aspx? CaseId = 100; World Bank Inspection Panel, *Nigeria: Lagos Metropolitan Development and Government Project*, http://ewebapps. worldbank. org/apps/ip/Pages/ViewCase. aspx? CaseId = 94.

4.2 幸运的少数：有结果的案例

2014 年 7 月 1 日至 2015 年 6 月 30 日一年间，12 个案件达成了处理结果：国际金融公司合规顾问/巡查官办公室 5 件，世界银行监察组 3 件，亚洲开发银行问责机制 1 件，日本国际协力机构指导原则检查官 1 件，荷兰开发银行和德国投资与开发有限公司的独立申诉机制 1 件，美国海外私人投资公司问责办公室 1 件。[①] 欧洲投资银行的申诉机制的 1 件也包括在内，因为申诉机制的公开案件登记最初提供的信息显示该案件已经达成了结果，但此后案件登记进行了更新，明确该案件没有达成任何结果。作者无法与申诉人取得联系，且考虑到一些现实的因素，我们无法对所有 12 个案件进行研究。接下来的章节对 7 个案件进行案例分析，在这些案件中，作者得以运用附件 4 列出的问题对申诉人进行访谈。

4.2.1 案例分析 1 申诉机制：乌干达新森林公司

这个案件最初被纳入本报告的原因是，报告草案撰写期间，欧洲投资银行的网站显示这个案件于 2014 年 11 月 20 日结案并且已经达成了调解解决方案。[②] 但是，如下文将要详细讨论的那样，申诉机制在其后发布了这个案件额外的公开信息，明确申诉机制从来没有进行过调解，也没有完成合规审查。相反，申诉由合规顾问/巡查官办公室处理。这个申诉的最后一个纠纷解决过程结束于 2014 年 5 月，不在本研究范围之内。不过，仍然在此进行简要背景介绍。

2004 年，新森林公司（NFC），一家伦敦的木材公司，与乌干达政府进行谈判，在乌干达建立木材种植园。新森林公司这个拟建项目的投资者包

[①] 美国海外私人投资公司问责办公室关于海外私人投资公司对布坎南生物可再生能源项目（Buchanan Renewables Biomass）投资的案件。问责办公室收到受该投资影响社区的申诉，由于该项目已经结束，申诉不予受理。美国海外私人投资公司管理层要求问责办公室对该项目进行独立审查。更多信息，参见 http://www.opic.gov/who-we-are/office-of-accountability/buchananrenewables。

[②] 欧洲投资银行申诉机制，新森林公司森林项目，乌干达，参见 http://www.eib.org/about/accountability/complaints/cases/nfc-forestry-project.htm。

括商业银行汇丰银行以及欧洲投资银行和国际金融公司投资的一个叫作农业竞争（Agri-Vie）农业基金的私募基金。乌干达政府为新森林公司颁发了开发位于乌干达中部的穆本德（Mubende）和基博加（Kiboga）区及东部的布吉里区的总面积约 2 万公顷的三个木材种植园的许可证。截至 2011 年，新森林公司已经在 9300 公顷土地上种植了约 1200 万棵松树和桉树，雇用劳工超过 1400 人。然而，种植园的建立导致穆本德和基博加地区总共 22500 多人被强制搬迁。①

就在本报告发送媒体之际，申诉机制公布了其 2014 年 11 月做出的该项目的《结论报告》，②详细介绍了其参与本案的情况。2011 年 10 月，作为对乐施会对这些强制搬迁的一份报告的回应，③欧洲投资银行行长要求申诉机制调查该指控。申诉机制在一个星期后暂停调查，称"等待不同的调查和调解程序的结果"，包括由合规顾问/巡查官办公室促成的调解的结果。④然而，直到申诉机制暂停其调查一个月后，合规顾问/巡查官办公室才收到关于新森林公司在穆本德和基博加地区的活动的申诉。合规顾问/巡查官办公室接受了这些申诉，虽然最初其考虑与欧洲投资银行整合资源来进行处理，但调解程序自始至终都没有申诉机制的正式参与。合规顾问/巡查官办公室的调解程序分别于 2013 年 7 月和 2014 年 5 月就穆本德和基博加地区的申诉达成了最终协议。协议包括了社区与新森林公司分别向合规顾问/巡查官办公室提交的申诉中提出的问题的"完全的和最终的解决方案"。⑤根据协议，新森林公司同意支持寻找一个本地的合作社并"与该合作社及其成员紧密合作以建立与社区之间更加坚实和持久的互惠关系"。⑥目前，合规顾问/巡

---

① 更多信息，参见乐施会国际，新森林公司及其乌干达种植园：乐施会案例研究（2011 年 9 月），http://www.oxfam.org/en/research/new-forests-companyand-its-uganda-plantations-oxfam-case-study。

② 欧洲投资银行申诉机制，新森林公司森林项目，申诉 MC/E/2011/13，《结论报告》（2014 年 11 月 20 日），见 http://bit.ly/2OROgh0（下称欧洲投资银行申诉机制，新森林公司森林项目结论报告）。

③ 乐施会国际，新森林公司以及乌干达种植园：乐施会案例研究，见第 55 页脚注①。

④ 欧洲投资银行申诉机制，新森林公司森林项目总结报告，见第 54 页脚注②。

⑤ CAO Cases, Uganda/Agri-Vie Fund-02/Mubende, http://www.cao-ombudsman.org/cases/case_detail.aspx?id=181.

⑥ CAO Cases, Uganda/Agra-Vie Fund-01/Kiboga, http://www.cao-ombudsman.org/cases/case_detail.aspx?id=180; CAO Cases, Uganda/Agri-Vie Fund-02/Mubende.

查官办公室正在对协议四年之内的执行情况进行监督，确保"顺利执行、可持续发展和成功"。[①]

合规顾问/巡查官办公室调解程序有了结论之后，申诉机制认为没有必要进行完整的调查并就此结案。[②] 根据申诉机制网站的信息，2015 年 11 月 20 日会有后续行动。[③] 申诉提起时有效的合规顾问/巡查官办公室《操作指南》排除了调解程序成功做出结论之后仍进行合规审查的可能性。因此，不会再有独立问责机制对本案进行调查以判定贷款人是否遵守了相关环境与社会标准，不会有贷款人会努力对社区受到的损害进行补救，也不会有任何一方从中吸取教训以改进往后的项目。

4.2.2 案例分析 2 合规顾问/巡查官办公室：哥伦比亚美洲大陆航空公司（哥伦比亚航空公司）

背景 哥伦比亚航空公司是拉丁美洲最大的商业航空公司之一，以哥伦比亚波哥大埃尔多拉多国际机场为中心运营。2009 年，国际金融公司为哥伦比亚航空公司及其子公司提供 5000 万美元公司贷款，为其实施更新机队的计划提供便利。贷款的目标是缩减成本、提高效率及安全性、更好的乘客服务。

申诉 2011 年 11 月，国际工会联盟（ITUC）/全球工会组织华盛顿办公室与国际运输工人联盟（ITF）共同提起了一项申诉。申诉反映了与国际运输工人联盟哥伦比亚分部［代表哥伦比亚航空公司工人的全国航空公司工人工会（Asociacion ColombianaDe Auxiliares De Vuelo，ACAV）与全国民航工会（Asociacion Colombiana De Aviadores Civiles，ACDAC）］进行的磋商。[④] 申诉人提出了哥伦比亚航空公司侵犯劳工权益及与自由结社权有关的

---

① CAO Cases, Uganda/Agra-Vie Fund-01/Kiboga; CAO Cases, Uganda/Agri-Vie Fund-02/Mubende.

② 欧洲投资银行申诉机制，新森林公司森林项目结论报告，第 6 页。

③ 欧洲投资银行申诉机制，新森林公司森项目，乌干达。

④ 写给国际金融公司合规顾问/巡查官的关于哥伦比亚航空公司的申诉信（2011 年 11 月 14 日），参见 http://www.cao-ombudsman.org/cases/document-links/documents/Avincacomplaint 111411 web.pdf。

侵权行为等问题。首先，哥伦比亚航空公司违反《国际金融公司社会和环境可持续性政策及绩效标准》标准 2（以下简称"标准 2"）（PS2）劳工与工作条件，尤其是通过歧视工会成员和采取各种措施对工会成员进行打击。第二，国际金融公司在项目周期的各个阶段都没能就客户遵守"标准 2"的问题进行恰当的管理。第三，国际金融公司或其客户未能按照"标准 2"及《信息获取政策》要求公布相关文件。最后一项指控是国际金融公司未能对中美洲航空（TACA）在与哥伦比亚航空公司合并之后遵守"标准 2"的情况进行严格评估。①

结果 评估过程中，本地工会表达他们愿意参与由合规顾问/巡查官办公室召集的讨论，并采纳与哥伦比亚航空公司解决纠纷的程序。然而，哥伦比亚航空公司并不愿意参与，因为其认为工会并没有穷尽所有内部沟通渠道。结果，案件转到合规顾问/巡查官办公室进行合规审查。合规顾问/巡查官办公室合规调查于 2015 年 5 月 18 日公布，这已是申诉提交近四年后及合规顾问/巡查官办公室审议认为有必要进行调查两年后。② 调查就国际金融公司对哥伦比亚航空公司处理尊重雇员结社自由问题的严重不足提出了尖锐批评。本报告认为，根据国际金融公司在哥伦比亚航空公司贷款审批前已从哥伦比亚工会及国际劳工组织获得的信息，其不应该于 2009 年发放贷款。③ 合规顾问/巡查官办公室还批评国际金融公司未能要求哥伦比亚航空公司公布其行动计划及关于其遵守国际金融公司劳工标准义务的评估，这违反了国际金融公司 2006 年《环境与社会可持续发展政策》。作为对本报告的回应，合规顾问/巡查官办公室将对国际金融公司的行动进行监督，并且希望在本报告出版一年内公布一份监督报告。④

---

① 国际金融公司合规顾问/巡查官办公室，国际金融公司对哥伦比亚航空公司审计的合规性评估：全球工会组织（Global Unions）代表哥伦比亚航空公司雇员于 1 月份提交的申诉案件（2013 年 1 月 8 日），见 http://bit.ly/2LZniX0。

② 国际金融公司合规顾问/巡查官办公室，合规顾问/巡查官办公室调查国际金融公司对哥伦比亚航空公司的投资（2015 年 5 月 18 日），见 http://bit.ly/2AFaTCZ。

③ 新闻稿，国际工会联盟－国际运输工人联盟（ITUC-ITF），哥伦比亚航空公司：国际金融公司应该遵循巡查官关于劳工标准合规的建议（2015 年 5 月 19 日）（http://www.ituc-csi.org/avianca-colombia-ifc-should-follow？lang＝es）（下称国际工会联盟－国际运输工人联盟哥伦比亚航空公司新闻稿）。

④ 同上。

结果满意度① 总的来说，申诉人对合规顾问/巡查官办公室合规审查表示满意，但对国际金融司对审查的回应并不满意。申诉人认为，合规顾问/巡查官办公室在 2015 年 5 月 18 日公布的调查报告"做得很好，资料翔实且进行了很好的研究"，他们"对调查发现和事实方面的文献记载非常满意，这些发现和文献记载确认了 2011 年提交的申诉中提到的问题中的 95%"。② 申诉人尤其对其中一个发现感到欣慰：合规顾问/巡查官办公室发现国际金融公司 2009 年 7 月做出向客户发放 3500 万美元贷款的决定没有足够的基础，不符合 2006 年《环境与社会可持续发展政策》关于"国际金融公司不资助不能期待在合理期限内达到"标准 2"的新的商业活动"的要求。他们相信，如果国际金融公司认真严肃对待这一发现，可能能够防止未来类似的违规行为。在哥伦比亚航空公司案件中，对申诉人来说很清楚的是，"公司收钱的那一刻，其态度是，满足"标准 2"并不会有什么不同"。③ 在其最近的一次公开声明中，国际工会联盟秘书长夏兰·巴洛（Sharan Burrow）表示："很明显，哥伦比亚航空公司收到国际金融公司贷款后就不再认真对待"标准 2"并且认为合规只是出于自愿。"④

申诉人对合规顾问/巡查官办公室调查报告的满意程度与他们对国际金融公司就报告做出的回应的看法截然不同，他们认为国际金融公司的回应非常软弱且令人很不满意。国际工会联盟华盛顿办公室主任彼得·巴克维斯（Peter Bakvis）表示，项目在工人权利方面没有做出重大的改变："文件资料记录的该公司在申诉提出时的那些做法今天仍在继续，工人权利仍然没有得到尊重。"⑤ 而且，申诉人在 6 月初致函世界银行行长金墉要求其对合规顾问/巡查官办公室的调查发现做出处理。但截至本报告访谈时，他们并没有收到世界银行的任何回复。提出申诉之后，申诉人看到的主要变化是哥伦比亚航空公司在 2013 年偿还了全部贷款，这甚至早于贷款到期日。因此，尽管现在有合规顾问/巡查官办公室调查报告中的这些发现，国际金

---

① 该评估是基于 2015 年 6 月 29 日与国际工会联盟/全球工会组织华盛顿办公室主任彼得·巴克维斯的电话访谈。彼得·巴克维斯表示，他代表其中一家机构提交的申诉不希望匿名，并同意记录访谈内容。与彼得·巴克维斯的采访记录（西班牙语）将在磋商时提供。
② 同上。
③ 同上。
④ 国际工会联盟－国际运输工人联盟，哥伦比亚航空公司新闻稿。
⑤ 与彼得·巴克维斯的电话访谈。

融公司也已经没有能力通过金融措施来促使哥伦比亚航空公司对其实践做法进行修正。

当被问到是否会建议其他人使用合规顾问/巡查官办公室，国际工会联盟华盛顿办公室主任巴克维斯回应说他会这样做，"但考虑到合规顾问/巡查官办公室的局限性、其修正客户行为能力的缺乏以及整个过程的漫长耗时，所以仅将建议作为最后救济手段"。总之，他们会建议使用这一机制获取资料翔实而且研究透彻的调查，但并不一定以此来解决当前具体问题。

过程满意度　总的来说，申诉人对申诉处理过程满意，即使许多的拖延令人沮丧并且处理过程给申诉人带来了更多的压力。

关于机制的可及性，申诉人强调说："合规顾问/巡查官办公室网站上的可用信息对提起申诉的过程解释得很清楚。"[①]　而且，他们感觉提起申诉的过程并不困难，在整个过程中他们也得到了合规顾问/巡查官办公室工作人员的支持。他们被告知申诉所需资料和其他相关信息。申诉人并没有在语言或者成本上遇到障碍。但是，申诉人感觉申诉处理过程使哥伦比亚航空公司工作人员本就已经承受的来自公司方面的压力更为沉重。[②]　关于合法性，申诉人感觉合规顾问/巡查官办公室尽了最大努力来很好地处理申诉。在他们的经验中，该机制具有建设性的态度。因此，总的来说这一过程是公平的。他们唯一认为不公平的地方是每一个阶段的不断拖延。申诉人反复表示，拖延带来了极大的困扰，但他们能与合规顾问/巡查官办公室分享对这一问题的意见。另外，前一版本的合规顾问/巡查官办公室《操作指南》中，案件必须首先经过合规顾问/巡查官办公室的规定被认为是对申诉人不必要的拖延和"浪费时间"[③]，因为公司从一开始就排斥对问题进行解决。

关于可预测性，申诉人在提交申诉前就充分意识到"这一过程不会很快，也不会导致贷款取消"。[④]　合规顾问/巡查官办公室向参与申诉的工会解

①　该评估是基于2015年6月29日与国际工会联盟/全球工会组织华盛顿办公室主任彼得·巴克维斯的电话访谈。彼得·巴克维斯表示，他代表其中一家机构提交的申诉不希望匿名，并同意记录访谈内容。与彼得·巴克维斯的采访记录（西班牙语）将在磋商时提供。
②　同上。
③　同上。
④　同上。

释了其局限并且提醒他们，这一过程可能不会解决与他们争取结社自由的目的有关的问题。[①]

关于公平性，申诉人对合规顾问/巡查官办公室的工作表示满意，因为提交申诉的要求解释得非常清楚。他们感觉得到了信息和建议方面的支持，这使他们能够充分理解整个过程及目标。最后，申诉人明确表达了透明度方面的一些困扰及处理过程中信息的缺乏。比如，"合规顾问/巡查官办公室向他们正式告知，在决定做出后的几个月内不会展开纠纷解决程序"。[②] 另外，彼得·巴克维斯表示，2014 年 8 月，一些合规顾问/巡查官办公室人员告诉他，合规顾问/巡查官办公室的最终调查报告已经做出，但到 2015 年 5 月合规顾问/巡查官办公室才最终公布这份报告，他们等了 9 个月。[③] 据彼得·巴克维斯称，一直到他与合规顾问/巡查官办公室副主席进行了一次私人会面并提出要求，合规顾问/巡查官办公室才公布了报告。[④] 申诉人还提到，对于合规顾问/巡查官办公室无法与申诉人分享的信息，合规顾问/巡查官办公室是知情的。[⑤] 总的来说，申诉人称，当申诉处理过程中出现特别的困难障碍或拖延时，合规顾问/巡查官办公室会进行告知，但这种告知并不是积极主动进行的。[⑥] 而且，仍然有一些信息并未上网公开。

由于国际金融公司未对合规顾问/巡查官办公室的调查发现进行回应，合规顾问/巡查官办公室的处理过程并未给申诉人带来权利兼容的救济。如前所述，申诉人认为"在作为申诉基础的工人权利方面并没有重大的改变或结果：申诉提出时公司有文献记录的做法今天仍在持续，而工人的权利仍旧没有得到尊重"，[⑦] 尤其是工人仍然没有结社自由。

国际金融公司的说法是它们已经从这个案件中吸取了教训。在其对

[①] 该评估是基于 2015 年 6 月 29 日与国际工会联盟/全球工会组织华盛顿办公室主任彼得·巴克维斯的电话访谈。彼得·巴克维斯表示，他代表其中一家机构提交的申诉不希望匿名，并同意记录访谈内容。与彼得·巴克维斯的采访记录（西班牙语）将在磋商时提供。

[②] 同上。

[③] 同上。

[④] 同上。

[⑤] 同上。

[⑥] 同上。

[⑦] 同上。

《合规顾问/巡查官办公室合规调查报告》进行回应时，① 国际金融公司称：

"国际金融公司对哥伦比亚航空公司投资八年来，已经采取了一些步骤强化我们在劳工问题上的做法，包括对环境与社会（E&S）专门人员进行与劳工相关的风险评估与管理能力的建设和训练、开发管理劳工问题的内部和外部指南、依靠独立国际劳工专家的支持及与全球劳工联盟进行定期交流。通过发布《2012 信息获取政策》，国际金融公司在信息公开方面的实践得到了改善。我们仍然致力于持续不断的学习和环境与社会风险管理实践的改进。国际金融公司在关注自身投资以外的国别和行业风险的重要性方面认同合规顾问/巡查官办公室的观察。正如国际金融公司管理层最近的其他一些回应中传递的那样，我们已经做出了程序和组织上的改变以在这方面进行改进。"②

然而，并没有任何制度来检查国际金融公司发布的有关其加强了对劳工问题的关注的声明。跟进追踪的唯一办法是下一个关于劳工问题向合规顾问/巡查官办公室申诉之后，我们才能看到实效。

4.2.3　案例分析 3　合规顾问/巡查官办公室：洪都拉斯金融商业银行（Ficohsa）

背景　洪都拉斯金融商业银行是洪都拉斯第三大银行和中美洲最重要的银行之一。2008 年国际金融公司对洪都拉斯金融商业银行进行了支持贸易融资、为住房及中小型企业（SMEs）贷款的投资；2011 年 5 月，董事会批准了一项对洪都拉斯金融商业银行的股权投资（3200 万美元）和次级债务投资（3800 万美元）。进行股权投资之前，国际金融公司已经确认洪都拉斯金融商业银行对具有重大的环境与社会（E&S）潜在风险的行业提供企业融资，如能源、建筑和农业。洪都拉斯金融商业银行与迪南公司（Corporación Dinant）之间的关系引发了合规顾问/巡查官办公室对国际金融公司对洪都拉斯金融商业银行投资的关切。迪南公司（迪南）是一家在洪

---

① IFC Response to CAO Compliance Investigation Report in respect of IFC's Investment in Avianca, Colombia（May 5, 2015）, http://www.cao-ombudsman.org/cases/document-links/documents/Avianca IFCPublicResponse InvReport May52015.pdf.

② 同上。

都拉斯北部拥有总面积超过 2 万公顷种植园的综合性的棕榈油与食品公司。2009 年，国际金融公司为迪南提供了 3000 万美元贷款，其中 1500 万美元于 2009 年 11 月已经发放。第二笔 1500 万款项的发放由于迪南自 2010 年中期在阿关谷（Aguán Valley）的植物园的安全与冲突问题受到关注而拖延。①

申诉　2012 年，合规顾问/巡查官办公室副主席发动了对国际金融公司在迪南投资的合规调查。② 这是合规顾问/巡查官办公室对迪南在阿关谷（洪都拉斯）的种植园及其周边针对农民的暴力行径的指控所做的回应，而这些暴力是迪南对所控制或影响的私人和公共保安力量的不当使用造成的。调查发现国际金融公司的风险评估及其环境与社会政策执行中存在重大失败——合规顾问/巡查官办公室意识到迪南是洪都拉斯金融商业银行最大借款人之一。鉴于此，国际金融公司通过对洪都拉斯金融商业银行的股权投资对迪南有重大影响。因此，合规顾问/巡查官办公室副主席启动了对国际金融公司在洪都拉斯金融商业银行投资的合规评估。2013 年 12 月发布的评估报告中，③ 合规顾问/巡查官办公室认为国际金融公司在洪都拉斯金融商业银行投资的环境与社会表现需要接受进一步调查，于是启动了合规调查。

结果　合规顾问/巡查官办公室调查的重点在于国际金融公司的表现，因此没有涉及洪都拉斯金融商业银行的作为与不作为。调查于 2014 年 6 月 13 日完成，合规顾问/巡查官办公室向国际金融公司提交报告要求其正式回应。在合规顾问/巡查官办公室主席的许可下，最终调查报告和国际金融公司的回应由合规顾问/巡查官办公室于 2014 年 8 月 11 日对外公布。④ 报告描述了国际金融公司在履行与洪都拉斯金融商业银行投资有关的环境与社会义务方面存在的重大缺陷。

报告批评国际金融公司未经适当审查即对洪都拉斯金融商业银行进

① IFC Compliance Advisor/Ombudsman, *CAO Investigation of IFC Environmental and Social Performance in relation to Investments in Banco Financiera Comercial Hondurena S. A.*（Ficohsa）（Aug. 6, 2014）, http://www. cao-ombudsman. org/cases/document-links/documents/CAOInvestigationofIFCRegardingFicohsa_C-I-R9-Y13-F190. pdf［hereinafter CAO Compliance Investigation Report - Ficohsa］.

② See CAO Cases, Honduras/Dinant-01/CAO Vice President Request, http://www. cao-ombudsman. org/cases/case_detail. aspx? id = 188.

③ 合规顾问/巡查官办公室，《合规顾问/巡查官办公室对国际金融公司对洪都拉斯金融商业银行投资的合规情况评估》（2013 年 12 月 4 日），见 http://bit. ly/2LOJfsm。

④ 合规顾问办公室合规调查报告——洪都拉斯金融商业银行。

行投资,因为合规顾问/巡查官办公室早前针对迪南的调查发现意味着国际金融公司再一次与一个被控煽动土地冲突和暴力的公司产生关联。洪都拉斯金融商业银行贷款甚至是在国际金融公司知道迪南贷款存在的问题之后通过审批。迪南公司不仅是贷款发生时洪都拉斯金融商业银行的第三大客户,合规顾问/巡查官办公室还注意到,2012 年洪都拉斯金融商业银行提到,其与 64 个 A 级客户——具有很高的导致负面环境与社会影响风险的客户——存在融资关系。其中,仅 48% 的客户遵守了其环境与社会政策。合规顾问/巡查官办公室发现,尽管这样,国际金融公司并没有确定其客户应当采取的消减风险的措施,这是其履行尽职调查义务的严重失败。

合规顾问/巡查官办公室的调查报告还指出:"通过查阅媒体上的可用信息,合规顾问/巡查官办公室发现了一些有关环境与社会问题的报告,与洪都拉斯金融商业银行在农业、旅游业、建筑行业和水电行业的一些客户有关。由于国际金融公司高风险客户的身份信息并不透明,不可能对这些失败的全部影响进行验证。"① 最后,报告确认,合规顾问/巡查官办公室将对国际金融公司回应其调查发现所采取的行动进行监督并在次年出具一份监督报告。②

结果满意度 如前所述,合规顾问/巡查官办公室对国际金融公司对洪都拉斯金融商业银行的投资的调查并非由受影响社区申诉而引发,而是由合规顾问/巡查官办公室副主席启动。在这个问题上表现活跃的组织之一阿关谷区域农业平台(the Plataforma Agraria Regional del Valledel Aguán)已就此案与合规顾问/巡查官办公室和国际金融公司进行了交流接触。关于洪都拉斯金融商业银行和迪南两案,尽管不能提供作为申诉人对处理过程的看法,这些组织可以就结果和它们参与(或没有参与)整个过程发表意见和看法。

---

① Oxfam Int'l, *The Suffering of Others*.

② CAO Communique, *Summary of Key Findings—Compliance Investigation of IFC Environmental and Social Performance in relation to Investments in Banco Financiera Comercial Hondureña S. A.* (Ficohsa) (Aug. 11, 2014) (available at http://www. cao-ombudsman. org/cases/document-links/ documents/CAOCommunique_ Ficohsa_ SummaryofFindings_ August112014. pdf).

用受访者的话来说，[①]"这是一个不寻常的案件，因为有在合规顾问/巡查官办公室副主席要求下进行的审计，但却没有人提起申诉，因此农民运动在这个过程中没有参与的空间。[②] 这就是为什么申诉没有考虑冲突解决阶段而直接进入了合规审查。同样的情况出现在国际金融公司对迪南和洪都拉斯金融商业银行案件的审计做出回应之后的行动计划的阐述中：既没有农民运动的参与空间也没有对农民参与权的确认。这反过来导致2014年向合规顾问/巡查官办公室提出的关于迪南和一个金融中介机构（OLEOPAL-MA）的两件申诉，直接由受影响社区提起"。[③]

关于申诉过程的结果，受访者同意，合规顾问/巡查官办公室参与迪南和洪都拉斯金融商业银行案件最好的结果是其做出的报告。总的来说，受访者认为，虽然有一些限制，这些报告"有助于支持农民运动的主张和要求"[④]。报告还"有助于提高国内和国际媒体及舆论对农民运动状况及阿关谷持续不断侵犯人权的关注"。[⑤] 合规顾问/巡查官办公室的报告作为国际层面的倡导工具也颇有益处。

尽管这样，受访者对"审计之前缺乏正式参与"以及总的来说"合规顾问/巡查官办公室向国际金融公司介绍这些报告之后的进展"并不满意。[⑥] 在这一点上，受访者表示，他们主要的不满与国际金融公司的参与有关："尽管很清楚阿关谷的人权侵犯情况及农民们一直在强调的土地流转方面的违规行为，该机构仍然决定对迪南进行资助，而这一情况恰恰是在合规顾问/巡查官办公室审计之后被发现的。"[⑦]

而且，受访者并不满意国际金融公司对合规顾问/巡查官办公室调查发

---

① Telephone interview with members of the Plataforma Agraria Regional del Valle del Aguán（Aug. 7, 2015）.

② 尽管在这个过程中没有正式的参与空间，被访者确认，合规顾问/巡查官办公室在审计期间曾与他们联系，就案件询问了相关信息，也提供了部分信息。

③ 参见合规顾问/巡查官办公室案件，洪都拉斯/ 迪南 – 03/阿关谷，http://www. caoombuds-man. org/cases/case detail. aspx？id = 223；合规顾问/巡查官办公室案件，洪都拉斯/金融中介（FI）– 01，http://www. cao-ombudsman. org/cases/case detail. aspx？id = 231。尽管被访者对这些案件表达了很多关注和看法，但考虑到本报告的目的，它们都没有被考虑进来。

④ Telephone interview with members of the Plataforma Agraria Regional del Valle del Aguán（Aug. 7, 2015）.

⑤ 同上。

⑥ 同上。

⑦ 同上。

现的回应，也对该机构没有承诺解决这一问题，尤其是更普遍地应对贫困问题表示不满："国际金融公司作为世界银行集团的一部分，正在破坏二战后该机构设立时肩负的使命：对抗贫困。因此，通过对管理土地及加剧农民搬迁的公司进行融资，国际金融公司实际上造成了更多的贫困，而不是与之进行抗争。"①

过程满意度 由于受访者并未作为申诉人参与这一过程，基本不可能进行这方面的评估。

国际金融公司吸取的教训：2014 年 4 月，合规顾问/巡查官办公室做出对国际金融公司向迪南贷款的调查报告之后，作为对来自公民社会和其自身董事会的压力的回应，国际金融公司制订了一份行动计划并聘请华盛顿的共识建设研究所（Consensus Building Institute）来决定是否有可能通过调解来解决政府、迪南和受影响社区之间的冲突。国际金融公司还聘请弗利·霍格律所就与迪南安全行动计划有关的人权问题为其提供意见。迪南本身已经承诺落实《安全与人权自愿原则》（Voluntary Principles on Security and Human Rights）。

2014 年 7 月 14 日，国际金融公司公布其《管理层对合规顾问/巡查官办公室关于洪都拉斯金融商业银行合规调查报告的回应》。② 在这份回应中，国际金融公司管理层认可了合规顾问/巡查官办公室的部分调查发现并提到其从报告中吸取的一系列机构性的教训，其中一部分内容包括：

"总的来说报告正确地指出了以往实践中的不足之处，尤其是国际金融公司在 2011 年对洪都拉斯金融商业银行进行投资之前的评估中存在的缺陷，以及对该银行投资组合中潜在的环境与社会风险缺乏应有的考量。我们当时的实践和程序没有要求我们将金融中介机构客户的主要风险与我们自己的直接投资组合项目进行交叉检查。从那以后，我们已经采取了措施来弥补这些缺陷并促进我们不同部门员工之间更好的信息共享。"

"国际金融公司已经采取了一些措施应对报告发现的许多问题，包括

---

① Telephone interview with members of the Plataforma Agraria Regional del Valle del Aguán (Aug. 7, 2015).

② *IFC Management Response to the CAO Compliance Investigation Report on Banco Financiera Comercial Hondurena S. A. (Ficohsa)* (July 14, 2014), http://www.cao-ombudsman.org/cases/document-links/documents/IFCResponsetoCAOregardingFicohsa_July142014.pdf.

2012 年《可持续发展框架》的更新及在合规顾问/巡查官办公室就国际金融公司对金融中介机构投资进行审计之后制订的行动计划。"

"国际金融公司环境与社会风险管理实践正在不断发展进步，我们努力不断在这方面做出改进。当我们的方式方法存在缺陷，如我们对洪都拉斯金融商业银行的投资涉及的这个案件反映出来的那样，我们一直致力于快速采取行动，从失误中学习，并为未来的探索进行必要的纠正调整。"

"同时，在与洪都拉斯金融商业银行共同努力加强其环境与社会风险管理体系及实践的过程中，我们已经看到了的积极进展。"

4.2.4　案例分析 4　合规顾问/巡查官办公室：乌干达布贾加利能源项目

背景　布贾加利能源项目包括 2007 年至 2012 年间在乌干达东南部的布贾加利瀑布修建一个水坝、水电站和电力传输线。传输线由乌干达的国家传输公司，即乌干达电力传输有限公司（UETCL）承建。国际金融公司对该项目发放 1.3 亿美元贷款，[①] 包括欧洲投资银行和非洲开发银行在内的几个金融机构也对此提供融资及贷款担保。

申诉[②]　2011 年 5 月 16 日，受项目影响的社区成员向合规顾问/巡查官办公室提出申诉，案件称为布贾加利 – 5。[③] 在布贾加利 – 5 申诉中，社区成员称其受到项目主要组成部分的影响，包括土地被传输线占用及爆破带来的

[①] 世行新闻稿，世行批准布贾加利水电开发项目以解决乌干达的能源短缺问题（2007 年 5 月 26 日），见 http://bit. ly/2n9MITL。

[②] The project has resulted in numerous grievances, and since the year 2000, seven complaints related to the project have been filed with the CAO alone. The CAO has given numerical designations to each of these complaints. Compliance Advisor/Ombudsman, CAO Cases, Uganda/Bujagali-02/Bujagali Falls, http://www. cao-ombudsman. org/cases/case_ detail. aspx? id = 114. See also National Association of Professional Environmentalists, *Unsettling Business: Social Consequences of the Bujagali Hydropower Project* 12 （2014）, http://nape. or. ug/wp-content/uploads/Bujagali_ unsettlingbusiness. pdf ［hereinafter "Unsettling Business"］.

[③] Complaint from the Bujagali Affected Community to the CAO （May 10, 2011）, http://www. caoombudsman. org/cases/document-links/documents/2011_ May16Complaint_ redacted. pdf. The Bujagali-5 Complaint is the fifth of seven complaints related to the dam that have been filed with the CAO starting in 2000. It is the second of four complaints filed against BEL, which all remain open. This is the first of two cases that went through the CAO Ombudsman; the other two went through the CAO compliance function.

房屋和健康损害。[1] 申诉还提出了若干与弥补社区所受影响的补偿程度有关的问题。2011 年 6 月，合规顾问/巡查官办公室认定布贾加利-5 申诉符合进入下一步评估的资格，这最终带来了由合规顾问/巡查官办公室主导的调解。

布贾加利-5 申诉之前，约 550 名社区成员于 2008 年将乌干达电力传输有限公司诉至乌干达国家法院，诉称社区未就项目造成的影响得到公平及足够的补偿。这一案件中提到的社区成员仅占数千名（可能为 5000 名[2]）受传输线影响的民众的一小部分。该案件的提起导致社区内部分化为两部分：案件中提到的社区群众（下称"第一组"）和案件中没有提到的社区群众（下称"第二组"）。这在合规顾问/巡查官办公室的调解中成了一个重要的问题，下文将就此展开讨论。

结果 合规顾问/巡查官办公室将布贾加利申诉目前的状态列为"促成问题解决"。[3] 调解的结果是，乌干达电力传输有限公司同意于 2015 年 7 月之前向第一组成员支付款项，每笔款项具体金额根据每个案件的不同情况另行决定。乌干达电力传输有限公司并没有在截止日期前支付款项，但在报告撰写之时，支付程序已经启动。关于处理第二组成员受到的损害的第二个调解程序何时开始，目前尚无官方消息。

结果满意度[4] 值得注意的重要一点是，乌干达电力传输有限公司愿意进行调解本身对于社区来说就是一个重要的里程碑，申诉人将其归功于合规顾问/巡查官办公室的参与。乌干达电力传输有限公司之前未能向社区提供足够的赔偿，之后又拒绝参与有意义的对话。案件在乌干达法院毫无进展，这让社区群众感到走投无路。所以，与乌干达电力传输有限公司新的

---

[1] 参见合规顾问/巡查官办公室，《巡查官评估报告：与布贾加利能源有限公司有关的第 5 例申诉》（布贾加利能源-05）。项目 6-7（2011 年 12 月）。

[2] 参见《扰乱社会的生意》。值得注意的是，布贾加利联网项目中，大约有 5000 人受到输电线路的影响。

[3] 合规顾问/巡查官办公室，合规顾问/巡查官办公室案例，乌干达/布贾加利能源-05/布贾加利，见 http://www.cao-ombudsman.org/cases/document-links/documents/2011 May16Complaint redacted. pdf。

[4] 案例研究基于参与布贾加利申诉的三位社区成员的访谈：汤姆·姆潘利、艾莎·潘德和文森特·潘卡莫儿（统称申诉人），以及国家专业环保主义者协会和帮助申诉人提交申诉的乌干达组织的意见。申诉人不希望匿名。他们说："我们希望公开我们的遭遇，因为我们的土地被抢走了。"另外，我们非常感谢文森特的贡献，但在该案例中没有进行更深入的讨论，因为他们主要关注另一个调解过程。

对话的机会是一个积极的发展。但是，申诉人对合规顾问/巡查官办公室调解的结果并不满意，理由主要有二。第一，他们感觉乌干达电力传输有限公司最终在调解中同意的赔偿额过低。第二，申诉人感觉第二组社区成员被"抛下了"，因为调解仅仅处理了第一组成员的诉求，但这些成员只占受传输线损害总人口的一小部分。

关于双方同意的赔偿，申诉人感觉，虽然乌干达电力传输有限公司同意进行调解，最后社区只能接受其提出的赔偿额，即使他们认为那并不公平。他们认识到，合规顾问/巡查官办公室不能强迫乌干达电力传输有限公司同意支付特定款项，并且感觉除了同意乌干达电力传输有限公司的条件外他们别无选择。对于第二组社区成员被排除在调解程序之外的问题，艾莎和汤姆（两位申诉人）表示不满。正如前面提到的，由于乌干达电力传输有限公司认为未在法院案件中提到的人员不能参与调解，大部分受影响社区成员未能参与调解。艾莎觉得"合规顾问/巡查官办公室抛下了我们"。对于艾莎和第二组社区成员来说，调解结果几乎没有什么意义，因为这一次他们不会得到任何赔偿。如汤姆所言，"我们并不都那么满意，因为还有一些成员可能被弃之不顾，而他们也需要帮助"。

过程满意度 关于可及性，申诉人感觉，一旦他们被告知合规顾问/巡查官办公室的存在，国家专业环保主义者协会（NAPE），一个乌干达民间组织，能够代表他们相对容易地提起申诉。从这个意义上讲，合规顾问/巡查官办公室是可及的。在申诉过程中，申诉人强调了国家专业环保主义者协会协助的重要性。然而，没有任何一位申诉人在国家专业环保主义者协会告知他们之前知道合规顾问/巡查官办公室的存在或提起申诉的可能性。另外，据申诉人所知，汤姆和艾莎都从来没有在项目进行过程中或调解进行过程中被国际金融公司联系过或与其有过会面。

然而，除了提起布贾加利申诉，在乌干达电力传输有限公司的坚持下，艾莎和第二组的其他成员无法进入合规顾问/巡查官办公室的调解过程。① 显然，乌干达电力传输有限公司认为如果社区成员没有参与这个诉讼案件，则意味着他们对最初提供的补偿是满意的，因此他们不能在另一个平台上

---

① 艾莎的确说过，尽管她没有参与调解，但合规顾问/巡查官办公室曾与她有过交流，因此她认为自己也参与了这个过程。

质疑那些赔偿数额。但是，艾莎注意到一个事实，许多社区成员没有出现在该诉讼案件中并不表示他们自己"决定"接受乌干达电力传输有限公司最初提出的赔偿。

最后，合规顾问/巡查官办公室调解仅解决由传输线造成的影响问题。申诉中提到的其他问题，如爆破造成的影响，并未在这一程序中得到处理。申诉人应该会更倾向于所有问题在同一个调解过程中处理。

过程的可预测性对申诉人来说同样是一个复杂的体验过程。如，一开始，合规顾问/巡查官办公室的重点放在第二组社区成员上，因为他们的冤屈合规顾问/巡查官办公室以前没有听说过。合规顾问/巡查官办公室动员第二组社区成员申诉，为他们进行登记并表示将确保其冤屈得到处理。然而，正如前面讨论过的那样，乌干达电力传输有限公司最终拒绝与第二组社区成员谈判。积极的一面是，尽管艾莎是第二组社区成员，她提到，合规顾问/巡查官办公室向她解释其功能职责及社区应当在调解中有什么样的期待，并在调解开始之后为她更新进展情况。

尽管调解没有带来令人满意的结果，汤姆和艾莎似乎都赞同合规顾问/巡查官办公室的合法性。主要原因在于，合规顾问/巡查官办公室参与之前，乌干达电力传输有限公司拒绝重新审议其最初提出的赔偿方案，而法院的案件几乎没有可能改变其立场。合规顾问/巡查官办公室能让乌干达电力传输有限公司坐到谈判桌前，如汤姆所言，"合规顾问/巡查官办公室尽了最大努力使双方会面并进行交谈"。艾莎表示，"合规顾问/巡查官办公室本身已经做得很好了"，而且她相信一旦第一组社区成员的调解结束，合规顾问/巡查官办公室会为第二组社区成员提供帮助。

申诉人关于合规顾问/巡查官办公室透明度的经历同样有好有坏。艾莎提到，合规顾问/巡查官办公室与社区共享信息的制度——包括在社区内部指定联络人——对她是有用的。她说，"他们帮助了我们，因为他们带来了来自调解各方的信息"。而另一方面，艾莎和其他第二组社区成员没有得到消息，不知道解决他们诉求的另一个调解程序何时开始。

关于过程的公平性，汤姆提到，社区代表觉得在调解过程中可以自由表达感受。然而，许多时候乌干达电力传输有限公司代表非常粗鲁并拒绝倾听社区的声音。汤姆也认为合规顾问/巡查官办公室"做了他们能做的"来为调解过程提供便利，而且他们并不一定能够控制乌干达电力传输有限公司的行为。

从 2015 年 8 月起，调解过程的权利兼容性是一个悬而未决的问题。虽然乌干达电力传输有限公司已经同意对第一组成员进行赔偿，最后实际赔偿如何还无法确定。汤姆认为乌干达电力传输有限公司同意的赔偿标准过低。汤姆觉得，经年累月的谈判之后，社区实质上不得不接受乌干达电力传输有限公司决定给予的赔偿额。另外，占受影响民众大多数的第二组成员不会从调解中得到任何赔偿。

将吸取到的教训融入调解过程并没有被优先考虑。汤姆提到，由于调解仅仅带来对已经发生的损害的赔偿，该公司将来可能会再次违规。

总之，对申诉人的访谈清楚显示，合规顾问/巡查官办公室调解的过程极其复杂。对于社区成员来说，乌干达电力传输有限公司能够同意进行谈判似乎已经是合规顾问/巡查官办公室参与的最大好处了。然而，那些谈判并没有带来申诉人希望得到的赔偿标准。而且，这些谈判仅仅解决布贾加利–5 申诉所代表的社区群众中的一小部分诉求。由于合规顾问/巡查官办公室并不一定在调解过程或谈判结果方面对各方行为具有控制力，本案例分析充分显示，试图让公司同意对社区成员因大型开发项目受到的损害进行赔偿这一举动本身就具有内在困难。

4.2.5 案例分析 5 独立申诉机制：巴拿马巴罗·布兰科水电项目

背景 2011 年 8 月，荷兰开发银行和德国投资与开发有限公司（FMO 和 DEG）各为南美伊斯特莫电力公司（GENISA）提供 2500 万美元，供其在巴拿马西部奇里基省的塔巴萨拉河修建巴罗·布兰科水坝。[1] 这个项目引发争议并在国内外受到关注。[2] 2015 年 2 月，巴拿马政府暂停了水坝的修

---

[1] FMO-DEG Independent Complaints Mechanism, *Panel Report No. 1: Barro Blanco Hydroelectric Project-Panama* 8（May 29, 2015），https://www. fmo. nl/l/en/library/download/urn: uuid: 963b97fd – 6f82 – 473d – b323 – 128a995130f5/150529_ barro + blanco + final + report + rev. pdf? format = save_ to_ disk&ext = . pdf［hereinafter ICM Barro Blanco Report］.

[2] See generally, United Nations Development Programme, *Presentan resultados del peritaje independiente al proyecto hidroeléctrico Barro Blanco*（Sept. 6, 2013），http://www. pa. undp. org/content/ panama/es/home/presscenter/articles/2013/09/06/presentan-resultados-del-peritajeindependiente-al-proyecto-hidroelectrico-barro-blanco-. html; James Anaya, *Declaración del Relator Especial sobre los derechos de los pueblos indígenas al concluir su visita oficial a Panamá*（July 26, 2013）http:// unsr. jamesanaya. org/statements/declaracion-del-relator-especial-sobrelos-derechos-de-los-pueblos-indigenas-al-concluir-su-visita-oficial-a-panama.

建，因为其认定项目未遵守项目自身的环评。① 贷款协议签订时，荷兰开发银行和德国投资与开发有限公司都没有独立问责机制。2014 年 1 月，它们共同设立了独立申诉机制。②

申诉 水坝一旦建成，将淹没 6.7 公顷恩各白·布各来原住民领地（被称为特区）的土地，这一领地于 1997 年依法得以确立。申诉由代表恩各白·布各来民众的最高民选官员加西卡将军和代表将受到水坝最直接影响的民众的草根组织"四月十号"行动（M-10）共同提起。申诉人要求进行合规审查。这是独立申诉机制处理的首例申诉。

申诉控诉，项目对环境及恩各白·布各来民众权利造成一系列影响。首要的是，申诉人声称，既没有人与他们就项目进行磋商，恩各白·布各来民众也没有按照创立特区的法律规定的程序自由、事前、知情地同意该项目。即将被淹没的地区是 6 个大家庭的家园，每个家庭有 40 到 50 个成员，而他们将全部搬迁。然而，这很可能仍然低估了受失地之害的人数。联合国开发计划署（UNDP）就水坝影响进行了一系列研究，发现由于恩各白·布各来民众内部的凝聚力，"在资源获取和利用方面的负面影响将不仅涉及那些土地被淹没的家庭，还将直接或间接涉及所有三个社区（Quebrada Caña，Kiad，和 Nuevo Palomar）的居民"。③

项目对恩各白·布各来自然资源和文化遗产的影响也需要征得民众同

---

① Press Release，*SOMO Human Rights and Grievance Mechanism Programme*，*Panama Suspends Construction of FMO-funded Barro Blanco hydroelectric dam over environmental and human rights abuses*（available at http://grievancemechanisms. org/news/panama-suspends-construction-offmo-funded-barro-blanco-hydroelectric-dam-over-environmental-and-human-rights-abuses）. See also Panama National Environmental Authority（ANAM），Order to Suspend Dam Construction（available at http://miambiente. gob. pa/index. php/homepage/ultimas-noticias/otrasnoticias/959-anam-ordena-paralizacion-de-obras-del-proyecto-hidroelectrico-barro-blanco-porincumplimientos-de-eia）.

② For more information on ICM，see DEG/FMO Independent Complaints Mechanism，*Annual Report*：*First Panel Report January* 2014 - 2015（Aug. 6，2015），https://www. fmo. nl/l/en/library/download/urn：uuid：a202083c - a943 - 47b3 - ab16 - 8375dc68885c/icm + annual + report + 2014 + - + hy + 2015. pdf? format = save_ to_ disk&ext = . pdf. For a CSO perspective on its establishment，see Press Release，*SOMO Human Rights and Grievance Mechanisms*，*Dutch development bank FMO now has a grievance mechanism*，（available at http://grievancemechanisms. org/news/dutchdevelopment-bank-fmo-now-has-a-non-judicial-grievance-mechanism）.

③ United Nations Development Programme，*Peritaje Al Proyecto Hidroelectrico Barro Blanco*，at 15（Sept. 2，2013），available at http://www. pa. undp. org/content/dam/panama/docs/documentos/undp_ pa_ barro_ blanco_ aspectos_ ecologicos. pdf.

意。那里第一个也是唯一一个教授恩各白·布各来语的学校正位于水坝建成后被淹没的位置。将被淹没的画廊森林是恩各白·布各来用于传统和手工产品的树木、药用植物和其他自然资源的重要来源。河中恩各白·布各来用于宗教和文化庆典的岩画也将被淹没。

结果 独立申诉机制于 2015 年 5 月公布了最终合规报告。尽管荷兰开发银行还要求其客户遵守《经济合作与发展组织（OECD）跨国公司指南》及其他一些政策，独立申诉机制仅依据《国际金融公司社会和环境可持续性政策及绩效标准》（以下简称"绩效标准"）进行合规评估。独立申诉机制发现，荷兰开发银行和德国投资与开发有限公司无法确保巴罗·布兰科项目完全遵守"绩效标准"1（社会与环境评估及管理制度）、5（征地与非自愿安置）、6（生物多样性保护与可持续自然资源管理）、7（原住民）和8（文化遗产）。

更进一步而言，独立申诉机制发现，"贷款协议在重大建设开始之前就已经签订，而与社会与环境影响有关的重大问题，尤其是与原住民权利有关的问题，在贷款协议签订之前并没有进行完整的评估"。[①] 荷兰开发银行和德国投资与开发有限公司未能对项目的潜在影响进行界定，使其未能要求客户采取行动减少这些影响。贷款协议所附的环境与社会行动计划"没有任何关于征地和安置及关于生物多样性和自然资源管理的条款。其中也没有提到文化遗产的问题"。[②]

关于遵守原住民政策的问题，独立申诉机制强烈质疑贷款人与受影响社区进行的磋商是否"按照'绩效标准'7 第 13 段要求的方式和强度（善意的谈判）进行"。小组认为，"贷款人并没有认真对待受影响社区的抵触情绪。在一定程度上，这可能是因为法律协议是在南美伊斯特莫电力公司与特区的区域理事会之间达成的，而贷款人认为这足以应对上述问题。但是，原住民报告清楚记载，直接受影响的社区对这些协议的合法性提出了质疑。这本应启动独立申诉机制报告里所确定的进一步行动步骤"。[③]

[①] 跨国企业研究中心（SOMO）和两端（Both ENDS），独立问责机制概述对巴罗·布兰科调研发现以及荷兰开发银行和德国投资与开发有限公司管理层的回应（2015 年 6 月 1 日），见：http：//bit. ly/2OL5M7o。

[②] 同上。

[③] ICM Barro Blanco Report.

荷兰开发银行和德国投资与开发有限公司在对独立申诉机制报告的回应中，仅做出了极少的承诺来应对尚未解决的违规行为。[①] 回应解释说，许多问题必须由巴拿马政府来解决，而且它们及其客户"在影响政府行为从而与所有利益相关者达成令人满意的协议方面，面对限制"。荷兰开发银行和德国投资与开发有限公司还承诺，就土地、安置及拆迁问题，"争取从具有丰富原住民权利方面的专业知识及当地法律背景的律师或其他专家那里，获得更加详尽的正式意见"。然而，并不清楚如果他们获得这样的意见，是否将与申诉人分享或者这些意见是否将带来任何后续行动。得到独立申诉机制的报告和荷兰开发银行和德国投资与开发有限公司的回应之后，申诉人及其民间组织同盟向荷兰和德国相关的部长致函，表达了他们对荷兰开发银行和德国投资与开发有限公司回应的不满。[②]

在申诉人的倡议下，一位"四月十号"行动的代表与荷兰开发银行和德国投资与开发有限公司的独立申诉机制的代表在 6 月底在荷兰海牙进行了会面。荷兰开发银行和德国投资与开发有限公司不同意要求其客户暂停水坝建设以进行对话，但他们承诺聘用一位调解人员与各方共同努力，就进行对话必需的条件达成一致。同时，巴拿马政府尝试与恩各白·布各来进行对话。据荷兰开发银行和德国投资与开发有限公司称，巴拿马政府并未接受他们提供一位调解人员，以推进上述进程的提议。目前，巴拿马政府仍在与原住民首领进行交谈，但"四月十号"行动并没有受邀参与。荷兰开发银行和德国投资与开发有限公司已数月未与申诉人进行沟通交流。

结果满意度[③]　据"四月十号"行动就此申诉的联系人马诺洛·米兰达称，"四月十号"行动对独立申诉机制的调查报告表示满意，因为报告显示项目并未得到受影响社区的同意。米兰达认为，因为这份报告是由独立专

---

① 荷兰开发银行和德国投资与开发有限公司对独立专家小组针对巴罗·布兰科水电项目的申诉所做的合规审查报告的回应。（2015 年 5 月 29 日），http：//bit. ly/2MeiwBO。

② Press Release, *SOMO Human Rights and Grievance Mechanisms Programme*, *Movimiento 10 de Abril presents letter of concern to Dutch and German embassies in Panama*（available at http：//griev-ancemechanisms. org/news/movimiento-10-de-abril-presents-letter-of-concern-to-dutchand-german-embassies-in-panama）。

③ 该案例研究基于与"四月十号"行动项目申诉的联系人马诺洛·米兰达所做的访谈，除公开获取的信息外，还有两端和跨国企业研究中心（SOMO）提供的信息，以及支持该案件申诉者的国际非政府组织提供的信息。

家做出，有助于使他们关注的问题更加令人信服，并有助于确保国际社会理解关于巴罗·布兰科水坝的冲突。

然而最终，荷兰开发银行和德国投资与开发有限公司的回应极其令人失望。米兰达说，"什么都没有改变……这两家银行和这家公司没有做出任何行动，来阻止对我们文化、领地和宗教的影响"。他会建议其他社区使用申诉机制，因为这将有助于引起对问题的关注。但是，为了让申诉对社区产生结果，开发性金融机构及国际机构的人权承诺不应该只停留在纸面上。他说："规则是一回事，执行是另一回事"。

"四月十号"行动捍卫权利的努力不是没有代价的。公司已经向公共事务部提出了针对社区领袖的申诉。有一件针对米兰达的未决法律诉讼称其擅闯水坝，对此他严词否认。针对这些指控捍卫自己的清白不仅耗时，而且对社区有经济方面的影响。

过程满意度 尽管米兰达总体上对他们与独立申诉机制小组成员的互动表示满意，提到小组成员"允许我们讲出真相"，但荷兰开发银行和德国投资与开发有限公司、独立申诉机制和公司为了在申诉过程中赢得客户合作而签订的秘密附属协议，却极大地破坏了他们对过程的信任。银行与南美伊斯特莫电力公司的贷款协议签订于独立申诉机制成立之前，因此协议中并没有要求公司与独立申诉机制合作的条款。这种情况并不是独立申诉机制独有。虽然每一个现有的独立问责机制都是在其所属的开发性金融机构建立以后才成立的，但是并没有证据显示，任何一个其他的独立问责机制或开发性金融机构做出特殊的安排，来处理就该独立问责机制开始运行之前受资助的活动提起的申诉。

正如申诉人理解的那样，在附属协议签订之前，公司拒绝在处理过程中进行合作，或不允许独立申诉机制小组成员接触项目文件。因此，小组成员在申诉提交后5个月内无法获知不对外公开的信息。申诉人仅在2014年10月向独立申诉机制致函后才被告知拖延的理由，他们在该信函中表达了对申诉处理进展的担忧。附属协议的内容从未与申诉人分享过。

附属协议取代了公开的独立申诉机制程序，并且允许南美伊斯特莫电力公司在调查报告初稿和最终文本分享给申诉人之前进行审阅。申诉人被告知，公司审阅的目的是确保独立申诉机制没有公布任何商业秘密。实践中，公司这样的审阅给处理进程带来了严重拖延，公司或开发性金融机构不允许独立申诉机制将报告分享给申诉人，直到申诉人以向媒体曝光为威胁。分享给申诉人的合规报告草稿中，已经包括荷兰开发银行和德国投资与开发有限公司及其客户的意见，尽管申诉人和他们的顾问认为按照独立申诉机制的议事规则他们可以与荷兰开发银行和德国投资与开发有限公司对同一份报告草稿进行审阅。尽管独立申诉机制小组成员请申诉人放心，公司审阅以及信息公开的先后顺序仍然摧毁了申诉人对报告内容的信心，"银行和公司是第一个知道这个报告的人，这很令人担忧，因为这给了它们对那些不利于它们的信息进行篡改的机会"。

荷兰开发银行和德国投资与开发有限公司已经表示，将来如果有针对独立申诉机制成立之前资助的活动的申诉，银行可能不得不签订类似的附属协议。这将严重危害独立申诉机制的合法性、透明度和可预测性。

"四月十号"行动将机制的可及性归功于他们从民间组织联盟那里得到的支持，包括奇里基自然（Chiriqui Natural）、两端及跨国企业研究中心。"四月十号"行动在有可能提起申诉的几年前，就与荷兰开发银行和德国投资与开发有限公司取得了联系。然而，米兰达自然地感觉到荷兰开发银行和德国投资与开发有限公司并不信任他们，或者说在两端介入之前并没有将他们视为直接受影响的利益相关者。独立申诉机制小组成员们也帮助"四月十号"行动理解荷兰开发银行和德国投资与开发有限公司的政策以及独立申诉机制的作用。尽管小组成员在一次实地走访中与申诉人见了面，并组织了几次电话会议，但由于上面提到的原因，很多时候很难获取关于案件状态的信息。

米兰达称，不仅处理结果没有权利兼容性，由于荷兰开发银行和德国投资与开发有限公司没有做出足够的回应，尽管荷兰开发银行和德国投资与开发有限公司的政策要求遵守国内法和国际人权标准，独立申诉机制的报告也并没有完全分析项目的人权影响。项目获批时，荷兰开发银行要求客户遵守《经济合作与发展组织跨国公司指南》（以下简称"指南"）。"指南"中有一个涉及《联合国商业与人权指导原则》（UNGP）的人权专章，该章规定，企业有责任尊重所有国际承认的人权，在适用的情况下，包括那些与原住民权利有关的人权。[①] 然而，小组仅仅按照"绩效标准"进行合

---

① 经济合作与发展组织（OECD），《经济合作与发展组织跨国公司指南》，第四章，第 1 页，"评论意见"，第 40 页（2011），见 http://www.oecd.org/daf/inv/mne/48004323.pdf。

规评估，并推理认为"贷款者对绩效标准的适用，是使项目绩效既符合《联合国商业与人权指导原则》又符合经合组织"指南"的恰当方式"。[①]然而，正如附件 12 描述的那样，"绩效标准"并没有像经合组织"指南"和《联合国商业与人权指导原则》期待的那样，要求进行人权影响评估，也没有明确将人权标准融入其中。

最后，"四月十号"行动感觉荷兰开发银行和德国投资与开发有限公司没有平等对待他们。用米兰达的话说，"知道银行认为公司比我们更加重要，这让我们非常不安。他们从来没有向我们询问过，从来没有与我们交谈，也从来没有为我们提供信息。但银行却为公司提供信息。这让我们感觉我们微不足道，而公司是重中之重"。

事实上，荷兰开发银行和德国投资与开发有限公司在申诉处理过程中一直代表公司在进行游说。巴拿马政府 2015 年 2 月暂停项目之后，荷兰开发银行和德国投资与开发有限公司给巴拿马副总统去信，表达他们对项目暂停的"重大关切和震惊"并要求项目建设获准恢复。[②] 他们还表示，政府这一决定"可能影响将来的投资决策，并且伤及进入巴拿马的长期投资流"。他们对政府这一决定的基础表示怀疑，声称他们的顾问并没有向其报告同样的不遵守相关标准的情况。政府的决定部分提及，公司没有与受影响社区达成合意，也没有经过批准的管理层行动计划来解决对文化遗产的影响。[③] 荷兰开发银行和德国投资与开发有限公司给副总统去信之时，他们已经看到了独立申诉机制的合规审查报告草稿，而草稿对这些问题确有提及。

4.2.6 案例分析 6 世界银行监察组：埃塞俄比亚基础服务促进项目

背景 世界银行设计了基础服务保护项目（PBS）用以支持埃塞俄比

---

① ICM Barro Blanco Report.
② 两端新闻稿，荷兰开发银行督促巴拿马继续巴罗·布兰科水坝的建设。（2015 年 5 月 18 日），见 http://www.bothends.org/en/News/newsitem/413/Dutch-FMOpushed-Panama-tocontinue-construction-Barro-Blanco-dam# ga = 1. 75074836. 742010282. 1427962178）。荷兰开发银行和德国投资与开发有限公司发给巴拿马副总统的信函已交给作者。
③ 巴拿马环境署（ANAM）要求搁置水坝建设。

亚。① 在基础服务保护项目下，整笔的拨款被转到地方政府预算，用作在下列五个行业扩展基础服务获取渠道及改进基础服务质量的经常性开支：教育、健康、农业、水资源与卫生及农村道路。自 2006 年，基础服务保护项目更新过两次，世界银行已总共为项目投入 20 亿美元资金。②

申诉 2012 年 9 月，生活在肯尼亚和南苏丹的难民营的阿努卡原住民代表向世界银行监察组提出一项关于基础服务保护项目的申诉。申诉声称，作为地区政府"公社发展计划"（又称为"村落化"）的一部分，他们被迫从埃塞俄比亚甘贝拉地区的祖先留下的肥沃的土地搬迁到集中的村子。申诉提到，村落化的官方目标是，更容易地改善基础服务保护项目目标行业中基础服务的获取渠道。③

申诉具体描述了阿努卡原住民如何被大规模强制性搬离他们祖先留下的肥沃的土地，而安置到不适合耕种而且缺乏学校、诊所和水井等基础服务的地方。④ 申诉称，安置地点食物获取很有限。⑤ 申诉强调，基础服务保护项目和甘贝拉村落化计划具有共同的目标，而且，按照世行文件，基础服务保护项目是甘贝拉地区政府融资的主要来源，尤其是负责执行村落化的公务员的工资。⑥

结果 在 2014 年 11 月发布的最终调查报告中，监察组"并没有试图验证关于村落化具体人权侵犯的指控"。⑦ 在认定村落化计划中民众搬迁并非是基础服务保护项目目标所必需的之后，监察组又发现，非自愿安置政策并不适用，因此世界银行遵守了 OP/BP4.12。然而，监察组发现，基础服务保护项目和村落化计划之间存在"业务上的联系"，因为它们都"具有为同样的人群提供更好基本服务的目标，都在同一地理区域运营，而且它们

---

① 世界银行项目信息文件，埃塞俄比亚基础服务促进项目，1（2006），第 3 页。
② 世行埃塞俄比亚基础服务促进三期项目概念阶段项目信息文件（2012 年 4 月 4 日）；世行埃塞俄比亚基础服务促进项目，执行董事讨论会议纪要（2012 年 9 月 25 日）。
③ 世行监察组的监察请求 1（2012 年 9 月 24 日），见 http://bit.ly/2AEQMFb。
④ 同上。
⑤ 同上。
⑥ 同上。
⑦ 世行监察组，《埃塞俄比亚：基础服务促进三期项目调查报告》，第 311 页（2014 年 11 月 24 日），http://bit.ly/2O765Io。

同时得以实施期间有超过三年（2010～2013）互相重合"。① 因此，监察组做出结论，银行的设计、评估、风险分析和项目监督不够，不符合OMS2.20、OP/BP10.00和OP/BP10.02的要求。② 监察组认为，内控的软弱增大了资金被转移的可能性，而银行关于能够完全追踪基础服务保护项目支出的说法"不能成立"。③ 监察组还发现，银行没有遵守原住民政策OP4.10，因为它未能在设计基础服务保护项目时考虑到阿努卡的生计、福祉和对基本服务的获取。④ 然而，监察组认定，银行不需对申诉人受到的损害负责。⑤ 由于对调查的严格性不满，国际包容性发展组织对监察组的调查发现提出了很详细的批评。⑥

2015年1月，作为对调查发现的回应，银行管理层制订了一份行动计划。⑦ 银行提到，自申诉提起，它已经开始将OP/BP4.10关于原住民的政策适用到埃塞俄比亚的相关项目中，而之前政府拒绝这样做。⑧ 银行承诺采取各种措施改进在埃塞俄比亚的开发项目的可问责性，包括为"埃塞俄比亚监察员机构"和地区申诉矫正官员的有效性给予支持，对地区公务员进行执行世行安保政策的能力建设。⑨ 它还声称将用一个结果导向型贷款取代基础服务保护项目整笔拨款。⑩ 在董事会批准了银行管理层行动计划之后的一个新闻稿中，银行进一步承诺，支持甘贝拉的小农户及确保旨在提高服务质量和减少饥荒的国家级项目惠及甘贝拉的所有民众。对已经在难民营住了好几年的申诉人来说很重要的是，作为世界银行新的《非洲之角倡议》的一部分，世界银行已经表示，将强化其工作，改善难民和其他生活在甘

---

① 世行监察组，《埃塞俄比亚：基础服务促进三期项目调查报告》，第311页（2014年11月24日），http://bit.ly/2O765Io，第309页。

② 同上，第31～32页。

③ 同上，第30～31页。

④ 同上，第208页。

⑤ 同上，第310页。

⑥ 国际包容性发展组织（Inclusive Development International），《埃塞俄比亚基础服务促进三期项目的监察要求：对世行监察组调研和发现的分析》（2015），见http://bit.ly/2KoJDZb。

⑦ 埃塞俄比亚：基础服务提升项目，管理层针对监察小组调研报告的报告和建议（2015年1月31日），http://bit.ly/2vAQjOx（下称《管理层的回应：埃塞俄比亚案件》）。

⑧ 同上，第36页。

⑨ 世行新闻稿，世行董事会讨论监察组关于埃塞俄比亚的案件（2015年2月27日），见http://bit.ly/2vDcRxQ（下称新闻稿：埃塞俄比亚案件）。

⑩ 《管理层的回应：埃塞俄比亚案件》，第53页。

贝拉这样的边境地区的人的发展前景。①

结果满意度② 尽管监察组发现了几处不合规的情况，申诉代表明确表示对处理结果不满意。

申诉人感到不平的是，监察组的最终调查报告没有对他们诉称的最严重的损害进行足够的记载。

申诉人感觉，他们向监察组申诉对政府行为有一定影响，也可能已经阻止了进一步的损害，但处理过程并没有带来对违规行为的纠正。

在 2015 年 1 月 30 日致世界银行行长金墉的一封公开信中，申诉人请求其支持他们"回到世代居住的土地而不用害怕遭到报复"，并要求银行和他们的民众进行磋商并拥有"我们的发展的所有权"。③ 但他们并没有感觉银行倾听了他们的声音，或者将他们的诉求反映在其行动计划中。

当被问到他们是否会建议其他人使用监察组时，申诉人回答说，即使他们对结果并不满意，为了寻求公正他们也"别无他途"。

过程满意度 申诉人在申诉处理过程经历了重重磨难。申诉人说，没有国际包容性发展组织等组织的协助，监察组对他们来说不会具有任何可及性。正是因为有了国际包容性发展组织的支持，他们才得以提起申诉。国际包容性发展组织为他们解释了世界银行的安保政策和申诉处理程序，并帮助他们准备和提交申诉。

申诉人不认为监察组在透明地运作。他们告诉本报告作者："从监察组（对申诉人进行了访谈以评估申诉资格之后）离开南苏丹的难民营那一刻起，我们就再没有从他们那里得到任何音讯。他们从未为我们更新过申诉处理进展，也没有与我们沟通；我们唯一的信息是从国际包容性发展组织那里得来的。"

申诉人还提到了对处理过程合法性、可预测性和公平性的担忧。最重要的是，尽管监察组在实地评估申诉资格的过程中与申诉人进行了交谈，但是并没有在调查过程中回去对其进行访谈："他们从来没有回来找我们，

---

① 新闻稿，埃塞俄比亚案件。

② 该评估基于对六位申诉者组成的访谈小组的访谈。2015 年 6 月 21 日，我们通过网络电话对他们进行了访谈。基于安全原因考虑，我们不能公开申诉者的身份。

③ 《埃塞俄比亚难民致世行行长金墉的公开信》（2015 年 1 月 31 日），见 http://bit.ly/2Kq5U8N。

他们在甘贝拉进行调查（但没有到难民营来），然后就回去了并且做出了报告。"因此，申诉人并没有感觉其观点被银行管理层考虑到了。这"不仅仅是他们跟我们说了什么，还有他们的身体语言。我们已经知道他们只是来展示他们的案件——行动计划——但并不期望来听取我们的意见或者听到我们的消息"。申诉人说："世界银行解释了其行动计划之后，我们完全拒绝。他们承诺做出一个更好的行动计划，但从此再也没有回来过。"

监察组的程序并没有为申诉人带来权利兼容的救济。尽管申诉人相信甘贝拉村落化由于向监察组提出的申诉以及倡导活动引起的国际关注而停止，他们并不相信自己或者甘贝拉的其他人得到了救济。他们说，"我们仍在等待结果"。申诉人仍然住在难民营里，缺乏医疗和教育资源，继续为他们的安全担惊受怕。一位申诉人评价到，在关于行动计划的磋商会议中，"我们甚至能够觉察到他们并不在乎我们，而且没有做出任何行动来保护我们"。

在《管理层报告和建议》中，世界银行谈及汲取的经验教训时称，"执行中主要的经验教训是增强民众的声音和可问责性的重要性"。[1] 管理层也发表意见称，它们学会了"确认计划目标达成中的障碍"，以及"需要不断进行培训和支持以加强（地方政府）层面的能力，无论它是关于监护、安保、市民的声音还是执行问题"。[2] 世界银行行长金墉在一份新闻稿中也表示，"我们从这个案件中吸取了重要的教训，以更好地预知保护穷人和更有效抗击贫困的道路"。[3]

国际包容性发展组织的法律总监娜塔莉·布加尔斯基表示，"人权侵犯和搬迁的强迫性质是《监察请求书》的中心议题，而监察组对相关的指控做出不予考虑的决定，这一决定，加之监察组无视大量违背政策的存在而做出的银行不对损害负责的调查，限制了银行从本案中吸取教训的可能性"。布加尔斯基表示，结果是"银行错过了对其现有环境与社会保护制度，及直接预算支持融资的可问责性存在的缺陷进行机构性反思的大好机会"。

---

① 监察组甘贝拉访谈，逐字翻译稿（2014年2月）（http://bit.ly/2n6l4pw），49页。
② 同上。
③ 新闻稿：埃塞俄比亚案件。

4.2.7　案例分析7　世界银行监察组：印度维什鲁加德皮帕科提水电项目

背景　2011 年 6 月，世界银行批准了对印度政府和北阿坎德邦地方政府一家叫作印度特里水电开发有限责任公司的联合企业的 6.48 亿美元贷款。① 贷款用以在恒河的主要支流阿拉克南达河修建一座水力发电站。

申诉　对当地社区的一些成员来说，水坝的修建引发了他们在环境、社会和文化方面的忧虑。他们于 2012 年 7 月向监察组提起申诉，② 阐述了许多方面的问题，包括对房屋、农地与森林的损害，水生生物多样性的丧失和沙子、鱼类和饮用水等河流提供的好处的丧失，泥石流和地震风险的增加，以及对森林砍伐和甲醛气体排放带来的日益增加的全球变暖的忧虑。另外，申诉人担心大量建筑工人的进入会减少当地妇女的自由。由于阿拉克南达河是宗教意义重大的恒河的支流，他们也对河流精神和文化价值的丧失忧心忡忡。监察组走访项目所在地之后，申诉人向监察组提供了补充信息。

结果　合规调查的结果是 2014 年 7 月的最终调查报告。监察组结论认为，世界银行"尽管仍然存在一些差距，但绝大多数情况下不仅遵守了自身的政策和程序，还在可能的情况下引入了最佳实践"。③ 这些差距与其发现的两处违规有关。第一处是违反世界银行的环评政策。调查发现，在社区是否丧失饮用水资源问题上，世界银行没有确定必需的措施。第二处则是违反银行的非自愿安置政策，调查发现，世界银行没有对当地社区的情况进行足够的评估。④ 这个问题并没有在最初的申诉中提出，但在监察组的资格审查走访之后增加到了申诉诉求中。

---

① 世界银行，项目及运营，维什鲁加德皮帕科提水电项目，见 http://www.worldbank.org/projects/P096124/vishnugad-pipalkoti-hydro-electric-project? lang = en（2015 年 6 月 11 日最后一次访问）。

② 对印度特里水电开发有限责任公司（THDC India Ltd）贷款的监察请求。监察组将有关维什鲁加德皮帕科提水电项目的信息提交给执行秘书（2012 年 7 月 23 日），见 http://bit.ly/2MgzRtA。

③ 监察组，调查报告：印度维什鲁加德皮帕科提水电项目（2014 年 7 月 1 日）。

④ 同上，第 95 页。

作为对调查报告的回应，管理层的行动计划于2014年9月公布。该计划通过承诺检测水源的改变来对第一处违规，即水源的丧失，进行处理。如果出现一处水源枯竭，银行将对印度特里水电开发有限责任公司建议的替换选项进行评估并监督执行。关于非自愿安置，管理层承诺，在社区成员从印度特里水电开发有限责任公司提供的两处安置地中做出选择之后对安置进行监督。①

结果满意度② 尽管监察组发现了两处违规，申诉人代表巴拉特·胡胡瓦拉（Bharat Jhunjhunwala）博士认为，申诉处理结果令人非常失望。

这主要有三个方面。第一，最终调查报告没有对提出的所有问题进行处理，"如果你认为我的请求不可行，那不进行处理是公平的，但得给我驳回的理由。你不能对请求的重要部分缄口不言"。第二方面的事实加剧了这种感觉，即申诉人没有途径表达对银行领导层的不满，"我已经写信给银行所有执行董事，也已经写信给银行行长。最后我收到荷兰执行董事的回复。他将我的申诉转发给了监察组。但我从他们那里得到的所有回复只是，我可以提起一个新的申诉。仅此而已"。加剧这种对申诉处理结果的不满情绪的第三方面事实是，申诉人相信银行管理层没有积极对违规发现进行应对。尤其是这一点，已经带给申诉人一个总的感觉，那就是整个申诉处理过程是不值得的，"我们花了大量的资源来提起这个申诉。银行即使是在监察组发现的小违规行为上也没有采取行动。这是穷人资源的巨大浪费。我们被欺骗了"。

过程满意度 虽然处理结果被认为非常不令人满意，胡胡瓦拉博士关于监察组在申诉处理过程中的作用的看法，总的来说，比较正面一些："我应该记住，整个过程，直到监察组走访，都挺令人满意。我对此没有什么抱怨。"

胡胡瓦拉博士认为监察组可获得且可预测，虽然这似乎主要得益于一个国际非政府组织银行信息中心（BIC）的帮助。银行信息中心为胡胡瓦拉

---

① Inspection Panel, *India-Vishnugad Pipalkoti Hydro Electric Project*, *Summary of Management Actions* (2014), http://ewebapps.worldbank.org/apps/ip/PanelCases/81-Summary%20of%20Management%20Actions（English）.pdf（hereinafter Inspection Panel, Summary of Management Actions: Vishnugad Project）.

② Although this case study is based on an interview with the complainants' representative, Dr. Bharat Jhunjhunwala, who consented to the publication of his name, two additional, unnamed complainants reviewed and approved the final text.

及其他申诉人就申诉处理过程答疑解惑并提出建议。

监察组的合法性也得到正面评价。胡胡瓦拉博士表示,他对监察组采取的在实体走访中保持独立性的措施表示赞赏。比如,他赞赏监察组在走访项目所在地过程中独立打理行程,也欣赏他们愿意与每一个人交流。然而,他表示,"内部人士"告诉他,最后的调查报告并非出自走访项目所在地的人员之手。在他的经验里,这极大地损害报告的合法性。他对世界银行人员走访过程中的行为的看法则更为负面。他感觉银行员工并不独立于印度特里水电开发有限责任公司。

申诉处理过程的透明度和公平性也存在问题。据胡胡瓦拉称,从走访到最终报告,他们等了 21 个月。对于申诉人来说,非常不清楚这期间发生了什么。这产生了关于银行管理层影响力的问题:"我们只是从监察组那里接到了一个电话,询问管理层是否联系了我们。我们告诉他们没有,仅此而已。所以为什么花了 21 个月?我想一定在某些地方有政治因素。"

权利兼容性是该案的主要关注点。首先,据申诉人称,银行承诺过要采取措施的那些地区其实情况没有改善。他们感觉,银行管理层做出的承诺被忽略了。另外,关于社区水源丧失的解决方案也令人心存疑虑。申诉人怀疑替代选择是不是实际可行。比如,由于艰难的山区地形,卡车送水将非常具有挑战性。最后,胡胡瓦拉博士表示,建立新的符合银行政策的非自愿安置一揽子措施的承诺没有兑现。

关于权利兼容性的忧虑并不仅限于合规审查结果。甚至在申诉提起之前,社区成员已经承受了来自印度特里水电开发有限责任公司的巨大压力。此外,自从监察组走访之后,印度特里水电开发有限责任公司似乎加剧了骚扰。有时,威胁已经升级到身体暴力。一位社区成员亲眼看见,因为抗议印度特里水电开发有限责任公司为清理土地修建道路而半夜拆毁她的窝棚和果树,她的儿子遭到袭击。虽然监察组被告知申诉人受到的骚扰,并已经在资格审查报告中记录了印度特里水电开发有限责任公司进行的恐吓,但这个问题没有在调查报告中得以解决,也没有在管理层行动计划中提到。

似乎没有关于这个申诉的学习过程。管理层行动计划中没有提到将来的项目中可以吸取的教训。[1]

---

[1] 监察组,管理行动概要:Vishnugad 项目。

5 建议

　　每一个申诉都讲述着一个故事：一个真实存在的人群的故事。这些人的生活受到本应造福他们的发展活动的负面影响。同时，每一个申诉都提供了一个机会给开发性金融机构来实现其愿景并改善人们的生活。这是开发性金融机构学习和理解发展如何服务于民众的机会。因此，虽然本报告的目的是确保被开发活动伤害的人群得到足够的救济，但是完成这个报告的组织的最终目标是，开发性金融机构追求以人权为基础而不造成伤害的发展模式。[①] 在这个目标实现之前，当务之急是问责体制得以强化，以确保每一个受开发活动伤害的人都得到救济。

　　本报告进行的研究最终形成了确保被发展活动损害的人们得到救济的两类建议。一类建议力求使现有的体制臻于完美。接下来的一节和表 2 中，包含了对开发性金融机构和独立问责机制提出的这一类的一般建议。附件 5-15（见 www.glass-half-full.org）包括对每一个机构提出的具体建议。不过，作者最终结论认为，现有机制不足以始终如一地为受开发性金融机构资助的活动影响的人们提供救济。要实现这样的目标，需要开发性金融机构可问责性的进一步发展进化。第二类建议则力求充实这一对话过程。

5.1　完善体系

　　以下建议将对现有问责体制进行改进。它们包括一个或多个机构的现有做法或容易整合进现有体制的措施。在许多个案中，这些建议是使问责

---

① 想要了解什么是真正的发展，见"摘要"第 1 页脚注②，国际问责项目（回到发展，Back to Development）。

体系更好地发挥作用的最低要求。

合法性

● 为选择独立问责机制负责人而组建的委员会应当包括外部利益相关者，包括公民社会的代表。

● 如果独立问责机制负责人之前曾为机制所属开发性金融机构工作，则应当被要求在加入该机制之前遵守一个冷却期。且这些负责人在任期届满之后应当被禁止为该开发性金融机构工作。

● 独立问责机制应当建立正式的外部利益相关者顾问团队，为其提供工作的反馈和指导。

可及性

● 开发性金融机构应当要求其客户在被要求公开开发性金融机构资助的活动的潜在环境与社会影响的同时，向受项目影响的人们公开独立问责机制的可用性。随后，该客户项目层面的申诉机制应当被要求为任何感兴趣的利益相关者提供关于独立问责机制的信息。

● 从开发性金融机构表示将考虑进行融资那一刻起，独立问责机制就应当接受要求进行合规审查或问题解决的申诉。只要贷款仍在偿还，或者开发性金融机构仍在投资，要求进行问题解决的申诉就应当被接受。要求进行合规审查的申诉在项目结束之后应当被接受。

● 开发性金融机构应当在其主页为其独立问责机制提供高度可见的网站链接。

● 独立问责机制应当允许申诉人以自己的语言提起的申诉，并且应当在其网站上提供多语种的信息。

可预测性

● 独立问责机制在处理申诉过程中必须始终遵守其期限限制。

● 开发性金融机构必须为独立问责机制提供足够的预算，使其有能力应对其接收的案件。

● 独立问责机制应当为申诉人提供定期案件状态更新。开发性金融机构应当制订附有受期限约束的执行规划的管理层行动计划，以处理独立问责机制调查发现的每一个违规现象。

● 所有独立问责机制都应当有权对纠纷解决过程中做出的承诺和在合规调查中发现的违规现象进行监测。必须指出的一个重要区分是，独立问责机制应当对这些违规现象是否得到了补救进行监测，而不是监测管理层行动计划是否得以执行，因为行动计划可能不足以解决违规现象。独立问责机制应当至少每年公布一次监测报告，且报告应包括由申诉人提供的开发性金融机构或其客户承诺履行情况的信息。

公平性

• 申诉人应当被给予与开发性金融机构同样的机会，对独立问责机制的报告进行审阅和评论。最终报告应当在发送给银行董事会的同时发送给申诉人，且应当将申诉人的观点包括其中。

• 开发性金融机构应当制订和落实程序，在管理层行动计划制订之前与申诉人进行充分的、有参与性的磋商。独立问责机制应当尊重申诉人的顾问及代表的作用。

• 对申诉处理过程不满，或对开发性金融机构或其客户的承诺落实情况不满的申诉人，开发性金融机构应当为其设立上诉程序。

• 开发性金融机构应当为其独立问责机制提供足够的资源，使其能够行使职权并确保申诉人能够有意义地参与到申诉处理过程中来。

透明度

• 独立问责机制应当确保其案件登记包括所有相关信息。

• 开发性金融机构应该以受其资助的活动影响的人群可及的形式和语言，公开这些活动的全面信息，包括环境与社会评估。它们还应当公开其金融中介机构客户支持的子项目的信息。

权利兼容性

• 明确承诺不资助将导致、促成或加剧人权侵犯的项目。为使这一承诺具有操作性，开发性金融机构应当要求客户进行人权影响评估。评估应当包括是否为人们提供足够的保护，使其能够对受资助的活动发出反对的声音。在其政策不能被遵守的情况下，开发性金融机构应当不对相关活动进行资助，这些政策包括磋商和信息公开的条款。

• 开发性金融机构及独立问责机制应当采纳规程，保护申诉人免遭报复并在报复发生时进行回应。

• 独立问责机制应当被赋予职权，在其相信迫在眉睫的损害可能发生时，建议暂停投资或暂停受资助的活动。

经验教训

- 开发性金融机构应当开发一个公开可用的管理追踪系统，记录其如何回应独立问责机制的调查发现和建议、从独立问责机制案件中吸取了什么教训以及如何将这些教训运用于未来的投资。

- 对已经被发现不遵守环境与社会标准的客户，在其纠正违规行为之前，开发性金融机构应当不对其类似活动提供资助。在对其他客户造成类似风险的活动提供资助之前，开发性金融机构应当确保已对在以往案件中汲取的经验教训加以运用。

- 独立问责机制应当对在其案件中汲取的经验教训进行记录，以促成开发性金融机构政策或实践的改善。

- 独立问责机制应当负有建立自身议事规则并对其进行改革的基本责任。只有那些会带来独立问责机制结构或职权发生重大改变的改革，才需要经过董事会批准。独立问责机制对议事规则或对这些建立议事规则的政策进行审议时，磋商程序应当标准化，且政策应当规定开发性金融机构和公民社会的提出意见的机会，并要求供审批的最终版本应当对外公开。

表格 2 包括附件 5 – 15（见 www.glass-half-full.org）中以对每一个独立问责机制/开发性金融机构进行的《联合国商业与人权指导原则》评估为基础提出的建议。这些建议描述了各个主体（独立问责机制和开发性金融机构）需要对其政策和实践进行的改革。不过，应当提到的是，落实其中一些关于独立问责机制的建议的权力掌握在开发性金融机构董事会手中。

表 2　完善体系的建议

合法性/可及性	机制	建议	独立审查机制 – 非洲开发银行	问责机制 – 亚洲开发银行	企业社会责任顾问 – 加拿大采掘业办公室	项目申诉机制 – 欧洲复兴开发银行	申诉机制 – 欧洲投资银行	独立申诉机制 – 荷兰开发银行/德国投资与开发有限公司	独立咨询与调查机制 – 美洲开发银行	合规顾问/巡查官办公室 – 国际金融公司/多边投资担保机构	指导原则检查官 – 日本国际协力机构/日本国际协力银行	问责办公室 – 美国海外私人投资公司	监察组 – 世界银行
合法性	独立问责机制	遵守机制负责人聘用前的"冷却"期和离职后禁令以防止与开发性金融机构管理层不断相互轮换	●	○	○	●	○	○	●	●	○	○	●
	开发性金融机构	建立定期会面的外部问责团队	○	○	○	●	○	○	○	●	●	○	○
	开发性金融机构	系统性地将外部利益相关者（如民间组织）纳人雇佣新的机制员工的选拔委员会中	○	○	○	●	○	○	○	●	●	○	○
可及性	独立问责机制	确保与申诉人和公众的沟通交流能用多种语言进行	○	○	○	●	○	○	○	●	○	○	●
	独立问责机制	消除提起申诉的障碍（从项目审批前到项目结束后）	●	●	×	○	○	○	○	○	●	○	○

续表

		独立审查机制-非洲开发银行	问责机制-亚洲开发银行	企业社会责任顾问-加拿大采掘业办公室	项目申诉机制-欧洲复兴开发银行	申诉机制-欧洲投资银行	独立申诉机制-荷兰开发银行/德国投资与开发有限公司	独立咨询与调查机制-美洲开发银行	合规顾问/巡查官办公室-国际金融公司/多边投资担保机构	指导原则检查官-日本国际协力机构/日本国际协力银行	问责办公室-美国海外私人投资公司	监察组-世界银行
可及性	开发性金融机构											
		要求客户公开机制的可用性 ○	●	○	○	○	○	○	○	○	○	○
		提高机构在开发性金融机构网站主页上的可见度 ○	●	○	●	●	○	●	○	○	●	●
	独立问责机制	坚持遵守期限限制 ○	○	○	○	○	○	○	○	●	●	○
		更好地就申诉处理过程及状态与申诉人进行沟通交流 ◎	●	○	○	○	○	○	○	●	○	○
		对纠纷解决中做出的承诺和合规调查发现的违规现象进行监测 ○	○	○	○	○	○	○	●	○	○	○
可预测性	开发性金融机构	任何时候发现违规现象均制订和执行有效的管理行动计划 ○	○	×	○	○	○	○	○	○	○	○

续表

		独立审查机制－非洲开发银行	问责机制－亚洲开发银行	企业社会责任顾问－加拿大采掘业办公室	项目申诉机制－欧洲兴复开发银行	申诉机制－欧洲投资银行	独立申诉机制－荷兰开发银行/德国投资与开发有限公司	独立咨询与调查机制－美洲开发银行	合规顾问/巡查官办公室－国际金融公司/多边投资担保机构	指导原则检查官－日本国际协力机构/日本国际协力银行	问责办公室－美国海外私人投资公司	监察组－世界银行
公平性	**独立问责机制**											
	允许申诉人对调查报告草案提出意见并将其送交纳入金融机构管理层的最终报告中						○					
	同时向申诉人和开发性金融机构董事会分享最终调查报告	●	○	●	○	○	○	○	○	●	○	○
	尊重申诉人选择的顾问/代表	○	○	○	●	○	●	●	○	●	○	●
	开发性金融机构											
	就管理层行动计划的制订与申诉人进行有意义的磋商	○	◎	×	○	○	○	○	○	○	○	
	为机制提供足够的资源	●	○	○	○	◎	○	○	○	◎	○	
	设立就开发性金融机构/独立问责机构决定向外部机构提出上诉的程序	○		○	○	●	○	○	○	○	○	○

续表

			独立审查机制 – 非洲开发银行	问责机制 – 亚洲开发银行	企业社会责任顾问 – 加拿大采掘业办公室	项目申诉机制 – 欧洲复兴开发银行	申诉机制 – 欧洲投资银行	独立申诉机制 – 荷兰开发银行/德国开发与投资有限公司	独立咨询与调查机制 – 美洲开发银行	合规顾问/巡查官办公室 – 国际金融公司/多边投资担保机构	指导原则检查官 – 日本国际协力机构/日本国际协力银行	问责办公室 – 美国海外投资公司	监察组织 – 世界银行
透明度	开发性金融机构	在网站上更新及公布完整的具体案件登记（包括案件登记、预算、不合格的申诉）	○	○	○	○	○	○	●	○	○	○	○
		以系统而可及的方式和语言公布更多所资助活动的信息（包括客户姓名、影响评估、贷款协议、金融中介机构的子项目）	○	○	○	○	○	○	○	○	○	○	○
权利兼容性	独立问责机制	采取额外措施保护申诉人不遭受报复	○	○	○	○	○	○	○	○	○	○	○
		在即将发生损害的情况下行使建议暂停项目的权力	●	○	×	●	●	○	●	○	○	○	○

续表

	独立审查机制 – 非洲开发银行	问责机制 – 亚洲开发银行	企业社会责任顾问 – 加拿大采掘业办公室	项目申诉机制 – 欧洲复兴开发银行	申诉机制 – 欧洲投资银行	独立申诉机制 – 荷兰开发银行/德国投资与开发有限公司	独立咨询与调查机制 – 美洲开发银行	合规顾问/巡查官办公室 – 国际金融公司/多边投资担保机构	指导原则检查官 – 日本国际协力机构/日本国际协力银行	问责办公室 – 美国海外私人投资公司	监察组 – 世界银行
权利兼容性 / 开发性金融机构 承诺不对可能导致、促成或加剧侵害人权的活动提供资助(并通过对人权影响评估使其更具有操作性)	○	○	○	○	○	○	○	○	○	○	○
采取措施应对针对申诉人进行的报复	○	○	○	○	○	○	○	○	○	○	○
独立问责机制 将政策/程序审查的磋商过程标准化	○	○	○	●	○	○	○	○	○	○	○
分析并记录案件中汲取的经验教训	●	●	○	○	○	○	○	●	○	○	●
吸取的经验和教训 / 开发性金融机构 建立并公布一个追踪工具,对承诺落实和政策/程序变更进行报告	○	○	○	○	○	○	○	○	○	○	○
在已经被发现违反社会标准和客户纠正违规行为之前,不对其类似活动提供额外融资	○	○	○	○	○	○	○	○	○	○	○

图释:○ = 表示该具体建议适用于该主体 ● = 表示该主体已经落实了该建议 × = 不适用 ◎ = 缺乏足够的信息以做出判定

5.2　21 世纪的可问责性

以下建议为问责绘制了一个大胆的新路线。它们愿景宏大，也因为这样，作者并不预期它们会被立即采纳。它们也并未穷尽。它们意在促成一个关于何为真正的发展及它对谁负责的、更大范围内的、十分必要的对话。

- 独立问责机制必须被赋予采取强制行动的职权。开发性金融机构问责机制，正如 20 多年前它被设立时那样，依赖于开发性金融机构的董事会及管理层，而这个董事会和管理层对资助的活动给受项目影响的人们带来的损害负有责任。然而，正如本报告展示的那样，开发性金融机构已经被证实不能或不愿承担这样的责任。其结果是，独立问责机制做出的调查发现或建议被置之不理，而申诉人的损害得不到救济。独立问责机制本应具有职权，引导开发性金融机构员工及客户采取行动应对违规现象，并对损害进行补救。

- 所有的发展融资都应当受某个独立问责机制管辖。这个建议适用于现有的和新成立的开发性金融机构。开发性金融机构提供的金融工具越来越复杂，而对其适用的环境和社会标准也已变得更加有限和灵活，如果存在这样的标准的话。独立问责机制要履行其问责职权，必须能够按照基于规则的标准对合规性进行评估，而不管被资助的活动如何。同样，开发性金融机构的图景也正在飞速变化，新的或不同的主体对发展活动进行资助。独立问责机制不能被视为发展的障碍，而应当被视为达到发展结果的关键因素。新的开发性金融机构，如亚洲基础设施投资银行和新开发银行，必须建立最先进的独立问责机制，以实现其发展使命。现有的还没有设立独立问责机制的双边开发性金融机构，可以考虑与另一个开发性金融机构共享一个独立问责机制，就像荷兰开发银行和德国投资开发有限公司已经实践的那样。

- 开发性金融机构应当为申诉人设立一个救济基金。申诉人如果受到开发性金融机构资助活动的损害，必须得到足够的赔偿。使开发性活动重新符合开发性金融机构的环境与社会标准，可能能够终止损害的继续发生，但可能无法对已经发生的损害进行补偿。同样，即使与开发性金融机构客户成功达成调解，也可能无法满足申诉人的需求。在那些案件中，作为造成或促成损害的负责方的一部分，开发性金融机构必须做好准备，动用自有资金来使申诉人得到赔偿，恢复他们未受损害时的状态。

- 开发性金融机构应当放弃要求其对环境和社会损害的豁免权。联合国人权事务高级专员办事处和经济合作与发展组织已经很清楚地表示，金融机构，包括国有企业和小股东，会造成或促成人权侵犯。① 不管是发展还是其他任何说法，都不能使开发性金融机构对损害责任享有豁免权的主张成立。当权利被拒绝而民众遭受损害，发展的结果也被破坏了。虽然独立问责机制将一直发挥重要的作用，但受项目影响的社区也应当有权选择向法院起诉或向仲裁庭提起仲裁。开发性金融机构实施这个建议的一种途径是，赋予受项目影响的人们作为机构与客户合同的第三方的权利。那样，受项目影响的民众就可以在开发性金融机构客户违背合同的环境与社会条款时，寻求合同救济。

- 案件在开发性金融机构董事会进行讨论时，申诉人应当参与会议。目前，董事会仅听取独立问责机制的观点（假设这些观点是中立的）和管理层的观点，但没有人出席会议陈述申诉人的看法。申诉人应当被邀请参加董事会会议，表达他们关于独立问责机制调查发现或建议以及管理层行动计划的充分的看法。这些会议应该上网直播，这样，受项目影响的民众就能够看到对他们造成影响的决定。

---

① 经济合作与发展组织（OECD），在金融部门内实施《经济合作与发展组织跨国公司指南》和《联合国商业与人权指导原则》的专家信函和声明（2014 年 6 月），参见 http://bit.ly/2MlKn2I。

| Contents |

Authors

Violet Benneker (SOMO), Natalie Bugalski (IDI), Juan Carballo (FUNDEPS), Caitlin Daniel (Accountability Counsel), Carla Garcia Zendejas (CIEL), Kristen Genovese (SOMO), Mariëtte van Huijstee (SOMO), Jennifer Ingram (Natural Justice), Pieter Jansen (Both ENDS), Erika Lennon (Program on International & Comparative Environmental Law, American University Washington College of Law), Jael Makagon (Natural Justice), Fidanka Bacheva McGrath (Bankwatch), Jocelyn Medallo (CIEL), David Pred (IDI), Nikki Reisch (Center for Human Rights and Global Justice, New York University School of Law), Anna Roggenbuck (Bankwatch), Gonzalo Roza (FUNDEPS), Sarah Singh (Accountability Counsel), Xavier Sol (Counter Balance)

Acknowledgements

The authors would like to thank a number of people for their invaluable contributions to this report. First of all, we would like to thank Kate Forrester (intern at Accountability Counsel) for her critical contribution in building the complaints database. Thanks to Taís Paiva Ludwig and Caitlin Buchanan (students at American University, Washington College of Law) for their help on the references throughout the report. Thanks to Emily Goldman (intern at Inclusive Development International) for her research support. Thanks to Lydia de Leeuw (SOMO) for her help in managing the review process of a draft of this report and to the following people for their valuable advice and contributions during the development of the report: Richard Bissell (National Academy of Sciences), Matthew Fischer-Daly (Cotton Campaign), David Hunter (American University, Washington College of Law), Gerhard Schuil (SOMO) and Daniel Taillant (Centre for Human Rights and Environment). The authors would also like to thank the complainants interviewed for the case studies and the survey respondents for sharing their experiences about how the IAMs and DFIs that are assessed in this research actually work in practice, and the IAMs themselves for their constructive comments on a draft of this report.

Acronyms

ADB	Asian Development Bank
AfDB	African Development Bank
BIC	Bank Information Center
CAO	Compliance Advisor Ombudsman
CM	Compliance Mechanism
CR	Compliance Review
CSO	Civil society organisation
CSRC	Corporate Social Responsibility Counsellor
DEG	German Development Bank
DFI	Development Finance Institution
EBRD	European Bank for Reconstruction and Development
EIB	European Investment Bank
E&S	Environmental and social
Exs.	The Examiners for the Guidelines
FMO	Dutch Development Bank
IAM	International Accountability Mechanism
ICM	Independent Complaints Mechanism
IDB	Inter-American Development Bank
IFC	International Finance Corporation
ILO	International Labour Organization
IP	Inspection Panel
IRM	Independent Review Mechanism
ITF	International Transport Workers' Federation

ITUC	International Trade Union Confederation
JBIC	Japan Bank for International Cooperation
JICA	Japan International Cooperation Agency
MICI	Independent Consultation and Investigation Mechanism
MIGA	Multilateral Investment Guarantee Agency
NAPE	National Association of Professional Environmentalists
NFC	New Forests Company
NJGM	Non-Judicial Grievance Mechanism
OA	Office of Accountability
OECD	Organisation for Economic Co-operation and Development
OPIC US	Overseas Private Investment Corporation
PBS	Protection of Basic Services
PCM	Project Complaint Mechanism
PS	Problem-solving
SEZ	Special economic zone
SPF	Special Project Facilitator
SME	Small-and medium-sized enterprise
UETCL	Uganda Electricity Transmission Company Ltd.
UNDP	United Nations Development Programme
UNGP	United Nations Guiding Principles on Business and Human Rights
WB	World Bank

Glossary

Complaint: An official, written submission to an IAM that describes an actual or potential harm that has or will occur as a result of an activity financed by a DFI. Several IAMs refer to this as a request.

Complainant: The person, people, or organization who have signed and filed the complaint. Most, but not all, IAMs require that the complainant be directly affected by the activity that is the subject of the complaint. Several IAMs refer to complainants as requestors. Filer, a more general term for complainant, is also used in this report. In addition to those that are directly affected by the activity, their representatives or CSOs, filers can also include corporations and IAM or DFI leadership.

Concluded cases: Concluded cases are those that are either closed or in monitoring.

Development Finance Institutions (DFIs): Also known as development banks or international financial institutions, DFIs invest in activities intended to contribute to economic development. These activities may include building hydro-electric dams, railway projects, or reform of laws and institutions.

Result: A complaint process that has produced a result is one in which there has been a settlement reached in problem-solving and/or a publicly disclosed compliance review report. Not considered a 'result' are settlements that concerned only procedural agreements regarding the conduct of the dialogue process or minor agreements about interim issues. Data concerning settlements was based on information reported by the IAMs themselves. Since researchers did not follow up with complainants to determine their perspective, it is important to note that recording a case as involving a settlement did not entail a judgement on the quality or acceptability of that settlement.

Substantive phase: A 'substantive' phase of a complaint process refers to either problem-solving or compliance review. Where the report refers to complaints reaching a substantive stage, what is being measured is how often a dialogue process or a full compliance investigation was initiated, not how often they were actually completed.

Supporting organisation: A CSO that provides assistance to a complainant, including undertaking research; reviewing complaints; advising complainants as they move through the IAM process; and/or assisting with advocacy at the relevant institutions. A supporting organisation is generally not named in the complaint or is named in a supporting capacity only.

User: This term is used to refer to a combination of two groups: 1) people who have been directly affected by the DFI-financed activities and have filed complaints to the IAMs (complainants); and 2) the CSOs that support them.

Executive Summary

Real development respects human rights and is shaped by the people it is designed to benefit. However, 'development' —the way it is currently practised by Development Finance Institutions (DFIs) —in many cases has been associated with the dispossession of land, loss of resources, diminished livelihoods and environmental degradation. Each of the 758 complaints submitted over the past 21 years to the 11 Independent Accountability Mechanisms (IAMs) administered by DFIs covered in this report, tells the story of a community whose lives were made worse by so-called 'development projects'. This number probably represents only the tip of the iceberg because most project-affected people are not aware of the availability of the IAMs.

While the aim of this report is to ensure that people who have been harmed by these development projects receive adequate remedy, the ultimate goal of the 11 organisations[①] that have authored this report is that DFIs should pursue a development model based on human rights. [②] The authors would like to see less need for the IAMs because fewer people are harmed. And they would also like to

---

① Accountability Counsel; Both ENDS; Center for International Environmental Law (CIEL); Central and Eastern European Bankwatch Network; Center for Human Rights and Global Justice, New York University School of Law; Centre for Research on Multinational Corporations (SOMO); Counter Balance; Foundation for the Development of Sustainable Policies (FUNDEPS); Inclusive Development International (IDI); Natural Justice; Program on International & Comparative Environmental Law, American University Washington College of Law.

② For a vision of what real development looks like, see International Accountability Project, *Back to Development: A Call for What Development Could Be* (2015), available at bit. ly/backtodevelopment [hereinafter IAP, Back to Development].

make sure that complaints are handled better in the future. Until then, the accountability systems at the DFIs provide a vital but crude backstop for those people and communities that have been harmed by the current development model.

The accountability system is made up of two halves—the IAM and the DFI, which in turn is composed of its management and board of directors. Each must fulfil its responsibility for the system to work and provide remedy to those who are harmed. The organisations that wrote this report undertook both quantitative and qualitative research to assess how well each functions. They drew on their own experiences as experts, as well as analysing the procedures and practices of the IAMs and DFIs, and, most importantly, the experiences of complainants.

What the authors found is that the glass of accountability is half full or half empty, depending on your perspective. Complainants are undoubtedly better off than they would be in the absence of any complaint procedure, as they often have nowhere else to turn to seek redress. However, the outcome rarely provides adequate remedy for the harm that people and communities affected by development projects have experienced. Their concerns may be validated, their issues may receive attention at the international level, and sometimes, though not often enough, their lives may be changed for the better as a result of their complaints.

What is preventing the system from working better for complainants? IAMs can and should do more to improve their practices. For example, they should provide complainants with regular updates on the status of their cases; they should develop procedures to prevent and respond more effectively to reprisals against complainants; they should meet their deadlines, publish complete information about their cases online, and recognise and take measures to overcome the power imbalance between complainants and the DFIs and their clients.

Ultimately, however, these accountability mechanisms operate in a constrained environment constructed by the DFIs that administer them. The DFIs impede the accessibility of the IAMs from the very beginning by failing to require their clients to disclose the IAMs' existence to project-affected people. They limit the window of time during which an IAM can accept a complaint. They do not contribute to solutions achieved through problem-solving processes. They do not consistently respond to the findings of non-compliance by their IAMs. And when they do develop an action plan to address the findings, they rarely consult adequately with the complainants.

These deficiencies combined result not just in a diminished outcome for complainants but in fewer complaints that produce an outcome at all. Of all 684 concluded complaints (complaints closed or in monitoring), [1] less than half (43%) were even found eligible. Just under 20% of concluded complaints resulted in a successfully negotiated settlement (8%) or a publicly disclosed compliance report (11, 5%). DFI management produced action plans in only 7% of concluded cases.

Whether you see the glass of accountability as half full or half empty, the authors hope there is agreement that the system can be improved. The current report provides two sets of recommendations. The first set seeks to perfect the current system by identifying best practices that should be adopted by all IAMs and DFIs. The authors of this report, however, have concluded that simply adopting best practice will not be enough to ensure that complainants receive remedy for the harms that have occurred. The current system was premised on the assumption that the DFIs would uphold their responsibility in the accountability system. However, more than 20 years after the first IAM, the Inspection Panel, was established by the World Bank in 1993, the DFIs have demonstrated that they are either unwilling or unable to fulfil their responsibilities.

A new accountability system must be established as a matter of urgency with mechanisms that are empowered to make binding decisions and DFIs that no longer claim immunity in national courts. DFIs will only revisit their development model when they are truly held accountable for the harms caused to people and communities around the world by the activities they finance.

---

[1] These are cases that have closed or are in monitoring, which make up 90% of all cases filed to IAMs (N = 758).

1　Introduction

1. 1　Background

Development Finance Institutions (DFIs, see Glossary), also known as development banks, invest in activities intended to contribute to economic development. These activities might include building hydro-electric dams, railway projects, or reform of laws and institutions. While these projects strive to alleviate poverty and create employment, experience has shown that DFI-financed projects may in fact harm the very people they are seeking to help. Despite the intention of DFI policies to prevent adverse environmental and social impacts, DFI-financed activities can cause, and in fact have resulted in, various harms. These include air and water pollution from coal-fired power plants, forced evictions to make way for mining and infrastructure projects, loss of biodiversity, and many others.

Independent Accountability Mechanisms (IAMs) were created to hold the DFIs and their clients accountable to the DFIs' own policies and to provide access to remedy for individuals and communities that are adversely affected by DFI-financed activities. The IAMs vary in their structure, functions and procedures. In 1993, the Inspection Panel of the World Bank was the first such mechanism created, and the first complaint (see Glossary) was filed in 1994. [1]Today, there

---

[1]　Int'l Bank for Reconstruction & Dev. & Int'l Dev. Ass'n, *World Bank Inspection Panel*, Resolution No. IBRD 93 – 10/IDA93 – 6 (Sept. 22, 1993), http://ewebapps. worldbank. org/apps/ip/PanelMandateDocuments/Resolution1993. pdf (establishing the Inspection Panel).

are more than a dozen. Over ten years ago, the mechanisms formed a network,[1] and since then, there have been several efforts to evaluate the effectiveness of one or more of the mechanisms. [2] In 2012, on the occasion of the twentieth anniversary of the UN Conference on Sustainable Development, the IAMs themselves published a report on their collective work. [3] What has been lacking to date, however, is a systematic, comparative analysis of the functioning of the DFIs' accountability systems, and an evaluation of their effectiveness from the perspective of users (see Glossary). This report aims to help fill that gap.

The majority of previous studies have focused exclusively on the effectiveness of the mechanisms themselves. However, IAMs make up only half of the accountability system at DFIs. The DFIs' boards of directors and management—the other half of the accountability system—must also be evaluated. At any given DFI, it is the board that grants the IAM its mandate. The board often selects the IAMs' personnel, provides its budget, imposes limitations on its functions, and ultimately, is responsible for the outcome of the activities it finances. The DFI's management also plays a critical role in the system by, inter alia, responding to the IAM's findings, consulting with complainants (see Glossary) on the development of an action plan to address instances of non-compliance, and applying lessons learned from cases to future projects. The system only functions if both halves of the mechanism work and work well.

1.2　Aim

The research presented in this report was guided by the following question: *To*

---

[1]　While it is unclear which IAMs officially belong to the network, a non-exhaustive list of IAMs can be found here: http://www. iadb. org/en/mici/partners, 8163. html.

[2]　See Martijn Willem Scheltema, *Assessing the Effectiveness of Remedy Outcomes of Non-Judicial Grievance Mechanisms*, Dovenschmidt Q. 2014, Feb. 12, 2014, at 190 – 97; Mathieu Vervynckt, An assessment of transparency and accountability mechanisms at the European Investment Bank and the International Finance Corporation (Eurodad, Oct. 2015), http://www. eurodad. org/files/pdf/560bbcee7a3d1. pdf; *see generally* Maartje van Putten, Policing the Banks (2009).

[3]　Kristen Lewis, *Citizen-driven Accountability for Sustainable Development: Giving Affected People a Greater Voice—20 Years On* (June 2012), < https://www. opic. gov/sites/default/files/files/citizen-driven-accountability. pdf >.

what extent are IAMs and the DFIs that administer them effective in providing remedy for human rights harm to complainants?[1] This research evaluates the policies and practices of 11 IAMs and corresponding DFIs from the perspective of the users— both those people who have been directly affected by the DFI-financed activities and have filed complaints to the IAMs (complainants) , and the civil society organisations (CSO_s) that support them.

The research team has used a variety of methods to solicit input from civil society networks and complainants in order to capture users' experiences. In the view of the report's authors, an important measure of how well an accountability system provides remedy is whether the individual or community member who has filed a complaint believes that they have been provided with adequate remedy. In other words: subjective satisfaction is an important criterion of effectiveness in affording remedy. The research also assesses the functioning of the accountability system through collection and analysis of publicly available data about the complaints submitted and their outcomes.

The insights developed through this research project are intended to help improve the accountability system—regarding both the DFIs and the IAMs—in order to provide adequate remedy for complainants. While the evaluation is critical and the recommendations are ambitious, they are offered in a constructive spirit. The organisations that contributed to this report all seek an effective, functioning accountability system that provides remedy for individuals and communities that have been adversely affected by development activities. Our ambition is to contribute to the strengthening of these systems and to efforts to ensure that the DFIs fulfil their responsibilities to those who are harmed by the activities they finance.

1.3 Methodology

This report seeks to analyse publicly available data on complaints filed to all

---

[1] Mechanisms use different terms to refer to complainants and the complaints they receive. Other terms used are "requests" or "requestors" . Throughout this report, the "complainant" and "complaint" concepts are used as a catchall for all similar terms.

IAMs. ① Consequently, the research on which it is based includes only those IAMs that publish information about complaints received and excludes those that have not made public any information about complaints received or that have not received any complaints to date. ② Thus the report assesses the following 11 IAMs and corresponding DFIs:

- The Independent Review Mechanism (IRM) of the African Development Bank (AfDB)

- The Accountability Mechanism (AM) of the Asian Development Bank (ADB)

- The Canadian Office of the Extractive's Sector's Corporate Social Responsibility Counsellor (Canadian CSR Counsellor) ③

- The Independent Complaints Mechanism (ICM) of the Dutch Development Bank (FMO) and German Development Bank (DEG)

- The Project Complaint Mechanism (PCM) of the European Bank for Reconstruction and Development (EBRD)

- The Complaints Mechanism (CM) of the European Investment Bank (EIB)

- The Independent Consultation and Investigation Mechanism (MICI) of the Inter-American Development Bank (IDB)

- The Compliance Advisor Ombudsman (CAO) of the International Finance Corporation (IFC) and the Multilateral Investment Guarantee Agency (MIGA)

- The Examiners for the Guidelines of the Japan International Cooperation Agency (JICA) and the Japan Bank for International Cooperation (JBIC).

- The Office of Accountability (OA) of the US Overseas Private Investment

---

① By doing this, the report builds on Accountability Counsel's report. *Accountability Counsel*, *Recent Trends in Accountability: Charting the Course of Complaint Offices* (2014).

② Like the Ombudsperson of the Brazilian Development Bank, the Compliance Officer of Export Development Canada, the Examiner of Nippon Export and Investment Insurance, and the General Counsel of the Australian Export Finance and Insurance Corporation.

③ The Canadian CSR Counsellor is an anomaly in this list because it is not a DFI, but rather a state-based mechanism with jurisdiction over the Canadian extractives sector. It is included in this report because it has participated in the IAMs network, which this report aims to engage.

Corporation (OPIC)

● The Inspection Panel (IP) of the World Bank (WB).

This report is the result of collaboration among civil society organisations (CSOs) that advocate for greater accountability at DFIs and improved remedy for complainants. The collaboration included shared data collection, online sharing of results and analysis, written contributions and peer reviews.

The data collection consisted of several components:

1. Quantitative analysis of the complaints filed to IAMs and the stages they reach, using a database consisting of all complaints filed to all 11 IAMs.

2. Qualitative process evaluation of the IAMs and their administering DFIs, using an assessment framework based on the United Nations Guiding Principles on Business and Human Rights (UNGP) effectiveness criteria for Non-Judicial Grievance Mechanisms (NJGMs).

3. Qualitative outcome evaluation of the IAMs and their administering DFIs based on complaints that have closed or reached a result (i. e. a settlement reached in problem-solving or a publicly disclosed compliance review report, see Glossary) during the period 1 July 2014 to 30 June 2015.

4. Review by mechanisms and experts.

Information that would not be available to users (such as information internal to the IAMs or DFIs) was not considered in the preparation of this report. The data were collected solely from information that was publicly available at the time of writing, combined with information provided directly by the users of the mechanisms. Information provided by the IAMs during the review period is explicitly referenced as such. The qualitative assessment of the IAMs and the corresponding DFIs is based on the effectiveness criteria for NJGMs described in Principle 31 of the UNGPs. [1] The effectiveness criteria apply to all State-based and non-State-based grievance mechanisms, and to both adjudicatory (eg. compliance review) and dialogue-based (eg. problem-solving) mechanisms. Although intended for use in the business and human rights arena, the authors consider the effectiveness criteria to be relevant

[1] The effectiveness criteria in Principle 31 are printed on the next page.

to a broader context and generally consistent with criteria used by CSOs prior to the development of the UNGPs. [1]

The qualitative sections of the present report incorporate the perspectives of the complainants and users, among whom are the report authors. Inherent to this qualitative method, the user experiences and perspectives captured in this study are theirs alone and are not representative of all IAM users. Similarly, because not all IAMs/DFIs had complaints that reached a result during the research period and because the report authors were unable to contact all complainants for the complaints that were concluded, the case studies in Chapter 4 are not intended to compare effectiveness across IAMs/DFIs in terms of providing remedy to complainants. More detail about the research methodology, including its limitations, can be found in Annex 1 of this report, available online at www. glass-half-full. org.

UNGP #31
Effectiveness Criteria for
Non-Judicial Grievance Mechanisms

In order to ensure their effectiveness, non-judicial grievance mechanisms, both State-based and non-State-based, should be:

A. Legitimate:

enabling trust from the stakeholder groups for whose use they are intended, and being accountable for the fair conduct of grievance processes.

B. Accessible:

being known to all stakeholder groups for whose use they are intended, and providing adequate assistance for those who may face particular barriers to access.

C. Predictable:

providing a clear and known procedure with an indicative time frame for each stage, and clarity on the types of process and outcome available and means of monitoring implementation.

---

[1] Principle 31 includes an eighth criterion. However, that criterion is only applicable to operational-level grievance mechanisms and, thus, is not relevant to the DFI accountability systems.

D. Equitable:

seeking to ensure that aggrieved parties have reasonable access to sources of information, advice and expertise necessary to engage in a grievance process on fair, informed and respectful terms.

E. Transparent:

keeping parties to a grievance informed about its progress, and providing sufficient information about the mechanism's performance to build confidence in its effectiveness and meet any public interest at stake.

F. Rights-compatible:

ensuring that outcomes and remedies accord with internationally recognised human rights;

G. A source of continuous learning:

drawing on relevant measures to identify lessons for improving.

Source: United Nations Human Rights Office of the High Commissioner. Guiding Principles on Business and Human Rights. Implementing the United Nations "Protect, Respect and Remedy", 2011 < http:// ww. ohchr. org/Documents/Publications/GuidingPrinciplesBusinessHR_ EN. pdf > .

1.4   Reading guide

The report is structured as follows:

Chapter 2 provides a quantitative analysis of complaints filed to the IAMs;

Chapter 3 evaluates the procedural aspects of the IAMs and DFIs against the UNGP effectiveness criteria for NJGMs;

Chapter 4 evaluates the outcomes of cases that have closed in the last year;

Chapter 5 makes recommendations to both IAMs and DFIs on two levels:

1. Reforms that would harmonise best practice within the current accountability system; and

2. More fundamental changes to the accountability system that would increase the likelihood that adequate remedy is provided to those who have suffered harm.

In addition, the following annexes are available online, at www. glass-half-full. org, for those who are interested in the assessments of the individual IAMs/ DFIs and the methodology used in the report:

Annex 1: Detailed Methodology

Annex 2: Assessment template based on United Nations Guiding Principles Effectiveness Criteria for Non-Judicial Grievance Mechanisms

Annex 3: Survey questions for users of the mechanisms

Annex 4: Interview questions for case studies

Annex 5: The Independent Review Mechanism of the African Development Bank

Annex 6: The Accountability Mechanism of the Asian Development Bank

Annex 7: Canadian Extractive Sector's Corporate Social Responsibility Counsellor

Annex 8: The Project Complaint Mechanism of the European Bank for Reconstruction and Development

Annex 9: The Complaints Mechanism of the European Investment Bank

Annex 10: The Independent Complaints Mechanism of the FMO and DEG

Annex 11: The Independent Consultation and Investigation Mechanism of the Inter-American Development Bank

Annex 12: The Compliance Advisor Ombudsman of the International Finance Corporation and Multilateral Investment Guarantee Agency

Annex 13: The Examiners of the Guidelines of the Japan International Cooperation Agency and the Japan Bank for International Cooperation

Annex 14: The Office of Accountability of the US Overseas Private Investment Corporation

Annex 15: The Inspection Panel of the World Bank

2 Functioning of the IAMs in Facts and Figures

2.1 Introduction and Key Findings

This chapter provides a comprehensive, quantitative analysis of complaints filed to all IAMs from their establishment until 30 June 2015. Explanatory remarks on the methods used are available in Section 2.2 below, with additional details available in Annex I ('Detailed Methodology', available at www. glass-half-full. org) and in footnotes throughout the text. The quantitative analysis presented here focuses on the progress of complaints through IAMs, particularly looking at whether cases are reaching and achieving results in the substantive phases of the complaints process. A 'substantive' phase refers to either problem-solving or compliance review (see Glossary).

A SUMMARY OF THE KEY FINDINGS IS AS FOLLOWS:

● More than half of complaints were about infrastructure projects, and the most commonly raised concerns related to inadequate consultation and disclosure, insufficient due diligence and the environmental repercussions of projects.

· Infrastructure projects were the subject of 57% of complaints for which such information is publicly available (see Figure 5).

· 42% of complaints for which such information is publicly available raised concerns about consultation and disclosure; 42% concerned due diligence, and 44% concerned specific environmental issues, such as pollution and biodiversity (see Figure 6; note that one complaint can involve several concerns).

• Steep attrition is visible at every phase of the complaints process, meaning many eligible complaints leave the process before they are able to achieve results. In the 684 concluded cases (see Glossary), complaint progress was as follows (see Figure 11) ;

· Nearly 43% of concluded complaints (complaints closed or in monitoring) were found to be eligible ;

· 28% reached a substantive phase ;

· Just under 20% produced results. This 20% of concluded complaints that produced results is broken down as follows: parties successfully negotiated settlements in 8% of concluded cases and publicly disclosed compliance reports were produced in slightly less than 12% of concluded cases ;

· DFI management produced action plans in 7% of concluded cases.

• Many complaints that have been found eligible never actually proceed to problem-solving or compliance review. This often occurs because of IAM decisions.

· Of the 291 eligible, concluded cases, only 66% reached a substantive phase. [1]

· In 59% of the 78 concluded cases eligible for (and where the complainant wanted) problem solving, but in which it did not occur, problem-solving did not proceed because the IAM decided that it was unnecessary or inappropriate.

· In 73% of eligible, concluded cases that could have proceeded to compliance review but did not, the compliance review was not initiated because the IAM decided it was unnecessary or inappropriate (see Figure 9).

· Slightly less than half (44%) of the 291 eligible, concluded complaints achieved results. [2] Of the 192 concluded complaints that reached a substantive phase, 67% achieved results.

· Of the 76 concluded cases that resulted in findings of non-compliance, 64. 5% resulted in a Management Action Plan.

---

[1] What is being measured here is simply how often a dialogue process or a full compliance investigation was initiated, not how often they were actually completed.

[2] A "result" was counted in any case that produced a settlement through problem-solving and/or a publicly disclosed compliance review report.

• Communities and individuals using IAMs without support from CSOs face higher attrition rates than cases involving CSOs. CSO involvement in cases appears to have a strong, positive effect on case outcomes (see Figure 13).

• Overall, of concluded cases filed without any CSO support, 62% were found eligible, 38% reached a substantive phase and only 19% achieved results. In contrast, of concluded cases that involved an international CSO, 87% were found eligible, 70% reached a substantive phase, and 63% achieved results.

• As compared to eligible complaints filed by individuals or community organisations without any CSO support, the odds that an eligible complaint will achieve results increase by nearly 40% when the case involves a domestic CSO. When an international CSO is involved in an eligible complaint, either alone or alongside a domestic CSO, those odds increase by nearly 175%.

2. 2　Additional Methodological Notes

The quantitative analysis that follows is drawn from a database compiled by the authors containing all publicly-reported cases filed with IAMs from their establishment until 30 June 2015. ① Information on the cases was collected from the mechanisms' websites and their annual reports or similar publications produced by the mechanisms. A few methodological points are worth emphasizing here.

First, instead of performing statistical analyses on all 758 cases filed, the pool of cases analysed was often limited to the 684 'concluded' cases, which are cases that are either closed or in monitoring. This limitation was imposed to balance simplicity, clarity and completeness. Restricting the analysis to these cases avoids inaccuracies resulting from the inclusion of active cases that have not had a chance to reach certain phases of the process. Additionally, including cases that are still at the monitoring phase, rather than limiting the analysis to only

---

① The authors last checked mechanisms' case registries and published annual reports on 8 October 2015. After that date, additional information about cases was only added to the database based on feedback from mechanisms on specific cases where new information had been recently publicly disclosed.

closed cases, ensures the inclusion of the most successful cases at IAMs: those that have produced a result needing to be monitored. When another subset of cases is analysed other than the two mentioned above, the total number is indicated in the text or footnotes.

Second, the analysis frequently references complaints that reach a 'substantive phase' of the process, which refers to either problem-solving or compliance review. A complaint 'reached a substantive phase' if a dialogue process or full compliance investigation was initiated, without regard to whether the complaint actually completed the dialogue process or compliance investigation. Complaints deemed by the mechanism to have entered a problem-solving or compliance review process, but where the process ended prior to initiation of a dialogue or a full investigation, were not counted as reaching a substantive phase. For example, complaints that ended at the appraisal stage of compliance review were not counted as having reached compliance review.

Third, in this analysis, a 'result' was counted in any case that produced a settlement in problem-solving and/or a publicly disclosed compliance review report. Where possible, the analysis attempted to report only on those settlements involving substantive agreements regarding issues raised in complaints. It did not include settlements that concerned only procedural agreements regarding the conduct of the dialogue process or minor agreements about interim issues. Data concerning settlements was based on information reported by the IAMs themselves. Since the researchers did not follow up with complainants to determine their perspective, it is important to note that recording a case as involving a settlement did not entail a judgement on the quality or acceptability of that settlement.

2.3   Facts and Figures

This section lays out a series of descriptive statistics concerning the main features of IAM complaints, such as: the year in which complaints were filed; the number of complaints IAMs received; the regions in which complaints originated; the current status of complaints; who filed them; what types of projects they concerned; and which issues they raised.

2. 3. 1 Complaints Over Time

In the 21 years since 1994, when the first IAM complaint was filed at the World Bank's Inspection Panel (one year after its establishment), IAMs have proliferated widely and have witnessed substantial increases in visibility and case volume. As of 30 June 2015, a total of 758 cases had been submitted to various IAMs.

Figure1 provides a graphical overview of the number of cases filed at IAMs per year. As a whole, the number of complaints filed at IAMs has increased substantially over the past two decades, with a record 130 complaints being submitted in 2013 alone. The largest increases in cases filed per year occurred between 2008 and 2013, when the number of cases per year jumped from 23 to 130.

This sharp increase is likely to have occurred in part because a number of new IAMs were established during those years, such as the International Development Bank (IDB)'s Independent Consultation and Investigation Mechanism (MICI) and the European Bank for Reconstruction and Development's Project Complaint Mechanism (PCM).

Trends shown in Figure 1 are generally encouraging. The steady rise in complaints each year until 2013 suggests an increase both in the number of pathways for remedy open to people negatively affected by international development projects, as well as an increase in the visibility and accessibility of existing mechanisms. While the number of complaints filed fell in 2014, it is unclear whether that drop represents a levelling off of an unusual spike or the beginning of a downward trend. The number of cases filed in 2014 was 82, close to 2012 levels, when 95 complaints were received. The spike in cases that occurred in 2013 seems to be due to corresponding spikes in the number of cases received by the Compliance Advisor Ombudsman (CAO) and the Asian Development Bank (ADB) 's Accountability Mechanism (AM). The drop observed in 2014 was accentuated by a decline in the number of complaints filed at the MICI, which had only eight cases filed in 2014, down from

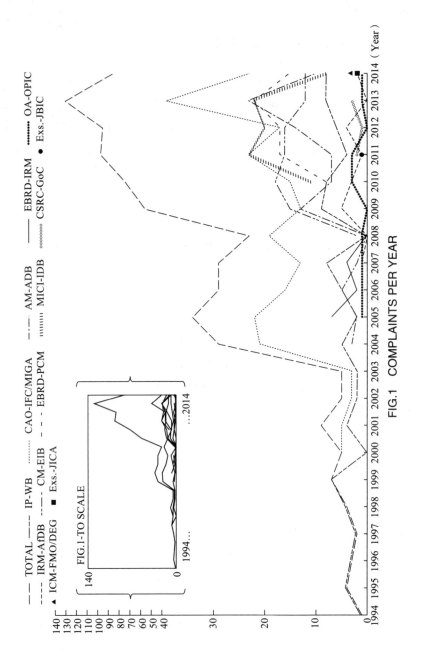

FIG.1 COMPLAINTS PER YEAR

more than 20 complaints per year from 2011 – 2013. The World Bank's Inspection Panel is the only mechanism that did not experience a drop in case filings between 2013 and 2014, with eight cases filed in each year.

The number of cases filed in 2015 may reveal whether the IAMs system as a whole is experiencing a downward trend in the number of complaints filed. According to publicly available information as of 8 October 2015, only 35 complaints were received from 1 January to 30 June 2015. If the second half of the year sees a similarly low number of complaint filings, total annual complaint filings for 2015 will fall to figures similar to those in 2010.

2. 3. 2　Where Are Complaints Filed?

Figure 2 shows the distribution of complaints by mechanism. The CAO is by

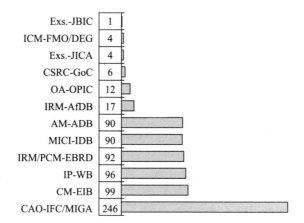

FIG. 2　COMPLAINTS FILED BY IAM[1]

---

[1] Methodological note regarding the European Investment Bank (EIB) Complaints Mechanism (CM): Although in total the EIB has received over 300 complaints, many of those complaints were not included in this analysis. The EIB CM's mandate is much larger than other IAMs. It accepts cases related to procurement and other issues raised by bank clients, in addition to cases related to project impacts on communities. For the purposes of this analysis, many of the EIB CM's cases were excluded to make the EIB CM more comparable to other mechanisms. Only cases relating to social or environmental issues, as well as a subset of those relating to disclosure, were included in this dataset. Complaints related to governance, procurement, human resources and customer and investor relations were not included because these generally do not relate to the impacts of EIB projects on local affected people.

far the most commonly used mechanism: since it first began receiving complaints in 2000, the CAO of the International Finance Corporation (IFC) and Multilateral Investment Guarantee Agency (MIGA) has handled 246 cases and overall has received 32% of all complaints filed at IAMs.

Despite the CAO's dominance in terms of total complaints received, other IAMs handle a comparable yearly caseload at times. The IAMs of certain regional development banks-notably the IDB's MICI, the ADB's AM, and the EBRD's PCM-have had case volumes nearly as high as the CAO's in some years. For example, in 2012, the CAO received 17 complaints, the MICI received 20, the AM received 14, and the PCM received 17. In other years, the number of complaints filed at the CAO as significantly higher than case volumes at any other mechanism. In 2014, for example, the CAO received 23 complaints, while the PCM received 15, the AM ten and the MICI only eight.

An important caveat to remember when interpreting this data is that IAMs have different levels of disclosure. Whereas some, like the MICI and the ADB's AM, report on all cases, even those that are unregistered, other IAMs-such as the African Development Bank (AfDB)'s Independent Review Mechanism (IRM) and the Japan International Cooperation Agency (JICA) Examiner-only report on cases that meet their criteria for registration.

2.3.3　Where Do Complaints Come From?

The greatest number of cases originates in Europe and Central Asia, making up 28% of the 679 cases for which information on region is available. Latin America and the Caribbean is a close second, with just under 28% of complaints. Only a small number of complaints originate from the Middle East and North Africa: less than 4% of all cases.

2.3.4　What is the Status of All Filed Complaints?

Figure 3 breaks down all complaints based on their status as of 30 June

2015. Of the 757 complaints whose status was known, [1] 87% of complaints had been closed and only 13% were active or in monitoring. Overall, 17% of cases have achieved results through the IAM process. [2] If one considers only concluded cases, this number jumps to 19%.

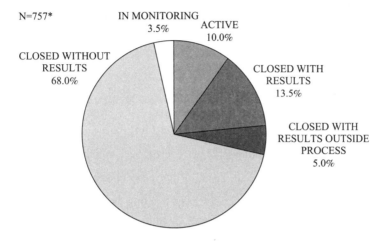

FIG. 3   COMPLAINTS BY STATUS

* Total number of cases for which status is known

Interestingly, IAMs reported 5% of complaints as having been "closed with results outside process". Most of those cases were filed at the World Bank's Inspection Panel (IP), which has two controversial practices that encourage resolution of complaints outside the mechanism's typical complaints process: the Pilot Program and Footnote 7. [4] Two of the cases in this category were handled through the IP's Pilot Program, and the majority of others were handled through the

---

[1]   There is one case at the CSR Counsellor for which the status is unknown.

[2]   This figure combines the cases closed with results and the cases in monitoring, all of which achieved results.

[3]   In this chart, the 'Other' category is made up of four complaints filed to the CAO from the United States. Little information is available on them since they were all ineligible (eligibility is the first hurdle at the CAO, since it does not have a registration stage).

[4]   Footnote 7 refers to the process set out in footnote 7 of the Inspection Panel's Operating Procedures. While both Footnote 7 and the Pilot Program are provided for in the Panel's Operating Procedures, results achieved through these processes are considered outside the Panel's process because they involve the Panel suspending its typical process to allow Bank Management an opportunity to resolve issues through its own actions. See Section 4.1.2 for more information about the Pilot Program and Footnote 7.

IP's Footnote 7 process or earlier variants of this practice, which provides World Bank Management with an opportunity to resolve the issues raised in the complaint before the Panel launches a formal investigation.

When the designation 'closed with results outside process' was used for cases filed at IAMs other than the IP, those cases were typically classified as such due to a successful outside negotiation between the complainants and the company or government involved.

2.3.5 Who Files Complaints?[1]

Figure 4 breaks down cases by the type of filer, based on the 456 complaints for which this information is known. Since each case could have multiple types of filers, Figure 4 shows each group based on the percentages of cases they filed.

Individuals were the most common filers, acting as sole or joint filer in 56% of cases. CSOs were the second most frequent filers, solely or jointly filing 48% of complaints. It is important to note that, when CSOs were filers, they usually filed with or on behalf of community members.

International CSOs were involved in a large percentage of complaints, although they often supported complaints rather than directly filing them. [2] Supporting activities that CSOs can undertake are more informal than serving as a filer and may include: assisting with research; reviewing complaints; advising complainants as they move through the IAM process; and/or assisting with advocacy at the relevant institutions. All told, international CSOs were involved in 26% of cases as

---

① This section includes data regarding the types of organizations and actors that file or otherwise support complaints. For these purposes, a filer is a party that formally signs the complaint or is formally identified in the complaint as a representative of complainants. Filers are also usually reported as such by IAMs. An organisation supporting a complaint is generally not named in the complaint, or is named in a supporting capacity only. While some of the information on supporting organisations is publicly available, much of it is not. Therefore, the data collected regarding supporting organisations relied heavily on self-reporting from CSOs themselves. This was the only aspect of the quantitative analysis that did not rely exclusively on publicly available information.

② The Detailed Methodology in Annex 1 (available at: www.glass-half-full.org) provides a detailed explanation of the distinction between filer and supporter and how information regarding supporting organizations was collected.

either a filer or as a supporting organisation（see Glossary）.

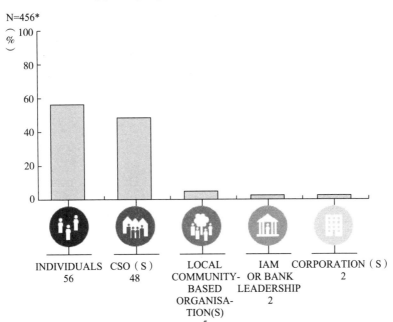

N=456*

FIG. 4　COMPLAINTS BY FILER

* Total number of cases for which filer is known

IAMs themselves or members of bank leadership filed 2% of complaints. ①
Almost all of these complaints, nine out of ten total, were CAO cases. Of these,
the IFC Executive Vice President requested one complaint, the President of the
World Bank Group requested another, and the CAO Vice President requested
seven. The only other complaint of this type was an EIB CM case that was
submitted by the EIB President.

2. 3. 6　What Types of Projects Lead to Complaints?

Figure 5 displays the sectors about which complaints have been filed, based
on the 502 cases for which such information was available. Many complaints relate
to more than one sector. For instance, a complaint regarding the construction of an

---

①　At some IAMs, the procedural rules do not allow complaints to be filed by the mechanism or bank
leadership, whereas at other mechanisms, such filings are permitted, but have never occurred.

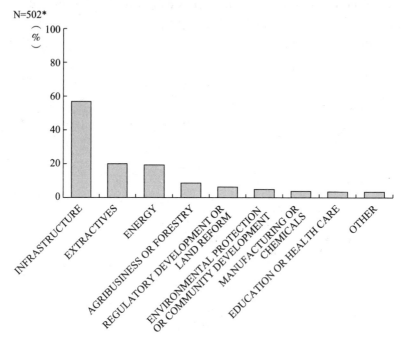

FIG. 5   COMPLAINTS BY SECTOR

* Total number of cases for which sector is known

oil pipeline would be recorded as involving both extractive industries and infrastructure. Figure 5 presents the percentage of cases related to each sector.

Three sectors stand out: infrastructure, extractive industries and energy. Of those three, infrastructure was by far the most common sector, with 57% of complaints relating to projects in that area. The energy and extractive industries sectors each accounted for approximately 20% of cases.

Unsurprisingly, these sectors are commonly associated with the types of concerns often referenced in complaints, such as displacement and pollution. However, complaints also arise from a broad range of other sectors, including from projects explicitly geared towards producing direct social or environmental benefits. For example, projects related to education or healthcare, both generally seen as socially desirable sectors, were the subject of 4% of complaints. Similarly, 6% of complaints related to projects designed to improve environmental protection and conservation or promote sustainable community development.

2. 3. 7   What Types of Concerns do Complainants Raise?

Figure 6 presents data concerning the issues raised in complaints, many of which are related to human rights, based on the 480 complaints for which such information was known. Most complaints raised multiple issues-some as many as ten. Therefore, just as for the two preceding charts, Figure 6 presents the percentage of complaints that raised each issue.

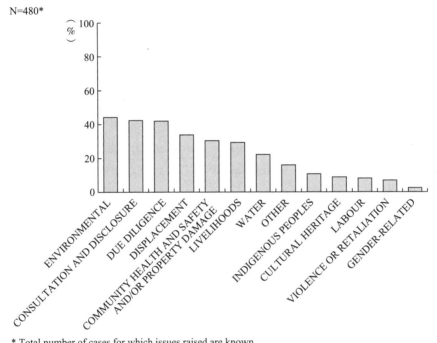

* Total number of cases for which issues raised are known

FIG. 6   COMPLAINTS BY ISSUES RAISED

The largest issue categories-consultation and disclosure, due diligence and environmental issues-were each raised in more than 40% of complaints. The 'environmental' category in this chart is a composite category created by combining mentions of pollution, biodiversity and other environmental issues, such as deforestation.

Several other issues also deserve to be highlighted. Violence and other retaliation was a concern in 7% of cases, a category which was composed of issues of violence (nearly 4% of cases) and issues of other retaliation (4% of cases). Gender-related issues-including gender-based violence, discrimination and other concerns-were only mentioned in 2.5% of cases.

The ‘ other ’ category in this chart encompasses a truly wide range of issues. Whereas some of the issues classified as ‘ other ’ were issues outside the mandate of IAMS, such as corruption or procurement, other complaints raised a broad array of specific issues that were difficult to categorise, such as faulty execution of the project in question, school closures and energy prices for consumers.

2.4 Complaint Progress Through Mechanisms

This section tracks the progress of cases through IAM processes-in particular, showing how far through the process they advance and how often results are achieved. The pool of cases analysed here is typically limited to concluded cases, which are cases that have closed or are in monitoring. In this dataset, 684 complaints were concluded, making up 90% of all cases filed to IAMs.

Since not all mechanisms involve a formal registration period, the phases of the process generally considered here are eligibility, problem-solving and compliance review. As noted earlier, problem-solving and compliance review are collectively referred to as ‘ substantive ’ phases. An important measure of case outcomes used in this section is what percentage of concluded cases achieved results. As noted above, cases were recorded as having achieved results if a settlement was reached in problem-solving and/or a compliance report was publicly disclosed.

2.4.1 Eligibility

Figure 7 illustrates the percentage of the 684 concluded complaints found eligible by IAMs. More than half of all concluded complaints were either not registered or found ineligible-only 42.5% of complaints were eventually found eligible.

The data collected on all complaints did not attempt to track the reasons why complaints were not registered or were found to be ineligible. It is therefore difficult

N=684

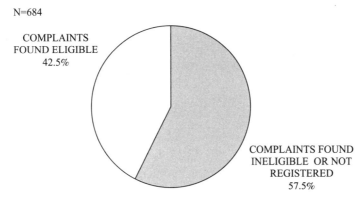

FIG. 7   COM PLAINTS found ELIGIBLE VS INELIGIBLE

to assess why less than half of complaints were found to be eligible. All of the IAMs for which such data is available have procedural rules governing their registration and eligibility decisions, some of which are straightforward to apply and some of which may require judgement calls on the part of the IAM. Presumably some percentage of unregistered and ineligible cases were indisputably ineligible based on these rules (e. g. complaints regarding procurement or corruption filed to a mechanism that does not accept such complaints). However, other cases may have been found ineligible or may not have been registered due to decisions by the mechanism about which there could potentially be disagreement. A separate analysis in Section 4. 1, focused on complaints closed without reaching or completing a substantive phase between 1 July 2014 and 30 June 2015, provides valuable insight into the reasons behind these decisions and discusses the controversy surrounding some eligibility and registration decisions.

2. 4. 2   Complaint Progress: Attrition

After a complaint has cleared the eligibility phase, it is still far from certain that it will reach a substantive phase of the IAM process. Overall, 33% of the 291 eligible, concluded cases failed to reach a substantive phase. An attrition rate of more than 30% between eligibility and substantive phases raises questions about the ability of IAMs to provide effective remedy, which need to be further explored.

Eligible complaints may not proceed to a substantive phase for a variety of reasons. Figures 8 and 9 present these reasons graphically, based on the 101 eligible, concluded cases that could have reached problem-solving but did not and the 128 eligible, concluded complaints that could have reached compliance review but did not. The most common reasons why an eligible complaint did not reach a substantive phase are that: the IAM independently decided that problem-solving or compliance review was unnecessary or inappropriate; the complainant chose not to pursue problem-solving or compliance review; the company or government carrying out the project in question refused to participate in problem-solving; or the institution's board refused to authorise a compliance investigation.

IAMs and bank leadership are behind a large portion of the eligible cases that do not reach a substantive phase. On the problem-solving side, in 59% of the 78 eligible cases, concluded cases that failed to reach problem-solving despite complainants' wishes, problem-solving did not occur because the IAM decided that it was unnecessary or inappropriate. Even more significantly, for eligible, concluded cases that did not go through compliance review, nearly 74% did not reach compliance review because the IAM deemed it unnecessary or inappropriate. An additional 5.5% of such cases did not proceed to compliance review because the DFI's board refused to authorise an investigation. This situation has occurred at only two institutions: the IDB, whose board has refused to authorise three MICI compliance investigations in the last five years, and the World Bank, whose board refused to authorise four Inspection Panel investigations during the Panel's first few years of operation. [1]

One additional point regarding Figure 9 deserves further explanation. The only complaints that did not reach compliance review because the 'complainant did not re-file' were those filed at the ADB AM during the earlier years of its operation, before its procedures were revised. Under the old procedures, problem-solving and compliance review were treated as separate complaint processes, and complainants had to explicitly refile with the compliance review function after undergoing or being found ineligible for problem-solving. However, this is a historical issue and under

---

[1] The World Bank Board has not blocked a Panel investigation since 1998.

the new procedures adopted in 2012, re-filing is no longer required.

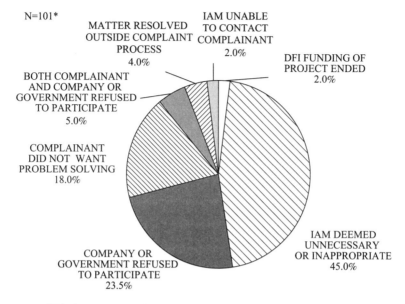

FIG. 8   why did eligible complaints not reach problem solving

 * Total number of eligible concluded cases which could have reached problem solving (they were found eligible at mechanisms that provide problem solving), but did not.

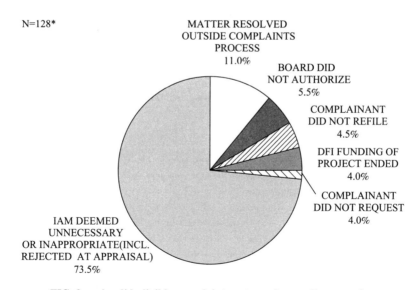

FIG. 9   why did eligible complaints not reach compliance review

 * Total number of eligible concluded cases which could have reached compliance review (they were found eligible at mechanisms that offer compliance review), but did not.

Figure 11 summarizes the percentages of the 291 eligible, concluded cases that reached problem-solving, compliance review, both, or neither. ① It was relatively uncommon for complaints to reach both problem-solving and compliance review: 34% reached problem-solving only and 36% reached compliance review only, whereas only 6.5% went through both. As was mentioned above, a substantial portion – 33% of eligible, concluded complaints-never reached either substantive phase. A further elaboration of the reasons why complaints may drop out of the complaint process before reaching a result is provided in Section 4.1.

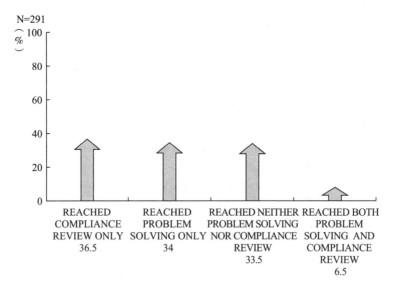

FIG. 10   **Progress of eligible concluded complaints**

---

①　Percentages for cases that reached problem-solving only, compliance review only, and both problem-solving and compliance review are controlled for the functions that were available to each complaint, depending on which IAM it was filed to and how it was filed. For example, the 'problem-solving only' percentage excludes all Inspection Panel cases (since it does not provide problem-solving); the 'compliance review only' percentage excludes all CSR Counsellor cases (because it does not provide for compliance review); and the 'both problem-solving and compliance review' percentage excludes Inspection Panel and CSR Counsellor cases. Exclusions also occurred because of the way certain complaints were filed-in particular, complaints that were brought to the CAO by bank or IAM leadership and those brought to the Project Complaint Mechanism (PCM) by CSOs who are not acting on behalf of directly affected people are only eligible for compliance review, and are therefore excluded from percentages for 'problem-solving only' and for 'both problem-solving and compliance review'. Because of these controls, these percentages add up to more than 100%.

2.4.3 Complaint Progress: Steps and Outcomes

Figure 11 (see next page) breaks down concluded cases based on which steps in the IAMs process were reached and what type of results were achieved. There is marked attrition at each phase of the process. Of all 684 concluded complaints, the following phases of the complaints process were reached: nearly 43% were found eligible; 28% proceeded to a substantive phase; and just under 20% produced results. This 20% of concluded complaints that produced results is broken down as follows: parties successfully negotiated settlements in 8% of concluded cases and publicly disclosed compliance reports were produced in slightly less than 12% of concluded cases. Further, DFI management produced action plans in 7% of concluded cases. This represents 64.5% of the 76 cases that led to findings of non-compliance. ①

Figure 11 should be interpreted as a descriptive rather than an evaluative figure, since not all complaints filed were qualified to reach a result. For example, not all filed complaints will meet eligibility criteria. Consequently, the drop outs between the different phases in Figure 11 do not imply a system failure per se, but they do require further analysis.

Focusing on the 291 concluded complaints that were found eligible, it can be observed that nearly half (44%) achieved results. It is important to remember, however, that the classification of cases that produced ' results ' does not take into account the findings of compliance reports, implementation of settlements or action plans or complainants' satisfaction with outcomes, as such information was generally outside the scope of the data available. Had this study been able to track such information for all concluded cases and include it within the definition of ' results ', it is possible that fewer cases would have been recorded as having achieved results. Chapter 4 provides insights into complainants' satisfaction with the results that were achieved in several cases between 1 July 2014 and 30 June 2015.

---

① This number includes all cases in which a mechanism made findings of non-compliance, regardless of whether the compliance report was publicly disclosed.

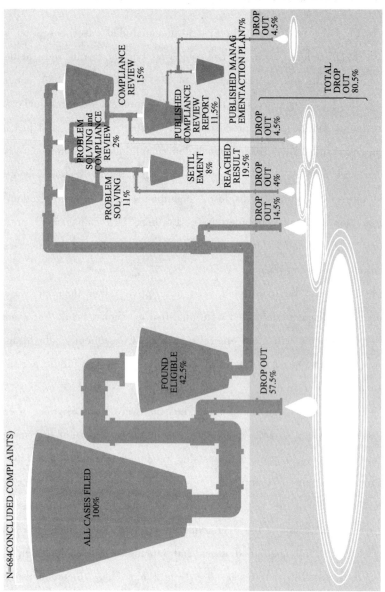

N=684 CONCLUDED COMPLAINTS

ALL CASES FILED 100%

FOUND ELIGIBLE 42.5%

DROP OUT 57.5%

PROBLEM SOLVING 11%

PROBLEM SOLVING and COMPLIANCE REVIEW 2%

COMPLIANCE REVIEW 15%

SETTLEMENT 8%

REACHED RESULT 19.5%

PUBLISHED COMPLIANCE REVIEW REPORT 11.5%

PUBLISHED MANAGEMENT ACTION PLAN 7%

DROP OUT 14.5%

DROP OUT 4%

DROP OUT 4.5%

DROP OUT 4.5%

TOTAL DROP OUT 80.5%

FIG.11 COMPLAINT PROGRESS AND ATTRITION

2. 4. 4　Progress of complaints By IAM

Figure 12 compares the progress of concluded cases through the major IAMs. ① There is significant variation among IAMs, both in terms of the percentage

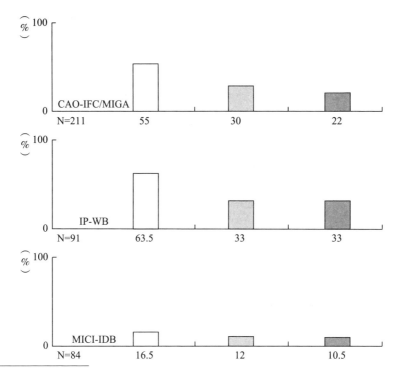

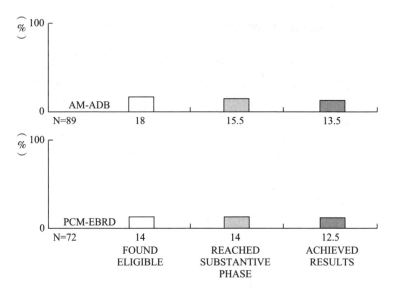

FIG. 12   Progress of complaints through IAMs

of complaints that reach each phase of the process and in terms of the ultimate outcomes of cases. The World Bank Group mechanisms-the CAO and the Inspection Panel-generally have lower case attrition rates throughout the complaint process compared to cases filed to the regional development bank mechanisms. However, an exception to this is the percentage of eligible complaints that achieve results, which is higher at the regional development bank mechanisms.

The Inspection Panel found 63. 5% of concluded cases eligible and 33% of concluded cases reached a substantive phase. Notably, all cases that reached a substantive phase went on to achieve results. This high rate of results in part reflects the Inspection Panel's procedures, which do not include a problem-solving phase and therefore remove from the complaint process the many uncontrolled variables involved in achieving a result through problem-solving. Of the Inspection Panel's eligible, concluded cases, 51. 5% achieved results.

The CAO, which has higher attrition rates of the two World Bank Group IAMs, found 55% of its concluded cases to be eligible, 30% proceeded to a substantive phase and 22% achieved results. Of the CAO's eligible, concluded cases, 40% achieved results.

Among the IAMs affiliated with regional development banks, the ADB AM shows the lowest rates of case attrition, with 18% of its concluded cases found eligible, 15. 5% reaching a substantive phase and 13. 5% achieving results. Of the ADB AM's eligible, concluded cases, 75% have achieved results. For the AM and the other regional development bank mechanisms, this statistic should be read taking into account the relatively small total numbers of concluded complaints found eligible, between ten and 16 complaints.

The PCM found only 14% of concluded cases eligible, but all of those found eligible then proceeded to a substantive phase and 12. 5% achieved results. Of the five mechanisms shown in figure 12, the PCM is the only one that does not show any case attrition between eligibility and reaching a substantive phase. This may be explained at least in part by the PCM procedures, which do not include steps that often lead to such attrition at other mechanisms, such as an appraisal process or a board approval requirement prior to proceeding with a substantive phase (see figures 8 and 9, showing why complaints do not reach substantive phases). Of the PCM's eligible, concluded cases, 90% achieved results.

At the MICI, a slightly higher 16. 5% of concluded cases were found eligible, but only 12% reached a substantive phase and 10. 5% achieved results. Of the MICI's eligible, concluded cases, 64. 5% achieved results.

2. 4. 5 Complaint Progress: With and Without CSO Involvement

Figure 13 . 1 & 13 . 2 illustrate the progress and outcomes of concluded cases based on whether or not an international or domestic CSO was involved in the complaint. ① A CSO is considered to be involved in a case if it either filed the complaint-solely or jointly with community-based complainants-or supported the

---

① The calculations in Figure 13. 1 and 13. 2 regarding the percentage of cases reaching problem-solving or compliance review, or achieving a result (an outcome that relies on a complaint first reaching a substantive phase) controlled for cases that were filed at a mechanism that did not offer both functions or were restricted to compliance review because of the type of filer. For example, the Inspection Panel only offers compliance review and the CSR Counsellor only offers problem-solving. Additionally, cases filed at the EBRD's PCM by CSOs that are not representing directly affected people are only eligible for compliance review.

complainants.

Complaints filed by individuals or community organisations without CSO support generally did not progress as far in the IAM process or achieve results as often as those whose cases were filed or supported by domestic CSOs. Cases that involved international CSOs (often, but not always, in tandem with community-based complainants and/or domestic CSOs) progress even further through the IAM process and reach results even more often than complaints involving domestic CSOs.

Of complaints filed by communities or individuals acting alone, without support from CSOs, 62% were found eligible, 38.5% reached a substantive phase, and 19% achieved a result. In contrast, 80% of complaints that involved a domestic CSO were found eligible, 53% reached a substantive phase and 41% achieved results. Complaints involving an international CSO performed even better: 87% were found eligible, 70% reached a substantive phase and 63.5% achieved results.

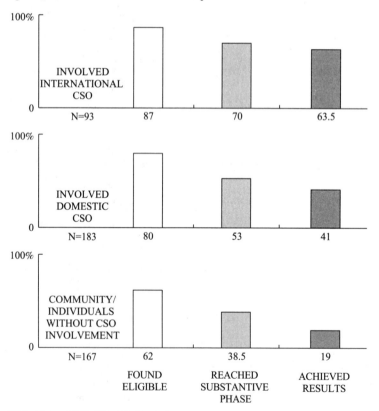

FIG. 13.1   PROGRESS OF COM PLAINTS BY CSO INVOLVEMENT

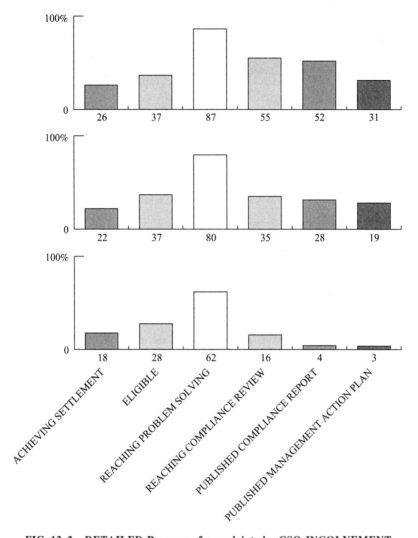

FIG. 13. 2 DETAILED Progress of complaints by CSO INCOLVEMENT

Additional results presented in Figure 13. 2 address percentages of each type of complaint reaching problem-solving and compliance review, as well as percentages that achieved a settlement, a publicly disclosed compliance report or a publicly disclosed Management Action Plan. Overall, a far greater percentage of complaints not involving a CSO reached problem-solving than compliance review (28% reached problem-solving, compared to 16% reaching compliance review). In contrast, a far greater percentage of complaints involving international CSOs

(again, often in tandem with local communities and/or domestic CSOs) reached compliance review than problem-solving (55% reached compliance review, as compared to 37% reaching problem-solving). Complaints involving domestic CSOs (often in tandem with or as representatives of local communities) reached problem-solving about as often as compliance review (37% reached problem-solving, as compared to 35% reaching compliance review).

Framed differently, the variance in percentages of complaints reaching problem-solving was much smaller than with compliance review. There is a wide disparity in the percentage of complaints that reach compliance review based on CSO involvement: only 16% of complaints filed without CSO support reached compliance review, whereas 55% of complaints supported by an international CSO reached that phase.

The difficulties that individuals and communities acting without the support of CSOs face when using the complaints process was substantiated using a regression analysis, which tested the effect that CSO involvement has on the odds that eligible complaints will eventually achieve results. Annex 1 ("Detailed Methodology", available at www. glass-half-full. org) contains detailed results of this regression, along with notes on methodology. This regression considered only concluded, eligible complaints and controlled for the IAM to which complaints were filed.

Complaints filed only by individuals or community organisations, without the support of any CSO, performed less well in the IAM process than those filed with additional organizational support. As compared to eligible complaints filed by individuals or community organisations without any CSO support, the odds that an eligible complaint will achieve results increase by nearly 40% when the case involves a domestic CSO. When an international CSO is involved in an eligible complaint, either alone or alongside a domestic CSO, those odds increase by nearly 175%.

2. 4. 6 Complaint Progress: How Much Time does the IAM Process Take?

Figure 15 presents the average time until the complaint process ended or monitoring began for the larger IAMs. Additional statistics, including durations for problem-solving and compliance review, are presented in Table 1. ① Overall, the average length of time until an eligible complaint exited the IAM process or entered monitoring was 17 months. The average length of the problem-solving and compliance review phases was the same: 12 months.

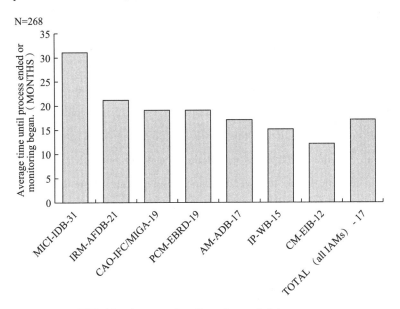

FIG. 14   Average duration of complaint process

Table 1   Additional Duration Statistics in Months (eligible cases only)

IAM	AVERAGE DURATION OF PROCESS*	AVERAGE DURATION PROBLEM SOLVING	AVERAGE DURATION COMPLIANCE REVIEW
TOTAL	17 (268)**	12 (63)	12 (92)
CAO-IFC/MIGA	19 (103)	14 (31)	16 (12)
IP-WB	15 (57)	N/A	17 (30)
MICI-IDB	31 (11)	13 (9)	23 (2)
AM-ADB	17 (14)	10 (12)	13 (7)
PCM-EBRD	19 (10)	2 (3)	12 (9)

① In order to prevent duration statistics for some IAMs from being artificially deflated due to high numbers of complaints that were not registered or found ineligible very shortly after being filed, the durations presented here were calculated using only data from eligible complaints.

续表

IAM	AVERAGE DURATION OF PROCESS*	AVERAGE DURATION PROBLEM SOLVING	AVERAGE DURATION COMPLIANCE REVIEW
CM-EIB	12 (51)	N/A***	2 (24)
IRM-AfDB	21 (5)	12 (5)	20 (2)

* The process measured here is the length of time before the complaints process ended or complaints went to monitoring.

** The number of cases that compose each statistic is listed in parentheses.

*** No data on duration of problem-solving is available for the CM-EIB.

Variation in duration among the mechanisms was quite limited-average durations for individual IAMs generally stayed within five months of the overall average. A notable exception to this general trend is the MICI. The average length of time until eligible MICI cases exited the process or entered monitoring was 31 months, more than double the overall average. Equally notable is the average length of compliance review for MICI cases—23 months. However, only two cases have completed compliance review at the MICI. ①

2.5 Discussion

Over the past two decades, IAMs have proliferated widely, offering a necessary forum for access to remedy for people and communities harmed by development projects. Both their proliferation and the growing number of complaints they have received over time is an encouraging sign that reflects well on their visibility and accessibility. However, IAMs may be experiencing a downward trend in the number of complaints being filed. Data regarding total complaints filed in 2015 should be watched closely, and if a downward trend is indeed occurring, the causes should be identified and corrected if needed.

---

① Although the MICI recently underwent a restructuring process, that restructuring does not appear to have affected the duration numbers presented here. Case durations at the MICI have been relatively consistent over time since the mechanism's establishment. However, several cases that have been delayed due to the restructuring were still active as of 30 June 2015. Once they close, they may increase the average durations at the MICI.

Moreover, despite the encouragement rightly provided by the rising number of IAMs and complaints received, the attrition that occurs at every phase of the IAM process is worrying. More than half of complaints do not proceed past the registration or eligibility phase, and a significant number of those found eligible never proceed to a substantive phase of the process. While it is a positive indicator that 44% of eligible, concluded complaints achieved results, IAMs should continue striving to strengthen their ability to produce useful outcomes on the ground for complainants. Additionally, more information is needed about why such a high percentage of cases are closed at registration or eligibility. [1]

Similarly, IAMs should focus on making the process more accessible and worthwhile for communities and individuals filing without support from CSOs. The struggles faced by individuals and communities filing without CSO support are a cause for concern, as these represent at least 24% of concluded complaints. Moreover, individuals and communities filing alone may be more vulnerable and isolated than those who have support from CSOs, making it even more imperative that the IAM process function well for these types of filers. For IAMs to be effective grievance mechanisms that are capable of providing remedy for those harmed by DFI projects, IAMs and DFIs must do more to ensure that their complaints processes are equally accessible to all complainants, regardless of their knowledge of the system or capacity to file complex and detailed complaints.

Major gains must be made towards consistently providing people affected by development projects with an effective process for securing remedy for harms suffered. Overall, the data analysed here suggests that IAMs and civil society should work together towards this end.

---

[1]   See Chapter 4 for a discussion of case attrition throughout various stages of the mechanism process.

3 Procedural Gaps: A Qualitative Analysis of Policy and Practice

The research team assessed the policies and practice of the IAMs and their DFIs against the effectiveness criteria of the UN Guiding Principles on Business and Human Rights (UNGPs). The evaluation of each mechanism and DFI can be found in Annexes 5 – 15, available online at www. glass-half-full. org. Below is a synthesis of the findings from those analyses. The research reveals several examples of best practice, but it does not appear that those practices are being widely replicated or adopted across all the IAMs and DFIs. On the contrary, the reforms adopted by DFI boards in recent IAMs reviews have decreased their effectiveness in a number of ways, as described in more detail below. Instead of a race to the top in which IAMs and DFIs vie to provide the most robust and fair process, it seems that many IAMs and DFIs are adopting policies and practices that accommodate their own interests and those of their clients, but not the people whom the accountability processes were designed to help.

3. 1 Legitimacy

IAMs face an uphill battle in establishing trust with CSOs and project-affected communities. After all, the mechanism is housed in the very institution that financed the project alleged to have caused harm. Often the mechanism staff will be the only individuals from the DFI whom the complainants meet. One way to establish trust and, as a result, enhance the legitimacy of the IAMs is to demonstrate the independence of mechanism staff from the DFIs by having a selection process that includes CSOs and other external stakeholders. Of the IAMs reviewed for this report, the Compliance Advisor Ombudsman (CAO) of the International Finance Corporation (IFC) and Multilateral Investment Guarantee Agency (MIGA) provides the best example. A nomination committee is established with representatives from CSOs, academia and the private sector to recommend a candidate for CAO Vice President (VP) to the President of the World Bank Group. The Project Complaint Mechanism (PCM) of the European Bank for Reconstruction and Development (EBRD) is another example in which external stakeholders—though not necessarily CSOs—are involved in the selection of the PCM Officer and Experts.

Having diverse perspectives represented in the selection process may result in greater diversity among IAM staff. While some IAMs, such as the World Bank's Inspection Panel, strive to ensure the geographical diversity of their staff, their professional backgrounds can be quite similar. Experience working at environmental, labour and human rights CSOs would serve IAMs well given the need for the mechanisms to interact regularly with local, national and international CSOs. Without access to the hiring process, it is impossible to determine whether that is the result of a lack of CSO applicants or that CSO candidates do not advance.

Another way for IAMs to solicit the views of CSOs and other external stakeholders is by establishing an advisory group to provide guidance and feedback. For example, the CAO has a seven-member Strategic Advisors Group made up of representatives from the private sector, academia and civil society. Conflicts of interest are avoided because none of the members are actively involved in supporting complaints to the CAO.

3. 2   Accessibility

Over the more than two decades since the first IAM was created, one of the biggest challenges to ensuring the effectiveness of these mechanisms remains one of the most fundamental: project-affected people are not aware of their existence. The users of the mechanisms and even the mechanisms themselves confirm this general lack of awareness. [1] A recent report, which surveyed 800 people affected by development activities[2] in eight countries, found that 83% had never heard of the World Bank Inspection Panel. Although the IAMs have made significant efforts to raise awareness by organizing CSO workshops and attending public events,[3] there is more that they can and should do to improve outreach, including providing information in multiple languages and improving their websites. However, the single most important measure to guarantee the accessibility of the IAMs is for the DFIs to require their clients to publicise the existence and availability of the mechanisms during consultation processes with project-affected people.

Increasingly, DFIs are requiring their clients to establish project-level grievance mechanisms. While these mechanisms may be useful in addressing discrete concerns, project-affected people may not trust that a project-level mechanism would adequately address their issues because they are often designed and operated by the same actor that may have caused the harm. [4] For that reason, project-level grievance mechanisms should also provide information about the availability of an IAM in the event that users are not satisfied with the result or when communities lack the confidence to use them. Failure to proactively provide

---

[1] Compliance Advisor/Ombudsman, *Review of IFC's Policy and Performance Standards on Social and Environmental Sustainability and Policy on Disclosure of Information* (May 2010), http://www.cao-ombudsman. org/documents/CAOAdvisoryNoteforIFCPolicyReview _ May2010. pdf; Edward S. Ayensu, Second Review of the Independent Review Mechanism (IRM) of the African Development Bank Group, Report of the Consultant (Sept. 2014), http://www. afdb. org/fileadmin/uploads/afdb/Documents/Compliance-Review/2nd_ IRM_ Review_ - _ Consultant_ s_ Report_ - _ ENG. pdf.

[2] For a vision of what real development looks like, see IAP, *Back to Development.*

[3] Inspection Panel, IAMs-CSO Outreach Workshop in Turkey (May 2015), http://ewebapps. worldbank. org/apps/ip/Lists/NewsFromThePanel/NewsFromThePanelDisp. aspx? ID =211&source = http://ewebapps. worldbank. org/apps/ip/Pages/News-fom-the-panel. aspx; Inspection Panel, CSO Outreach Workshop in Zagreb, Croatia (July 2015), http://ewebapps. worldbank. org/apps/ip/Lists/NewsFromThePanel/NewsFromThePanelDisp. aspx? ID = 217&source = http://ewebapps. worldbank. org/apps/ip/Pages/News-fom-the-panel. aspx.

[4] Centre for Research on Multinational Corporations (SOMO), *The Patchwork of Non-Judicial Grievance Mechanisms* (Dec. 2014), http://grievancemechanisms. org/resources/brochures/non-judicial-grievance-mechanisms-apatchwork-1/at_ download/file.

such information creates a de facto eligibility requirement for complainants-namely, that complainants have sufficient resources and capacity to discover the mechanism on their own.

The IAMs were created to serve project-affected communities, and yet, the DFIs currently rely on chance to ensure that those who need them will actually find them. The Asian Development Bank (ADB) is unique among the banks in requiring its staff to work with clients to disclose information about the mechanism. While not explicitly referenced in the loan agreement, it is understood that the ADB's disclosure and safeguard policies require the clients to disclose this information. [1]

The World Bank recently included a reference to the Inspection Panel in its project documentation, which is available online. However, it is unclear whether it is translated and actively provided to project-affected people. Moreover, the text also makes reference to the World Bank's Grievance Redress System and project level grievance mechanisms. Both of those processes are operated by Bank management and clients, respectively, and as such are not considered independent grievance mechanisms. Reference to them in project documents may confuse project-affected communities and divert them from the Inspection Panel.

Once the complainants have found the appropriate mechanism, they may face barriers to filing a complaint. Both the Independent Consultation and Investigation Mechanism (MICI) of the Inter-American Development Bank (IDB) and the EBRD's PCM have recently adopted changes to their procedures that prevent complainants from requesting problem-solving and/or compliance review regarding a project that is being considered for financing but for which final approval has not yet occurred. A substantial number of client requirements precede project approval, including environmental and social due diligence and consultation with project-affected people, for which DFIs can and should be held accountable. In general, the earlier people can raise their concerns about a project, the easier it will be to accommodate them by modifying the design or improving mitigation measures, which can be addressed through a compliance review or via problem-solving. Such

---

[1] Based on review comments provided by ADB's AM, received 19 October 2015.

approves a budget increase. As seen in the case studies in the following chapter, delays, whatever the cause, can lead complainants to believe that there has been interference in what should be an independent process. This is especially true when the mechanism does not communicate adequately with the complainants about the status of their complaint, which is a widely occurring practice.

Lack of communication with complainants is an issue that arises not only when complainants experience delays in the process. Users express a desire for the mechanisms to be more proactive about providing status updates to complainants, even if it is only to say that the complaint is proceeding according to plan. Frequent communication helps complainants know what to expect from the process. The extent to which mechanisms communicate with complainants appears to vary not just between mechanisms but also from case to case.

Endowing mechanisms with the mandate to monitor the outcomes of their investigations and dispute resolution processes improves the predictability of the process by helping to ensure that commitments are implemented and measures are taken to address instances of non-compliance. However, not all mechanisms have a monitoring mandate, and many that do have only limited authority. For example, in the case of compliance reviews, many IAMs are limited to monitoring the implementation of the Management Action Plan prepared by the DFI to address the instances of non-compliance found by the mechanism's investigation. If the Management Action Plan is not adequate to address the findings of the mechanism, however, then full implementation of the Plan might still leave instances of non-compliance unaddressed and complainants without a response to their concerns.

3. 4　Equitability

An equitable complaint process would allow complainants the same rights of participation as the DFI and its client, but few do. The rules of procedure of many IAMs allow the DFIs to review and comment on draft reports, but do not afford the same opportunity to complainants. For example, the CAO shares a draft of its investigation with IFC for its comments, but does not provide the same opportunity to the complainants. At the conclusion of the process, when the IAM and the DFI management discuss the report and the appropriate response with the DFI's board of directors, the complainants are never in the room and they seldom have the opportunity to present their perspectives in writing. The procedures of the PCM and the AM provide good practice in this regard by including the complainants' comments when the final report is submitted to the relevant board.

Similarly problematic is the frequent failure of DFIs to respond adequately to the findings of non-compliance made by the IAMs in their investigation reports. This issue crops up repeatedly in the case studies detailed in the next chapter and in the user survey (see Annex 3). In general, complainants are not satisfied with the steps taken by DFIs and their clients to respond to complainants' concerns, either with regard to process or content. Complainants report that DFIs fail to consult with them when developing Management Action Plans (MAPs) that are intended to address the IAMs' findings. In order for meaningful consultation to occur, the complainants must first have access to the findings of the IAMs. In eight DFIs, the complainants do not have access to the IAM report prior to being consulted by DFI staff on the MAP. That means that complainants do not know whether and to what extent the mechanism has found instances of non-compliance, if and when they are asked by DFI staff about what measures to include in the MAP to correct them. The IFC is not even required to consult with complainants at all. Instead, both the CAO's investigation report and the IFC's proposed action plan are sent to the World Bank Group President for review and approval. The first time complainants see either document is after the President has approved them. This failure to consult explains, in part, complainants' dissatisfaction with the measures that DFIs and their clients propose to take to address their concerns.

More often than not, when IAMs find that DFIs have failed to comply with their own policies or procedures, causing harm to individuals or communities, the response of the DFI does not contemplate actions that are proportional to the violations, nor do they address the needs and concerns of the very people the DFIs seek to benefit. As seen in the next chapter, for those complainants who request or are limited to compliance review, after investing resources and several years going through the process, they might not-and often do not-see any concrete benefits or changes in their circumstances because of the failure of the DFI to respond meaningfully to the issues they have raised.

This inadequate response by DFIs is compounded by the absence of any appeals process. Complainants must accept a decision handed down by the same body—namely, the board of directors—that approved the project at issue. Complainants cannot appeal to a truly independent entity if they are dissatisfied with the outcome. The one striking exception is the EIB's Complaints Mechanism. If complainants are dissatisfied with the process or EIB's response, they can appeal to the European Union Ombudsman, who can determine if there has been maladministration, interpreted by the Ombudsman to include compliance with law and respect for human rights. [1] However, there are too few cases that have gone through the appeals process to determine whether it improves the complainants' chances of a successful outcome (see Annex 9 for more information). For the other DFIs to establish a similar appeals process, they would have to delegate power to or submit to the jurisdiction of an external body.

3.5 Transparency

IAMs must operate transparently in order to remain accountable to stakeholders, build confidence in their effectiveness, and respect the public interests at stake. The authors' analyses reveal wide variation in the kinds and amounts of information that the IAMs disclose regarding the complaints they receive. At one extreme, some IAMs provide no information regarding the content of past or pending complaints, the outcomes of closed cases or the rationale for determinations regarding individual complaints. [2] At the other extreme are those mechanisms that

---

[1] At your service, European Ombudsman, http://www. ombudsman. europa. eu/atyourservice/couldhe-helpyou. faces (last visited Nov. 12, 2015).

[2] For example, the following IAMs do not post any information regarding past or existing complaints on their respective websites, and are therefore excluded from the present research: Ombudsperson of the Brazilian Development Bank, www. bndes. gov. br/SiteBNDES/bndes/bndes_ en/Navegacao_ (转下页注)

publish a list of all past and pending complaints along with a description of the status of each, links to documentation submitted by the complainant, the DFI's response to the allegations raised in the complaint, other documents related to the complaint process and a reasonably detailed analysis of the IAM's decision regarding its treatment of the complaint. [1] Even within that group, not all mechanisms publish ineligible complaints. Approximately half of the IAMs fall somewhere between these two extremes. For example, the EIB's CM has only this year published online a complete registry of complaints received. However, due to EU privacy laws, it has yet to provide documentation or information regarding most of those cases. [2] Other IAMs post the text of complaints and disclose some information

---

(接上页注②) Suplementar/Ouvidoria); Compliance Officer of Export Development Canada, http://www. edc. ca/EN/About-Us/Management-and-Governance/Compliance-Officer/Pages/default. aspx); Examiner of Nippon Export and Investment Insurance, http://www. nexi. go. jp/en/environment/objection. html); or Australian Export Finance and Insurance Corporation, http://www. efic. gov. au/about-efic/our-organisation/complaints-mechanism/.

[1] The Independent Review Mechanism of the African Development Bank, http://www. afdb. org/en/about-us/structure/independent-review-mechanism-irm/requests-register/, Inspection Panel of the World Bank, http://ewebapps. worldbank. org/apps/ip/Pages/AllPanelCases. aspx, Compliance Advisor/Ombudsman of the International Finance Corporation and Multilateral Investment Guarantee Agency, http://www. cao-ombudsman. org/cases/, Office of Accountability of the Overseas Private Investment Corporation, https://www. opic. gov/who-we-are/office-of-accountability/public-registry-cases, and Independent Complaints Mechanism of FMO, https://www. fmo. nl/project-related-complaints, and DEG, https://www. deginvest. de/International-financing/DEG/Die-DEG/Verantwortung/Beschwerdemanagement/#4, provide most of this information for each case, including the text of the complaint, management's response, and the analysis undertaken by the respective IAM.

[2] The website of the Complaints Mechanism of the European Investment Bank contains an index listing the names of complaints received along with limited information concerning the nature of the allegations. See European Investment Bank, Complaints Mechanism Cases, http://www. eib. org/about/accountability/complaints/cases/index. htm. However, except in a few recent instances, see, e. g. , Belgrade By-Pass, Serbia, http://www. eib. org/about/accountability/complaints/cases/belgrade-by-pass. htm, the index generally does not provide copies of related documentation and for many cases lacks a description of the CM's analysis of complaints received. The CM publishes an annual Complaints Mechanism Activity Report, which provides (1) casework statistics, including an overview of the number of complaints received, deemed inadmissible, closed, or registered; (2) descriptions of some closed and pending cases; and (3) an annex containing a full list of all complaints received, their general subject matter, status within the complaint procedure, and outcome, where relevant. *See, e. g.* , European Investment Bank, Complaints Mechanism Activity Report 2014 (Nov. 2014), http://www. eib. org/infocentre/publications/all/complaints-mechanism-annual-report – 2014. htm.

about their own analyses and the status of cases, but in varying degrees of detail. ①

For a complaint process to work, complainants not only need information about and from the IAMs; first and foremost, they need access to information regarding the activities financed by DFIs. The amount of information available and the format in which it is available varies across DFIs and even across activities. For example, the AfDB posts project documents but not all in one place, requiring potential complainants to search through the DFI's database for all relevant information. The Dutch Development Bank FMO only recently started disclosing some of the activities it finances. However, the information provided is extremely limited, even for projects with the highest environmental and social risk. For each project disclosed, FMO publishes three paragraphs identifying the client, the objective and FMO's justification for the project. There is no link to an environmental and social impact assessment.

DFIs not only support traditional project finance where the funds are destined to one particular activity or project, but now also make use of many different types

---

① For example, the Independent Consultation and Investigation Mechanism (MICI) of the Inter-American Development Bank (http://www. iadb. org/en/mici/public-registry, 1805. html) and the Project Complaint Mechanism (PCM) of the European Bank for Reconstruction and Development (http://www. ebrd. com/workwith-us/project-finance/project-complaint-mechanism/ pcm-register. html) provide the complaint as well as a reasonably detailed analysis of the determination made in respect of the complaint, but do not consistently provide DFI management's response to the allegations raised in the complaint as a separate and independent document. The Examiner for Environmental Guidelines of the Japan International Cooperation Agency (http:// www. jica. go. jp/english/our_ work/social_ environmental/objection/index. html) provides a link to requests for examination, an indication of the phase of assessment, and a link to a document setting forth the ultimate determination made by the Examiner for the Guidelines, but provides very limited or no analysis of the reasoning that led to its determination. The Special Project Facilitator (SPF) of the Asian Development Bank (http://www. adb. org/site/accountability-mechanism/problem-solving-function/complaint-registry-year) posts complaints and analysis of complaints accepted for review, but does not provide a detailed analysis when complaints are rejected for further handling. However, the ADB's Compliance Review Panel (CRP) does publish comprehensive information about the complaints it handles (http://compliance. adb. org/dir0035p. nsf/alldocs/ BDAO – 7XGAWN? OpenDocument). The Canadian Office of the Extractive Sector's Corporate Social Responsibility Counsellor provides only limited analysis of its assessment of complaints that are rejected or do not proceed to full review (http://www. international. gc. ca/csr_ counsellor-conseiller_ rse/Registry-web-enregistrement. aspx? lang = eng).

of financing vehicles that make it more difficult for those affected to discover the source of the financing. One example is financing through other ' financial intermediaries', such as private equity funds or commercial banks. DFIs that fund financial intermediaries, like the IFC, will identify their direct client, but often not the final recipients of the funds. In other words, the identities of their clients' clients are rarely disclosed and nor are the location and purpose of the sub-projects supported by their clients. Although those affected by these sub-projects are entitled to file a complaint to the relevant IAM should they experience harm, in practice it is almost impossible for project-affected people to know that a DFI is involved in a project at all. [1]

3. 6   Rights-compatibility

The outcomes of complaints processes can only be rights-compatible if the standards against which the mechanisms are measuring DFI performance are themselves rights-compatible. Unfortunately, very few of the DFIs make explicit commitments to human rights. Those DFIs that do so—like the US Overseas Private Investment Corporation (OPIC) and the European Investment Bank (EIB) — fail to operationalize them in the form of enforceable policies and guidance notes, integrated into project design. The UN Special Rapporteurs have urged the World Bank to adopt human rights standards in its environmental and social safeguards, currently under review. [2]

DFIs and their IAMs can do more to protect the security of everyone involved in the complaint process-including complainants, consultants and CSOs. Beyond offering to keep complainants' identities confidential, IAMs have no other system in

---

[1]   Kate Geary, Oxfam. Int'l, *The Suffering of Others: The Human Cost of the International Finance Corporation's Lending Through Financial Intermediaries* (Apr. 2015), https://www. oxfam. org/ sites/www. oxfam. org/files/file_ attachments/ib-suffering-of-others-international-finance-corporation – 020415 – en. pdf [hereinafter OxfamInt'l, The Suffering of Others].

[2]   Letter from UN Special Mandate Holders, to Jim Yong Kim, World Bank Pres. (Dec. 12, 2014) (*available at* http://www. ohchr. org/Documents/Issues/EPoverty/WorldBank. pdf).

place to prevent or respond to reprisals when they occur. Because DFIs often have country or regional offices—unlike the IAMs, which are located at DFI headquarters—their staff may be in the best position to intervene in the event of reprisals against complainants. However, DFIs seemingly have no system or protocol in place to address security risks to those who criticise DFI-financed activities. The ability to raise concerns about DFI-financed activities, without fear for one's safety or security, is critical to ensuring sustainable development, not to mention the adequate implementation of DFI consultation requirements. Without adequate guarantees of protection, the risk of reprisals may prevent people from filing complaints to IAMs, thus limiting access to remedy. Unfortunately, the Inspection Panel's Ethiopia case described in the next chapter, demonstrates what can happen when DFIs and IAMs lack the systems to assess, prevent and address security risks.

None of the IAMs has the authority to compel action to prevent or end adverse human rights impacts caused by DFI-financed projects. That authority currently rests only with the entity that initially approved the project, and often that is the DFI's board of directors. Some mechanisms, however—including the PCM, IRM, CM and MICI—may at any time during the complaint process, recommend to the DFI that it suspend financing or processing of the project at issue if they believe that serious, irreparable harm will be caused. It appears, however, that this power has never been invoked. All other IAMs could benefit from having (or asserting) the same authority, although the extent to which it helps ensure respect for human rights depends on their willingness to use it.

3.7 Lessons Learned

The frequency with which IAMs find the same policy violations in their investigations demonstrates that DFIs are not sufficiently and systemically learning lessons from IAMs' cases to improve the implementation of their policies. One of the most striking pieces of evidence of this failure is the World Bank's recent Involuntary Resettlement Portfolio Review, which found " significant potential failures in the Bank's system for dealing with resettlement". [1] This dysfunction, and the attendant harms to those displaced, has continued despite the Inspection Panel's repeated findings of noncompliance with the involuntary resettlement policy over the years. [2] Improving the integration of IAM findings and lessons into future project design and implementation could be achieved through a management tracking system, perhaps similar to that used at the ADB with regard to ineligible complaints, [3] which records the measures taken by the DFI to address the concern (s) raised by complainants and the lessons the DFI has learned and will apply in the future.

Many DFIs invest repeatedly in the same client or sector, despite complaints filed related to those clients or activities. DFIs should not provide financing to clients found to be in non-compliance for activities likely to have similar environmental and social impacts unless and until those clients have remedied the situation and demonstrated their commitment and capacity to fully implement the environmental and social standards and prevent future harm.

Having an advisory mandate, like the CAO's, can also help IAMs shine a light on where DFI policy or its implementation should be improved. But even those IAMs without an official advisory mandate have found creative ways to identify and highlight trends in their own caseloads, often including their analyses in annual reports or, in the case of the ADB's AM, a 'Learning Report', which it publishes every three years. Regardless of the form it takes, however, this advice too often

---

① Social Development Department, World Bank, Involuntary Resettlement Portfolio Review: Phase II: Resettlement Implementation, (June 16, 2014).

② Submission to the World Bank's Safeguard Review and Update Process from the Inspection Panel, *Lessons from Panel Cases: Inspection Panel Perspectives* (May 2013), http://ewebapps. worldbank. org/apps/ip/Documents/IPN_ Inputs _ SafeguardsReview _ May2013. pdf [hereinafter Inspection Panel Comments on World Bank's Safeguard Review].

③ Asian Dev. Bank, *Accountability Mechanism Policy* 37, 196 (2012), http://www. adb. org/sites/ default/files/institutional-document/33440/files/accountability-mechanism-policy-2012. pdf. (stating "At the end of the process of addressing the ineligible complaints forwarded to the operations departments by the OSPF or CRP, the operations department will produce a report summarizing the complaint, issues, actions taken to address the problems or issues, decisions or agreements by parties concerned, results, and lessons. ")

seems to go unheeded by the DFIs. For example, it should be obvious that lessons learned from the Inspection Panel's cases should inform the update of the World Bank's environmental and social safeguard policies. The cases provide a rich source of information about implementation challenges and policy gaps. Nonetheless, in the initial approach paper outlining the consultation process for the World Bank's safeguard review, the Inspection Panel was not mentioned. [1] In the absence of CSO demands and the Panel's own initiative, it is unclear whether the World Bank would have benefited from the Panel's insights. [2]

---

[1] World Bank, The World Bank's Safeguard Policies Proposed Review and Update: Approach Paper (Oct. 2012), http://consultations. worldbank. org/Data/hub/files/consultation-template/review-and-update-world-banksafeguard-policies/en/materials/safeguardsreviewapproachpaper. pdf.

[2] Inspection Panel Comments, Comments on the Second Draft of the Proposed Environmental and Social Framework from the Inspection Panel (June 17, 2015), http://ewebapps. worldbank. org/apps/ip/Style% 20Library/Documents/Inspection% 20Panel% 20Comments% 20on% 202nd% 20Draft% 20ESF% 20 – % 2017% 20June% 202015. pdf.

4 Reflections from the Ground: A Qualitative Outcome Analysis

Using the UNGP effectiveness criteria to assess the IAMs and DFIs presents a challenge because the criteria are focused primarily on the process, not the outcome. The true test of the effectiveness of a complaints process, however, is whether the grievance is resolved. Are complainants better off for having submitted a complaint? In this chapter, the authors examine the results produced by the IAMs and DFIs. Because the effectiveness of the IAMs and DFIs varies over time, the authors have focused on cases that have concluded during the year period from 1 July 2014 to 30 June 2015. As a result, the current chapter provides a snapshot of the recent performance of the IAMs and DFIs.

As discussed in Chapter 2, the majority of complaints filed to date have been closed prior to achieving any results. While many of these complaints are closed because they fail to meet the minimum registration and eligibility criteria, a substantial number are found eligible, but still fail to proceed to a substantive phase of the complaints process. The first section of this chapter takes a look at all complaints that failed to reach or complete a substantive phase of the process during the research period and why, according to the IAMs, they failed to do so.

There are relatively few IAM complaints that reached a result, as defined in Chapter 2 in 2015. The case studies that follow in the second section of this chapter are presented from the complainants' perspectives, describing how they experienced the process and what they think of the result. Because the cases are unevenly distributed across institutions, it is not possible to undertake a comparative analysis. Rather, the case studies present complainants' recent experiences from which to benefit when considering reforms to make the accountability system more responsive to the needs of rights-holders.

The theme emerging from the case studies mirrors what the authors heard from the broader spectrum of users: on the positive side, complainants generally report that they are treated fairly by the IAMs and appreciate that their concerns are taken seriously. In the Avianca case, for example, the CAO's compliance review validated the complainants' grievances. In terms of real changes on the ground, however, there is little to be seen. Half of the complainants in the Bujagali case received a commitment of compensation, although this has yet to be realised. However, the other half are still waiting to see if they can obtain a similar commitment.

The case studies also confirm complainants describe feeling pressure and receiving threats after filing complaints. In the following cases, neither the DFI nor the IAM seemed to respond adequately, confirming the need for both to develop systems to better protect complainants and respond to reprisals, if they occur.

One conclusion that repeats itself throughout the case studies and the surveys that informed the previous chapter is that the failure to ensure redress for complainants is the result of the DFI's inability or unwillingness to commit to and implement measures that address complainants' grievances. Too often, complainants are left with a strong, compelling report by the IAM detailing significant deficiencies in the implementation of the DFI's environmental and social standards, but without an equally robust response from the DFI. Similarly, even where the DFI's client has made meaningful commitments to complainants through a dialogue process, the DFI rarely, if ever, contributes to the remedy, although it has contributed to the harm.

4.1　End of the Road: Cases that Close Prior to Achieving a Result

The authors have no expectation that every complaint can or should complete the complaint process. For example, complaints that relate to activities in which the

DFI is not involved are rightly dismissed. The significant number of complaints that have closed prior to achieving a result, however, merits a closer look in order to determine whether there are any unnecessary barriers or burdens that could be removed or alleviated.

Section 2.4 provides an overview of the percentage of complaints that fail either to meet eligibility requirements or reach a substantive phase of the complaint process. As indicated in Figures 8 and 9, some complaints do not advance through the substantive phase of the complaint process for reasons beyond the control of the mechanisms. This section focuses on the reasons why complaints do not advance that are the result of decisions made by the IAMs. ① The report authors analysed the information provided on each IAM website regarding complaints closed prior to achieving a result during the period 1 July 2014 until 30 June 2015. That information (or the lack thereof) gave rise to the following seven broad categories:

1. No explanation: The mechanism provided no explanation for closing or dismissing the complaint.

2. Withdrawn: The complaint was withdrawn by the complainant (s).

3. Complaint incomplete: The complaint did not provide all of the requisite information to be eligible for consideration by the mechanism.

4. Resolution outside IAM process: The mechanism deemed the complaint resolved or in the process of resolution between complainant (s) and the DFI or borrower/ client, outside the IAMs process, either: 1) through dialogue, consultation, mediation or similar dispute-resolution activities; or 2) through other actions undertaken by the DFI or borrower/client independently.

5. Outside the mechanism's mandate: The complaint fell outside the mechanism's mandate, 'jurisdiction', or authority because: 1) the activity or conduct that is the subject of the complaint is not part of the DFI's active or proposed portfolio (i. e. , it is not financed by, and/or is not being considered for

① Specifically, this section focuses on the reasons for ineligibility in Figure 7, the reasons why IAMs deemed problem-solving and compliance review were "unnecessary or inappropriate" in Figures 8 and 9, and the reasons why the IAMs deemed complaints resolved outside the complaint process in Figures 8 and 9.

financing from, the DFI); 2) the harm alleged in the complaint is not of the type that the mechanism is empowered to review; 3) the complainants failed to comply with one or more procedural prerequisites; and/or 4) the activities at issue otherwise fall outside of the substantive jurisdiction of the mechanism (for example, see Box 1).

6. Parallel proceeding: The mechanism declined to proceed to the substantive phase of the complaint process because there was pending litigation or other ongoing formal proceedings external to the financial institution regarding the subject of the complaint.

7. Insufficient causal link: The mechanism determined that the challenged conduct and/or alleged harm were too spatially or temporally attenuated from activities financed by the DFI or that the complaint had otherwise failed to assert a sufficient causal link between the conduct or harm in question and institutional financing.

Box #1:
Mining Dialogue Technical Assistance, Haiti

DFI / IAM: World Bank/Inspection Panel

DDICILENT: Government of Haiti

FILER: Kolektif Jistis Min an Ayiti (Haiti Justice in Mining Collective) and affected communities

SUPPORTING CSO : NYU CHR&GJ and Accountability Counsel

DATE OF FILING: 7 January 2015

DATE OF CLOSURE: 6 February 2015

REASON FOR FILING: The World Bank provided technical assistance to help the government of Haiti to draft a new national mining law. Complainants raised concerns that: 1) the mining law does not contain adequate protections for local communities and the environment; 2) the government lacks the capacity to adequately enforce any regulations in the new law anyway; and 3) the people of Haiti (and especially communities likely to be directly impacted by mining) have not been provided with adequate information about the new law and have not been adequately consulted about its development.

REASON CLOSED: Despite finding that the concerns were 'serious and legitimate', the Panel determined that reviewing the case would be outside its operational mandate, because the project was financed through a Bank-Executed Trust Fund to which the Bank's operational policies (including the safeguard policies) do not apply.

Among the reasons why cases closed without reaching or completing a substantive phase of the complaint process, at least two merit further examination. The first is that DFIs and some IAMs are narrowly defining the scope of the project, which may exclude potential complaints that seek to challenge that definition through complaint processes. The second is that barriers to compliance review, due to narrow project definitions or discretion by the mechanisms, are exacerbated when IAMs pursue alternative processes that deviate from their procedures.

4. 1. 1 Defining the Scope of the Project

How a DFI—and its IAM—defines the scope of a given project can determine the availability of redress for project-related grievances. One reason several IAMs gave for not advancing certain cases to the substantive phases of the complaint process was the absence of a sufficient causal link between a project supported by the relevant DFI and the alleged conduct or harm. The IAMs' reliance on this rationale underscores the importance of how a project's scope is defined and how its impacts are understood. Defining the boundaries of a project always involves a judgement call: does the project encompass only those activities directly financed by the DFI or does it extend to other activities, not financed by the institution, but necessary to the viability of the project, or which would not occur but for the existence of the DFI-financed project? Does the project scope encompass the consequences of DFI-financed activities, and if so, what are the temporal or spatial limits on attribution of responsibility for adverse impacts to a project? These hotly contested questions[①] are particularly thorny when a DFI provides budget support for broad, sector-wide reforms or activities (especially at the national level), but not necessarily specific activities undertaken within that sector pursuant to the reforms. Similar questions arise when a DFI finances the early, preparatory stages of a project, such as mineral exploration or large-scale infrastructure feasibility studies, but not the production or implementation phase, such as mineral extraction or the construction of a hydropower dam or other infrastructure installation.

Some IAMs appear more willing than others to question DFIs' definitions of their own projects. In one example, the CAO did not accept the IFC's narrow definition of a project's scope. IFC had provided support for the development of a legal framework for special economic zones (SEZ) in Papua New Guinea, and a complaint raised concerns about one of the SEZ's governed by the framework. [②] The IFC asserted that the alleged harms were not causally related to its project, which did not finance individual SEZs. [③] Although the CAO ultimately closed the case before undertaking a compliance review, it did not do so based on the IFC's project definition but because the IFC's advice had not yet been incorporated into Papua New Guinea's legal framework. The CAO thus left open the possibility that the IFC could be held accountable for the consequences of its advice once implemented.

Not all IAMs adopt this approach, however. In another case, complainants asserted that the EBRD's investment in a gold mining company, Lydian

---

① *See, e. g.*, Alf Jerve, Chairperson, World Bank Inspection Panel, Defining the boundaries of a project: Where does Bank accountability stop? Lessons from Panel cases and beyond, Presentation at World Bank Spring Meetings (Apr. 18, 2013) (presentation *available at* ewebapps. worldbank. org/apps/ip/Documents/IPN_ SpringMeetingsAreaofInfluence_ session_ Apr2013. pdf).

② Before being appraised for compliance review, this case had gone to the CAO's problem-solving phase, resulting in a signed agreement between the parties. Consequently, according to the methodology described in Chapter 2, the case is considered to have reached a substantive phase, but because the agreement was not implemented, it is not considered to have reached a result. Following the ultimately unsuccessful problem-solving phase, the CAO considered whether to pursue compliance review and ultimately decided against it. Thus, while this case did reach a substantive phase (dispute resolution) the project provides a useful illustration of an IAM closing a case prior to compliance review because of an insufficient causal link between the harm alleged and the project.

③ International Finance Corporation, Compliance Advisor/Ombudsman, Papua New Guinea/PNG SEZ – 01/Madang Province, http://www. cao-ombudsman. org/cases/case_ detail. aspx? id = 175.

International, could lead to environmental and social harms from mining activities at the Amulsar Gold Mine, due to the inadequacy of social and environmental assessments. [1] The EBRD maintained that its equity investment in the mining company was approved for use only in mineral exploration and project preparation, not mining extraction or production activities. Accepting this narrow framing of the project, the PCM determined that the complaint was ineligible for compliance review because it focused on the potential impacts of the eventual mine, which the EBRD had not yet committed to fund. [2] This interpretation of the project scope fails to take into account the singular purpose of mineral exploration and project preparation activities—that is, to lay the groundwork for eventual mining-and the fact that, if successful, such activities would lead to a variety of environmental and social impacts associated with mineral extraction.

A determination about a project's boundaries relates to the substance of the complaint, and cannot be made without due consideration of the allegations or a thorough appraisal by the IAM. Unquestioning reliance by the IAMs on the DFIs' own descriptions of their projects undermines the IAMs' ability to fulfil their role of providing relief to complainants when a DFI violates either the letter or the spirit of applicable policies and guidelines. Moreover, DFIs may be unwittingly limiting their own effectiveness by narrowly defining their projects and thereby excluding potential benefits as well as adverse impacts from their scope.

4. 1. 2   Balancing Compliance Review and Problem-Solving

Data regarding cases that have closed before reaching or completing a substantive phase of the complaint process this past year reflect persistent obstacles for complainants seeking a full compliance review. As highlighted in Chapter 2, of the 128 eligible, concluded cases that did not reach compliance review, in 73%

---

[1]   European Bank for Reconstruction and Development, Project Complaint Mechanism, DIF Lydian (Amulsar Gold Mine), Request Nos. 2014/03 and 2014/3, http://www. ebrd. com/work-with-us/project-finance/projectcomplaint-mechanism/pcm-register. html.

[2]   See Letter from CEE Bankwatch & SOMO to the EBRD Board of Directors (Feb. 24, 2015) (*available at* http://grievancemechanisms. org/ltronAmulsarfinal. pdf).

the compliance review was not initiated because the IAM decided it was unnecessary or inappropriate. Even after a complaint had been deemed eligible, if problem-solving was unavailable or had proven unsuccessful, or if complainants sought compliance review directly, IAMs still retained significant discretion in deciding whether to evaluate the DFI's adherence to its own policies. That discretion may be exercised in unclear and unpredictable ways.

At some mechanisms, like the CAO, which have both a problem-solving function and a compliance function, there were notable discrepancies in the types of issues that the IAM was willing to address through each function. Although IAM procedures may indicate that the same complaint can be pursued through problem-solving, compliance review, or both,[1] that is often not the case. Some types of grievances may in fact be too individual or specific to be addressed through a formal compliance investigation aimed at addressing systemic problems or patterns. But it is not always clear where that line is drawn.[2] For example, in some cases in which problem-solving was unsuccessful, the CAO went on to determine that the grievances at issue were not of the type amenable to compliance review because, even though they related to the social impacts of an IFC-finance

---

[1] *See, e. g.*, European Inv. Bank, The EIB Complaints Mechanism-Principle, Terms of Reference and Rules of Procedures (Oct. 2012), http://www. eib. org/attachments/strategies/complaints _ mechanism_ policy _ en. pdf; European Bank for Reconstruction and Dev. , *Approval of New Governance Policies*, http://www. ebrd. com/whatwe-do/strategies-and-policies/approval-of-new-governance-policies. html (linking to the 2014 updates of the Environmental and Social Policy, Public Information Policy, and PCM Rules of Procedure); Dutch Development Bank [FMO], Independent Complaint Mechanisms (2013), https://www. fmo. nl/l/en/library/download/urn: uuid: e15d0940 – 2f57 – 4dd8 – be94 – cfe11101218a/independent + complaints + mechanism + fmo. pdf? format = save_ to_ disk&ext = . pdf; German Development Bank [DEG], Independent Complaints Mechanism (2013), https://www. deginvest. de/DEG-Documents-in-English/About-DEG/Respon sibility/DEG_ Complaints-Mechanism_2014_05. pdf.

[2] It is not clear, for example, what the CAO means by " substantial concerns " or " systemic importance ," in the following oft-repeated phrases: " complaints ···indicative of substantial concerns regarding the environmental and social outcomes of the project or issues of *systemic importance* for IFC such that would merit a compliance investigation. " IFC Compliance Advisor/Ombudsman, Compliance Appraisal: Summary of Results, Yanacocha, Complaints 04 – 07 (May 29, 2015), http://www. cao-ombudsman. org/cases/document-links/documents/CAOAppraisalofYanacocha _ May 292015_ forweb_000. pdf (emphasis added).

project, they were not of sufficient magnitude or severity. ① This is a particularly troubling outcome when the client is the one whose unwillingness to engage in dispute resolution or preference for compliance review is what triggers the complaint's transfer to the IAM's compliance function—only to then have the complaint closed without a full investigation. ② In such cases, complainants are left without any meaningful response by the IAM/DFI to their grievances.

In other instances, the IAMs' use of alternative procedures or discretion authorized by their standard procedures forecloses compliance review while simultaneously falling short of problem-solving. For example, the World Bank's Inspection Panel (IP) handled two complaints under its new 'Early Solutions approach' (or 'Pilot Program'). ③ In another case closed this past year, the IP used a controversial interpretation of its standard procedures by first suspending consideration of the complaint while World Bank Management sought to address the concerns raised by the complaint and subsequently recommending against investigation after determining that Management's actions sufficiently addressed the substance of the complaint. The use of these procedures, especially when it is unclear how they will apply, threatens predictability for complainants.

Complainants have a right to opt for problem-solving as an alternative to compliance review or as a first step in addressing their grievances. Indeed, directing complaints to mediation or other negotiated dispute resolution as a first step may prove to be an effective way to prevent or mitigate harms. But the approach taken in

---

① *See, e. g.*, IFC Compliance Advisor/Ombudsman, Compliance Appraisal Report: Appraisal of IFC investment in Harmon Hall, Mexico (Apr. 8, 2015), http://www. cao-ombudsman. org/cases/document-links/documents/CAOCompliance_ AppraisalReport_ Mexico_ HarmonHall02 – 06and08_ Apr082015. pdf.

② *See, e. g.*, CAO Cases, Chile: Hidromaule-01/San Clemente, http://www. cao-ombudsman. org/cases/case_ detail. aspx? id = 226; IFC Compliance Advisor/Ombudsman, Compliance Appraisal: Summary of Results, IFC Investment in Hidromaule, Chile (June 22, 2015), http://www. cao-ombudsman. org/cases/document-links/documents/CAOCompliance _ AppraisalReport _ Chile _ Hidromaule-01_ 06222015_ forweb. pdf.

③ World Bank Inspection Panel, Paraguay: Sustainable Agriculture and Rural Development Project, http://ewebapps. worldbank. org/apps/ip/Pages/ViewCase. aspx? CaseId = 100; World Bank Inspection Panel, Nigeria: Lagos Metropolitan Development and Government Project, http://ewebapps. worldbank. org/apps/ip/Pages/ViewCase. aspx? CaseId = 94.

the IP's Early Solutions approach does not qualify as mediation or problem-solving. The pilot programme lacks any procedural safeguards to counteract the inherent power imbalance between the complainants and bank management, as well as other project actors. The absence of a mediator, for example, or any of the other protections, checks and balances that mediation would have, sets the pilot programme apart from formal problem-solving processes. The pilot programme is not well suited to ensuring that complainants meaningfully participate in the design and implementation of measures to address their own grievances.

The sequencing of IAM functions may affect the ability of the complaint to reach the other phase, or the outcomes of either or both phases. Complainants should be allowed to choose which phase they want to go to first (problem-solving or compliance), or to pursue both simultaneously. The efficacy of dialogue and negotiated dispute resolution depends greatly on the complainants' knowledge of and capacity to assert their rights. Sometimes, having the benefit of the information and analysis of an IAM's compliance review may help to rectify power imbalances between the complainants and the DFI or its client. At other times, the substance and process of the problem-solving phase (including its successes and failures) may actually bring to light systemic issues that require review through a compliance phase. At a minimum, whatever the sequence in which complaints are examined, IAMs should ensure that the results of problem-solving are no less protective than what is required by the DFI's environmental and social standards.

4. 2   The Lucky Few: Cases that Achieved Results

Twelve cases achieved results during the year period from 1 July 2014 to 30 June 2015: five at the CAO of the International Finance Corporation (IFC); three at the IP of the World Bank; one at the AM of the Asian Development Bank (ADB); one at the Examiners of the Japan International Cooperation Agency (JICA); one at the ICM of the Dutch Development Bank (FMO) and the German Development Bank (DEG); and one at OA of the US Overseas Private

Investment Corporation (OPIC). ① One further case is included here, at the CM of the European Investment Bank (EIB), because information initially provided on the CM's public registry indicated that it had achieved a result, but the case registry has since been updated, which clarified that no result had been achieved. Inability to contact complainants and practical considerations prevented the authors from researching all 12 cases. What follows are case studies for the seven cases in which the authors were able to interview the complainants, using the questions listed in Annex 4.

4. 2. 1　CASE STUDY#1　CM: New Forests Company, Uganda

This case was originally included in this report because, at the time of drafting, the EIB website indicated that it was closed on 20 November 2014 and had achieved a mediated solution. ② However, as discussed in more detail below, the CM has since released additional public information about this case clarifying that the CM never undertook a mediation process, nor did it complete a compliance review. Instead, complaints were addressed by the CAO, and the last process of dispute resolution associated with this complaint closed in May 2014, outside the research window. Nevertheless, a brief background is provided below.

In 2004, the New Forests Company (NFC), a London-based commercial timber company, began negotiating with the Ugandan Government to establish timber plantations in Uganda. NFC's investors in the proposed project included the commercial bank HSBC as well as the EIB and the IFC through its investment in a private equity fund called the Agri-Vie Agribusiness Fund. Uganda granted NFC a licence to develop three timber plantations totalling around 20,000 hectares in the Mubende and Kiboga districts in central Uganda and the Bugiri district in eastern Uganda. By 2011, NFC had planted around 12 million pine and eucalyptus trees

---

① The OA/OPIC case relates to OPIC's investment in Buchanan Renewables Biomass. The OA received a complaint from affected communities regarding this investment, but it was declared inadmissible because the project had already closed. OPIC management then requested that the OA should perform an independent review of the project. For more information, see: https://www. opic. gov/who-we-are/office-of-accountability/buchananrenewables.

② EIB Complaints Mechanism, NFC Forestry Project, Uganda, http://www. eib. org/about/accountability/complaints/cases/nfc-forestry-project. htm.

on 9,300 hectares and was employing more than 1,400 people. However, the establishment of the plantations led to the forced removal of around 22,500 or more people in Mubende and Kiboga districts combined. [1]

As this report was going to press, the CM posted its Conclusions Report on this project, [2] dated November 2014, which detailed its engagement in the case. In October 2011, in response to a report by Oxfam that documented the evictions, [3] the EIB President requested that the CM should investigate the allegations. The CM suspended its investigation after one week, "pending the results of different investigation and mediation processes" including the mediation facilitated by the CAO. [4] However, the CAO did not receive complaints about NFC's activities in Mubende and Kiboga until a month after the CM suspended its investigation. These complaints were accepted, and while initially the CAO considered pooling resources with the EIB, the mediation process began and ended without the formal involvement of the CM. The CAO mediation process resulted in final agreements being reached in July 2013 and May 2014 in the Mubende and Kiboga district complaints, respectively. The agreements represent the 'full and final settlement' between the communities and NFC on the issues set out in their respective complaints before the CAO. [5] Pursuant to the agreements, the NFC agreed to support the founding of a local cooperative society and to "work closely with the co-operative and its members to build more solid and lasting mutually beneficial relations with the community". [6] Currently the CAO is monitoring the

---

[1] For more information, *see generally* Oxfam Int'l, The New Forests Company and its Uganda Plantations: Oxfam Case Study (Sept. 2011), https://www.oxfam.org/en/research/new-forests-company-and-its-uganda-plantations-oxfam-case-study.

[2] EIB Complaints Mechanism, NFC Forestry Project, Complaint MC/E/2011/13, Conclusions Report (Nov. 20, 2014), http://www.eib.europa.eu/attachments/complaints/2014 – 11 – 20 – letter-from-eibsg-nfc-forestry-project-final-reply-annex-conclusions-report.pdf [hereinafter EIB Complaints Mechanism, NFC Forestry Project Conclusions Report].

[3] Oxfam Int'l, *The New Forest Company and its Uganda Plantations: Oxfam Case Study*.

[4] EIB Complaints Mechanism, NFC Forestry Project Conclusions Report.

[5] CAO Cases, Uganda/Agri-Vie Fund – 02/Mubende, http://www.cao-ombudsman.org/cases/case_detail.aspx? id = 181.

[6] CAO Cases, Uganda/Agra-Vie Fund-01/Kiboga, http://www.cao-ombudsman.org/cases/case_detail.aspx? id = 180; CAO Cases, Uganda/Agri-Vie Fund – 02/Mubende.

implementation of the agreements over the course of four years to ensure their "smooth implementation, sustainability and success" . ①

After the conclusion of the CAO's mediation process, the CM determined that a full investigation was unnecessary and closed the case. ② According to the CM's website, a follow-up is scheduled for 20 November 2015. ③ The CAO's Operational Guidelines that were in effect at the time the complaints were filed precluded the possibility of a compliance review following the successful conclusion of a mediation process. As a result, there will be no investigation of this project by either IAM to determine whether the lenders complied with relevant environmental and social standards, no contribution by the lenders to redress the harms the community suffered, and no lessons learned to improve future projects.

4. 2. 2 CASE STUDY#2 CAO: Aerovías del Continente Americano S. A. (Avianca), Colombia

BACKGROUND: Avianca (*Aerovías del Continente Americano S. A.*) is one of the largest commercial airlines in Latin America and operates from its main base at El Dorado International Airport in Bogotá, Colombia. In 2009, the IFC provided a US $50 million corporate loan to Avianca and its subsidiaries to facilitate the company's plans to renew its fleet. The aim was to reduce costs, improve efficiency and safety, and to provide a better passenger service.

THE COMPLAINT: In November 2011, a complaint was submitted by the International Trade Union Confederation (ITUC) /Global Unions Washington Office in cooperation with the International Transport Workers' Federation (ITF). The complaint also reflected consultation with Colombian affiliates of ITF: the national airline workers' union (*Asociacion Colombiana De Auxiliares De Vuelo-*

---

① CAO Cases, Uganda/Agra-Vie Fund-01/Kiboga, *supra* note 72; CAO Cases, Uganda/Agri-Vie Fund-02/Mubende.

② EIB Complaints Mechanism, NFC Forestry Project Conclusions Report, at 6.

③ EIB Complaints Mechanism, NFC Forestry Project, Uganda.

ACAV) and the national civil aviation union (*Asociacion Colombiana De Aviadores Civiles*-ACDAC), representing workers at Avianca. ① The complainants raised various concerns related to labour rights violations at Avianca, as well as violations surrounding the right to freedom of association. First, that Avianca violated IFC Performance Standard 2 (PS2) —Labor and Working Conditions—in particular by discriminating against union members and taking various measures to discourage union membership. Secondly, that IFC failed at various stages in the project cycle to properly manage issues related to its client's compliance with PS2. Thirdly, that IFC and/or its client failed to disclose documents as required by the IFC Performance Standards and Access to Information Policy. The final allegation was that IFC failed to conduct a rigorous assessment of PS2 compliance of Taca Airlines subsequent to its merger with Avianca. ②

THE RESULT: During the assessment process, local unions expressed their willingness to engage in a dispute resolution process with Avianca convened by the CAO. However, Avianca was not willing to engage as they believed the unions had not yet exhausted the internal channels of communication. As a result, the case was transferred to CAO compliance. The CAO compliance investigation was disclosed on 18 May 2015, nearly four years after the complaint was submitted and over two years after the CAO appraisal determined that an investigation was warranted. ③ It is sharply critical of IFC's handling of serious deficiencies at Avianca in respecting its employees' freedom of association. The report states that, in light of information IFC had received from Colombian unions and the ILO prior to approval of the

---

① Letter of complaint regarding Avianca, Colombia. to the IFC Compliance Advisor/Ombudsman (Nov. 14, 2011) (*available at* http://www. cao-ombudsman. org/cases/document-links/documents/ Aviancacomplaint_111411_web. pdf).

② IFC Compliance Advisor/Ombudsman, Compliance Appraisal for Audit of IFC regarding Avianca S. A. , Colombia: Case of Complaint from Global Unions on behalf of unions representing employees of Avianca January (Jan. 8, 2013), http://www. cao-mbudsman. org/cases/document-links/ documents/CAOAppraisalReport_ Avianca_ January82013. pdf.

③ IFC Compliance Advisor/Ombudsman, CAO Investigation of IFC Investment in Avianca, Colombia (May 18, 2015), http://www. cao-ombudsman. org/cases/document-links/documents/CAOInvesti-gationReportAvianca-May182015. pdf.

Avianca loan, it should not have made loan disbursements in 2009. ① The CAO also criticises IFC for its failure to require Avianca to disclose its action plans and assessments regarding compliance with IFC's labour standard obligations, in violation of IFC's 2006 Environmental and Social Sustainability Policy. CAO will monitor IFC's actions in response to this report and expects to issue a monitoring report within one year of the date of publication. ②

OOTCOME SATISFACTION③: In general terms, the complainants are satisfied with CAO's compliance review, but dissatisfied with IFC's response to it. The complainants think that CAO's investigation report published on 18 May 2015 "was very well done, well documented and researched" and they are "really satisfied with its findings and the documentation of the facts, which is a 95% confirmation of the concerns presented in the submission of 2011 " . ④ The complainants are particularly pleased with one specific finding: CAO finds that IFC's decision to disburse US $35 million to the client in July 2009 was made without sufficient basis to meet the requirement of the 2006 Sustainability Policy that "IFC does not finance new business activity that cannot be expected to meet the Performance Standards over a reasonable period of time" . They believe this may prevent comparable violations in the future, if the finding is taken into serious consideration by the IFC. In the Avianca case, it was clear for the complainants that "at the moment the company received the money, its attitude was that meeting the Performance Standards made no difference" . ⑤ In a recent public statement,

---

① Press Release, ITUC-ITF, Avianca-Colombia: *IFC should follow ombudsman's recommendations for labour standards compliance, say unions* (May 19, 2015) (available at http://www. ituc-csi. org/ avianca-colombia-ifc-should-follow? lang = es) [hereinafter ITUC-ITF Avianca Press Release].

② *Id.*

③ This assessment is based on a telephone interview with Peter Bakvis, Director of the International Trade Union Confederation (ITUC) /Global Unions-Washington, DC office on June 29, 2015. Peter Bakvis, who speaks on behalf of one of the organisations that submitted the complaint did not wish to remain anonymous and agreed to have the interview recorded. The recording of the interview with Bakvis (in Spanish) is available for consultation. Telephone interview with Peter Bakvis, President, Int'l Trade Union Confederation (ITUC) /Global Unions-Washington, DC office (June 29, 2015).

④ *Id*

⑤ *Id.*

Sharan Burrow, ITUC General Secretary, said, "It is obvious that once Avianca received the payments on its IFC loan it ceased to take the standards seriously and saw compliance as voluntary". [1]

The complainants' satisfaction with the CAO's report is in strong contrast to their opinion about the IFC's response to it, which they consider to be very weak and unsatisfactory. According to ITUC Director Peter Bakvis, there were no significant changes made to the project with regards to workers' rights: "The company practices that were documented when the complaint was submitted, continue today and workers' rights are still not being respected". [2] Moreover, the complainants wrote a letter to the World Bank's president, Jim Yong Kim, at the beginning of June, asking him to address the CAO's findings. However, at the time of the interview they had not received any response from the Bank. A major change that the complainants did see as a result of submitting the complaint was that "Avianca repaid the whole loan in 2013, even before the term had expired. Thus, now despite the findings of CAO's report, the IFC has no capacity to leverage the company by financial measures to modify its practices. "

When asked whether they would advise others to use this mechanism, ITUC's Director Bakvis responded he would do so "but as a last resort, taking into consideration the limitations of the CAO and its lack of capacity to modify the client's practices and the length of time of the whole process". In summary, they would recommend the use of the mechanism to obtain a well-documented and thoroughly researched investigation but not necessarily to resolve concrete immediate problems.

PROCESS SATISFACTION: On the whole, the complainants are satisfied with the complaint process, even though the many delays were frustrating and the process put further pressure on the complainants.

In terms of accessibility of the mechanism, the complainants highlighted that "the information available on the CAO's webpage explains quite well the process to

---

[1] ITUC-ITF Avianca Press Release.
[2] Telephone interview with Peter Bakvis.

submit a complaint". [1] Moreover, they feel that the process to file the complaint was not difficult and they were also supported throughout the process by the CAO's staff. They were informed about the documents they required for the submission and other relevant information. The complainants did not encounter any obstacles regarding languages or costs. Nonetheless, the complainants feel that the complaint process added to the already existing pressure on Avianca workers by the company. [2]

With regard to legitimacy, the complainants feel that the CAO made their best efforts to handle the complaint well. In their experience, the mechanism had a constructive attitude. Consequently, they considered the process, in general, to be fair. The only aspect that they identify as unfair, were the constant delays at each stage of the process. The complainants repeatedly expressed the view that the delays caused significant frustration, but they were always able to share that with the mechanism. Also, the requirement in the previous version of the CAO's Operational Guidelines that the case must first go through the Ombudsman process was seen as an unnecessary delay and a "waste of time"[3] for the complainants, because the company had been reluctant to solve the problems from the very beginning.

In terms of predictability, the complainants were well aware before submitting the complaint, "that the process was not going to be quick, and that the process would not result in a cancellation of the loan". [4] The CAO explained its limitations to the unions involved and warned them that the process would probably not resolve their problems regarding their objective to allow freedom of association. [5]

Regarding equitability, the complainants were satisfied with CAO's work, as the requirements for submitting the complaint were explained well. They felt supported with information and advice to fully understand the whole process and its objective.

---

[1] Telephone interview with Peter Bakvis.

[2] *Id.*

[3] *Id.*

[4] *Id.*

[5] *Id.*

Finally, the complainants expressed some frustrations regarding transparency and the lack of information during the process. For example, "the CAO officially informed them about the decision of not carrying out a dispute resolution process several months after the decision was made" . ① Also, Bakvis stated that some CAO staff informed him in August 2014 that the final CAO investigation report was ready, but they had to wait nine more months until the CAO finally published the report in May 2015. ② According to Bakvis, this only happened after a personal meeting with the CAO's Vice-President, when he requested the publication of the document. ③ The complainants also mentioned that the CAO was privy to information it could not share with complainants. ④ In general terms, the complainants reported that the CAO informed them when there were particular obstacles or delays during the process, but did not do so proactively. ⑤ Moreover, there is still some information that has not yet been published on the webpage.

Because of IFC's failure to respond to the CAO's findings, the CAO process did not result in rights compatible remedies for the complainants. As stated before, complainants considered that "in terms of workers' rights, which were the basis of the complaint, there were no significant changes or outcomes: the company practices that were documented when the complaint was submitted, continue today and workers' rights are still not being respected," ⑥ specifically workers still do not have freedom of association.

According to the IFC, they have learned lessons from this case. In its response to the CAO Compliance Investigation Report, ⑦ the IFC states that:

"in the eight years since IFC's investment in Avianca, we have taken a

---

① Telephone interview with Peter Bakvis.

② *Id.*

③ *Id.*

④ *Id.*

⑤ *Id.*

⑥ *Id.*

⑦ IFC Response to CAO Compliance Investigation Report in respect of IFC's Investment in Avianca, Colombia (May 5, 2015), http://www. cao-ombudsman. org/cases/document-links/documents/ Avianca_ IFCPublicResponse_ InvReport_ May52015. pdf.

number of steps to strengthen our practice regarding labor issues, including through capacity building and training of environmental and social (E&S) specialists on assessing and managing labor-related risks, developing internal and external guidance on managing labor issues, relying on the support of independent international labor experts, and having regular interaction with the Global Unions. IFC has also improved its disclosure practice as a result of the 2012 Access to Information Policy. We remain committed to continuous learning and improvement of our E&S risk management practice. IFC also agrees with CAO's observations regarding the importance of looking at country and sector risks beyond the scope of IFC's investment. As communicated in other recent IFC Management responses, we have made procedural and organizational changes to improve in this area. " ①

However, there are no systems in place to verify IFC's claims of improved attention to labour issues. The only way to follow this up is after the next complaint to the CAO regarding labour issues.

4.2.3　CASE STUDY #3　CAO: Banco Financiera Comercial Hondureña (Ficohsa), Honduras

BACKGROUND: *Banco Financiera Comercial Hondureña* (Ficohsa) is the third largest bank in Honduras and one of Central America's most important banks. Following earlier investments in Ficohsa in 2008 to support trade finance, housing and loans to small—and medium—sized enterprises (SMEs), in May 2011 the IFC Board approved an equity investment (US $32 million) and sub-ordinated debt investment (US $38 million) in Ficohsa. Prior to making its equity investment, IFC identified that Ficohsa provides corporate financing in sectors that have significant, potential environmental and social (E&S) risk, such as energy, construction and agribusiness. It was the relationship between Ficohsa and *Corporación Dinant* that triggered CAO's concerns about IFC's investment in

---

① IFC Response to CAO Compliance Investigation Report in respect of IFC's Investment in Avianca, Colombia (May 5, 2015), http://www. cao – ombudsman. org/cases/document – links/documents/ Avianca_ IFCPublicResponse_ InvReport_ May52015. pdf.

Ficohsa. Corporación Dinant (Dinant) is an integrated palm oil and food company with plantations totalling over 20, 000 hectares in northern Honduras. In 2009, IFC committed a US $30 million loan to Dinant of which US $15 million was disbursed in November 2009. A second disbursement of US $15 million has been delayed due to concerns regarding security and conflict issues around Dinant's plantations in the *Aguán Valley* since mid - 2010. [1]

THE COMPLAINT: In 2012, the CAO Vice-President triggered a compliance investigation on IFC's investment in Dinant. [2] This was in response to allegations about violence against farmers on and around Dinant's plantations in the Aguan Valley (Honduras) as the result of inappropriate use of private and public security forces under Dinant's control or influence. In the course of this investigation—the findings of which demonstrated significant failures in the IFC's assessment of risk and implementation of its environmental and social policies—CAO became aware that Dinant is one of Ficohsa's largest borrowers. As a result IFC had a significant exposure to Dinant through its equity stake in Ficohsa. As a result, the CAO Vice-President initiated a compliance appraisal of IFC's investment in Ficohsa. In its appraisal report, released in December 2013, [3] CAO concluded that IFC's environmental and social performance with regard to its investments in Ficohsa merited further enquiry and initiated a compliance investigation.

THE RESULT: CAO's investigation focused on IFC's performance, and, as such, does not make findings about Banco Ficohsa's action or inaction. CAO completed the investigation on 13 June 2014 and submitted the report to IFC for official response.

---

① IFC Compliance Advisor/Ombudsman, CAO Investigation of IFC Environmental and Social Performance in relation to Investments in Banco Financiera Comercial Hondurena S. A. (Ficohsa) (Aug. 6, 2014), http://www. cao-ombudsman. org/cases/document-links/documents/CAOInvestiga tionofIFCRegardingFicohsa_ C-I-R9-Y13-F190. pdf [hereinafter CAO Compliance Investigation Report-Ficohsa].

② See CAO Cases, Honduras/Dinant-01/CAO Vice President Request, http://www. cao-ombudsman. org/cases/case_ detail. aspx? id = 188.

③ IFC Compliance Advisor/Ombudsman, CAO Compliance Appraisal of IFC investments in Banco Ficohsa (Dec. 4, 2013), http://www. cao-ombudsman. org/cases/document-links/documents/CAO_ Appraisal_ Ficohsa_ C-I-R9-Y13-F190. pdf.

Following clearance by the President, the final investigation report and IFC's response was released by CAO on 11 August 2014. [1] The report describes material shortcomings in the way that IFC discharged its environmental and social obligations in relation to the Ficohsa investment.

Thus, the report criticized the IFC for supporting Ficohsa without proper vetting, as its earlier findings against Dinant meant the IFC was now re-exposed to a company accused of fomenting land conflict and violence. The approval of the Ficohsa loan went ahead even after the IFC knew about the problems with the Dinant loan. Not only was Dinant Ficohsa's third largest client at the time of the loan, but the CAO also noted that, in 2012, Ficohsa reported a financial relationship with 64 Category A clients-those at high risk of causing negative environmental or social impacts. Of these, only 48% were in compliance with its environmental and social policies. The CAO found that despite this, the IFC did not identify measures its client should take to mitigate these risks: a large-scale failure of due diligence. The CAO investigation report also notes that, "Reviewing information available through the media, CAO notes reports of E&S concerns in relation to a number Ficohsa clients operating in the agribusiness, tourism, construction and hydropower sectors". IFC's lack of transparency regarding the identity of Ficohsa's high-risk clients makes it impossible to verify the full impact of these failures. [2] Finally, the report established that CAO will monitor IFC actions in response to the CAO findings and issue a monitoring report within the next year. [3]

OUTCOME SATISFACTION: As described above, the CAO's investigation of IFC's investment in Ficohsa was triggered not by a complaint from affected communities, but by the CAO VP. One of the organisations active on the issue— the Plataforma Agraria Regional del Valle del Aguán—has engaged with the CAO

---

[1] CAO Compliance Investigation Report-Ficohsa.

[2] Oxfam Int'l, The Suffering of Others, at 7 – 10.

[3] CAO Communique, Summary of Key Findings-Compliance Investigation of IFC Environmental and Social Performance in relation to Investments in Banco Financiera Comercial Hondureña S. A. (Ficohsa) (Aug. 11, 2014) (available at http://www. cao-ombudsman. org/cases/documentlinks/documents/CAOCommunique_ Ficohsa_ SummaryofFindings_ August112014. pdf).

and the IFC on this case. While they are not able to provide input about the process as complainants, they were able to express their views and perceptions about the outcomes and the way they were (or not) involved in the whole process, regarding both the Ficohsa and Dinant cases.

In the words of the interviewees,[①] "this is an unusual case because there was an audit at the request of CAO's Vice President but there was no complaint, so the campesino movements didn't have a participation space in the process. [②] That's why the conflict resolution phase was not contemplated and the complaint went directly to compliance. The same happen with regards the elaboration of the action plans to follow up on the IFC's responses to the audits in the Dinant and Ficohsa cases: there was neither space nor recognition for the participation of the campesino movements. This, in turn, led to the presentation of two complaints to the CAO in 2014, this time directly by the affected communities, regarding Dinant and a Financial Intermediary (OLEOPALMA)." [③]

In terms of the outcomes of the process, interviewees agreed that the best outcome of CAO's involvement in the Dinant and Ficohsa cases were the reports produced. Generally, and with a few caveats, the interviewees thought the reports "helped support the claims and demands of the campesino movement."[④] The reports also "helped raise concern in the national and international media and public opinion about the situation of the campesino movement and the constant violations of human rights in the Aguán". [⑤] The CAO's reports were also useful as

---

① Telephone interview with members of the Plataforma Agraria Regional del Valle del Aguán (Aug. 7, 2015).

② Despite not having a formal participation space in the process, the interviewees affirmed that the CAO contacted them to get and provide information about the case when they were working on the audits.

③ See CAO Cases, Honduras/Dinant-03/Aguan Valley, http://www. cao-ombudsman. org/cases/case_ detail. aspx? id = 223; CAO Cases, Honduras/Financial Intermediary (FI) – 01, http://www. caoombudsman. org/cases/case_ detail. aspx? id = 231. Even though the interviewees expressed a series of concerns and views regarding these cases, they were not considered for the purpose of this report.

④ Telephone interview with members of the Plataforma Agraria Regional del Valle del Aguán.

⑤ *Id.*

advocacy tools at the international level.

Despite this, interviewees were not satisfied with "the lack of formal participation before the audits" and, above all, "with the process following CAO's presentation of the reports to the IFC". [1] In this sense, interviewees expressed the view that their main dissatisfaction is related to IFC's involvement: "even though the institution was well aware of human rights violations in the Bajo Aguán and the irregularities that the campesinos had been highlighting regarding land transfer, they decided to finance Corporación Dinant anyway, and it was only after CAO's audits that this situation was unmasked." [2]

Moreover, interviewees were also dissatisfied with IFC's responses to the findings of CAO's investigations and the institution's lack of commitment to solving the problem, specifically, and addressing poverty more generally: "IFC, as part of the World Bank Group, is breaking the mandate for which it was created after the Second World War: to fight poverty. Thus, through financing of corporations that manage lands and promote the displacement of campesinos, it is actually promoting more poverty, not fighting against it." [3]

PROCESS SATISFACTION: Since interviewees were not involved as complainants in the process, this evaluation is mostly not possible.

IFC 's lessons learned: In April 2014, in response to pressure from both civil society and its own Board following the CAO's investigation report on the IFC's loan to Dinant, the IFC formulated an Action Plan and hired the Washington, DC-based Consensus Building Institute to determine whether mediation to resolve the conflicts between the government, Dinant and affected communities is possible.

The IFC also contracted the law firm Foley Hoag to advise it on human rights issues related to Dinant's Security Action Plan. Dinant has committed itself to implementing the Voluntary Principles on Security and Human Rights.

On 14 July 2014, the IFC published its *Management Response to the CAO*

---

[1] Telephone interview with members of the Plataforma Agraria Regional del Valle del Aguán.

[2] *Id.*

[3] *Id.*

Compliance Investigation Report on Banco Financiera Comercial Hondurena S. A. (*Ficohsa*). ① In its response, IFC management recognized some of CAO's findings and mentioned a series of institutional lessons learned from the report, including, inter alia:

"Overall the report correctly identifies shortcomings in previous practice, particularly as regards gaps in IFC's appraisal, prior to the IFC investment in Ficohsa in 2011 and a lack of due consideration of the potential environmental and social risks in the Bank's portfolio. Our practices and procedures at that time did not require us to cross check our FI client's key exposures against our own direct investment portfolio projects. Since then we have taken steps to close these gaps and facilitate better information sharing among staff working in different parts of the institution. "

"IFC has been taking a number of steps that address many of the report findings, including through the 2012 Sustainability Framework updates and the Action Plan developed as a result of CAO's audit of IFC investments in Financial Intermediaries. "

"IFC E&S risk management practice is constantly evolving and we seek to continually improve in this regard. When there are gaps in our approach, as was the case with our investments in Ficohsa, we remain committed to acting quickly, learning from our mistakes, and making the necessary course corrections for our future endeavours. "

"We are also seeing positive progress in our work with Ficohsa to strengthen its E&S risk management systems and practices. "

4.2.4   CASE STUDY#4   CAO: Bujagali Energy Project, Uganda

BACKGROUND: The Bujagali Energy Project involved construction of a dam, hydropower plant and transmission lines at Uganda's Bujagali Falls, in

---

① IFC Management Response to the CAO Compliance Investigation Report on Banco Financiera Comercial Hondurena S. A. (Ficohsa) (July 14, 2014), http://www. cao-ombudsman. org/cases/document-links/documents/IFCResponsetoCAOregardingFicohsa_July142014. pdf.

southeastern Uganda, between 2007 and 2012. The transmission line was built by the Uganda Electricity Transmission Company Ltd. (UETCL), Uganda's national transmission company. The IFC contributed US $ 130 million in loans to the project,[1] and several other financial institutions, including the EIB and the AfDB also provided financing and loan guarantees.

THE COMPLAINT[2]: On 16 May 2011, community members impacted by the project filed a complaint with the CAO, designated Bujagali-5.[3] In the Bujagali-5 complaint, community members alleged impacts caused by the main components of the project, including land taken for the transmission line, and damage to houses and health caused by blasting.[4] The complaint also alleged numerous problems with the level of compensation offered to the community to offset these impacts. The CAO found the Bujagali-5 complaint eligible for further assessment in June 2011, which subsequently resulted in a CAO-led mediation process.

Prior to filing the Bujagali-5 complaint, a complaint naming approximately 550 community members was filed in 2008 in the Uganda national court against UETCL,

---

[1]   Press Release, World Bank, World Bank Group Approves Support for Bujagali Hydropower Project That Will Address Uganda's Power Shortages (Apr. 26, 2007) (*available at* http://web. worldbank. org/WBSITE/EXTERNAL/PROJECTS/0, contentMDK: 21315008 ~ pagePK: 41367 ~ piPK: 279616 ~ theSitePK: 40941, 00. html).

[2]   The project has resulted in numerous grievances, and since the year 2000, seven complaints related to the project have been filed with the CAO alone. The CAO has given numerical designations to each of these complaints. Compliance Advisor/Ombudsman, *CAO Cases*, *Uganda/Bujagali-02/Bujagali Falls*, http://www. cao-ombudsman. org/cases/case _ detail. aspx? id = 114. See also National Association of Professional Environmentalists, Unsettling Business: Social Consequences of the Bujagali Hydropower Project 12 (2014), http://nape. or. ug/wp-content/uploads/Bujagali _ unsettlingbusiness. pdf [hereinafter "Unsettling Business"].

[3]   Complaint from the Bujagali Affected Community to the CAO (May 10, 2011), http:// www. caoombudsman. org/cases/document-links/documents/2011_ May16Complaint_ redacted. pdf. The Bujagali-5 Complaint is the fifth of seven complaints related to the dam that have been filed with the CAO starting in 2000. It is the second of four complaints filed against BEL, which all remain open. This is the first of two cases that went through the CAO Ombudsman; the other two went through the CAO compliance function.

[4]   See Compliance Advisor/Ombudsman, Ombudsman Assessment Report: Fifth Complaint (Bujagali Energy-05) Regarding the Bujagali Energy Ltd. Project 6 – 7 (Dec. 2011).

alleging that community members had not received fair and adequate compensation for impacts caused by the project. Those named in the court case represented only a fraction of the several thousand people (possibly as many as 5,000[1]) who were impacted by the transmission line. The filing of the court case resulted in the creation of two groups within the community: those who were named in the court case (hereinafter ' Group 1 ') and those who were not named (hereinafter ' Group 2 '). This became an important issue in the CAO mediation, as discussed below.

THE RESULT: The CAO lists the current status of the Bujagali-5 complaint as "facilitating settlement" . [2] The mediation process resulted in UETCL agreeing to make payments to Group 1 members no later than July 2015, with the exact amount of each payment to be decided on a case-by-case basis. UETCL did not meet its July 2015 deadline to make payments, but at the time of writing, it had started the process. There has been no official word yet on when another mediation process will begin to address the Group 2 members.

OUTCOME SATISFACTION[3]: It is important to note that UETCL's willingness to mediate at all—which the complainants attribute to the involvement of the CAO—was itself an important milestone for the community. UETCL had previously offered inadequate compensation to the community and then refused to engage in meaningful dialogue thereafter. Lack of progress in the Ugandan courts left the community feeling that they were out of options. Therefore, a new opportunity for dialogue with UETCL was a positive development. Nevertheless,

---

[1] See *Unsettling Business*, noting that approximately 5, 000 individuals were affected by the transmission lines in the Bujagali interconnection project.

[2] Compliance Advisor/Ombudsman, *CAO Cases, Uganda/Bujagali Energy-05/Bujagali*, http://www. cao-ombudsman. org/cases/case_ detail. aspx? id = 172.

[3] The case study is based upon interviews with three members of the community named in the Bujagali-5 complaint: Tom Mpandi, Aisha Pande and Vincent Kamoga (collectively "complainants"), as well as inputs from the National Association of Professional Environmentalists (NAPE), the Ugandan organisation that helped the complainants to file their complaint. The complainants did not wish to remain confidential. They said, " *We want our stories to be public, because our land was taken* ". Additionally, although Vincent's contributions are greatly appreciated, they are not discussed in detail in this case study because they focused mainly on a different mediation process.

the complainants were not satisfied with the outcome of the CAO mediation process for two main reasons. First, they felt that the schedule of rates of compensation that UETCL ultimately agreed to in the mediation were too low. Second, the complainants felt that the Group 2 members had been "left behind" because the mediation only addressed the claims of the Group 1 members, who made up a small fraction of the total population who suffered damages caused by the transmission line.

With regard to the agreed compensation, the complainants felt that, although UETCL did agree to mediation, in the end the community had to accept UETCL's offer of compensation even though they did not consider it to be fair. They recognized that the CAO could not force UETCL to agree to pay a particular amount and felt that they had no choice but to agree to UETCL's terms. With regard to the exclusion of the Group 2 community members from the mediation, both Aisha and Tom (two of the complainants) expressed dissatisfaction. As noted above, a large percentage of the impacted members of the community were not a part of the mediation because of UETCL's position that those not named in the court case could not participate. Aisha felt that the "CAO left us out". For Aisha and the other Group 2 members, the outcome of the mediation means little because they will not be receiving any compensation at this time. As Tom stated, "we are not all that satisfied because there are still some members who may be [left] behind, and they also need assistance".

PROCESS SATISFACTION: With regard to accessibility, the complainants felt that the CAO was accessible in the sense that, once they were informed of its existence, the National Association of Professional Environmentalists (NAPE), a Ugandan CSO, was able to file a complaint on their behalf with relative ease. In filing their complaint, the complainants stressed the importance of NAPE's assistance. However, none of the complainants knew about the CAO or the possibility of filing a complaint until NAPE informed them of that option. Additionally, to their knowledge, neither Tom nor Aisha had ever been contacted by or met with the IFC during the course of the project or during the mediation process.

However, beyond the filing of the Bujagali-5 complaint, at the insistence of

UETCL the CAO mediation was inaccessible to Aisha and the other people in Group 2. ① It was apparently UETCL's position that, if community members did not join in the court case, that meant they were satisfied with the compensation that had initially been offered, and therefore were barred from challenging those amounts in another forum. However, Aisha noted that the fact that many community members were not named in the court complaint was not a "decision" on their part to accept the compensation that UETCL initially offered.

Finally, the CAO mediation only addressed impacts caused by the transmission line. Other issues raised in the Bujagali-5 complaint, including impacts caused by the blasting, were not addressed in this process. The complainants would have preferred for all issues to have been handled in the same mediation.

The predictability of the process was also a mixed experience for the complainants. For example, initially, the CAO focused on the Group 2 members because they had grievances that were not yet being heard. The CAO mobilized the Group 2 members, registered them and said they would ensure that their grievances would be addressed. However, as discussed above, UETCL ultimately refused to negotiate with the Group 2 members. On the positive side, despite being a Group 2 member, Aisha noted that the CAO explained to her what it does, what the community should expect in the current mediation and provided updates on the process after the mediation began.

Despite the lack of satisfactory outcomes from the mediation, both Tom and Aisha seemed to agree on the legitimacy of the CAO. The main reason for this is that, prior to the CAO's involvement, UETCL refused to revisit its initial offers of compensation, and there was little prospect that the court case would change that position. The CAO was able to bring UETCL to the table, and according to Tom, the "CAO tried its best to make us meet and talk". Aisha stated that "the CAO itself has done good work" and she believed that the CAO would help the Group 2 members once the Group 1 mediation was finished.

---

① Aisha did state that, although she could not participate in this mediation, the CAO had been communicating with her so she felt involved in the process.

The complainants' experience with the transparency of the CAO was also mixed. Aisha noted that the CAO's system for sharing information with the community—which involved designated contact people within the community-worked for her.

She stated, "they have helped us, because they were bringing information from the mediation parties". On the other hand Aisha and the other Group 2 members have no information on when another mediation that will address their claims might begin.

With regard to the equitability of the process, Tom noted that the community representatives felt free to present their feelings during the mediation. However, at times the UETCL representatives were rude and refused to listen to what the community was saying. Tom also recognized that the CAO "did what they could" to facilitate the process and did not necessarily have control over UETCL's behaviour.

The rights compatibility of the mediation process is an open question as of August 2015. While UETCL has agreed to compensate Group 1 members, it remains to be seen what compensation will actually be paid. Tom is already of the view that the range of rates agreed to by UETCL is too low. Tom's sense was that, after years of negotiations, the community essentially had to accept whatever UETCL decided to offer. Additionally, the Group 2 members, who make up a majority of those who were impacted, will not see any compensation as a result of this mediation.

The integration of lessons learned in the mediation process was not prioritized. Tom noted that since the mediation only resulted in compensation for past harm, there may be violations by the company again in the future.

In conclusion the interviews with the complainants made clear that the process of mediating a complaint with the CAO is extremely complex. For the community members, the fact that UETCL would even agree to negotiate seemed to be the greatest benefit of the CAO's involvement. However, those negotiations did not lead to the level of compensation that the complainants sought for the damages they suffered. Furthermore, the negotiations only addressed the claims of a small percentage of the community represented in the Bujagali-5 complaint. While the

CAO does not necessarily have control over the behaviour of the parties regarding the mediation or the outcome of negotiations, this case study highlights the difficulties inherent in trying to get companies to agree to compensate community members for damage caused by large-scale development projects.

4.2.5 CASE STUDY #5 ICM: Barro Blanco Hydroelectric Project, Panama

BACKGROUND: In August 2011, the Dutch and German development banks, FMO and DEG, each provided a US $25 million loan to Generadora del Istmo S. A. (GENISA) for the construction of the Barro Blanco dam on the Tabasará River in the Province of Chiriquí in western Panama. [1] The project has been the subject of controversy and has garnered attention at the national and international levels. [2] In February 2015, the Government of Panama temporarily suspended construction of the dam after determining that the project was not in compliance with its own environmental impact assessment. [3] At the time of the loan agreement, neither FMO nor DEG had an independent accountability mechanism.

---

[1] FMO-DEG Independent Complaints Mechanism, Panel Report No. 1: Barro Blanco Hydroelectric Project-Panama 8 (May 29, 2015), https://www. fmo. nl/l/en/library/download/urn: uuid: 963b97fd-6f82-473d-b323-128a995130f5/150529_ barro + blanco + final + report + rev. pdf? format = save_ to_ disk&ext =. pdf [hereinafter ICM Barro Blanco Report].

[2] See generally, United Nations Development Programme, Presentan resultados del peritaje independiente al proyecto hidroeléctrico Barro Blanco (Sept. 6, 2013), http://www. pa. undp. org/content/panama/es/home/presscenter/articles/2013/09/06/presentan-resultados-del-peritajeindependiente-al-proyecto-hidroelectrico-barro-blanco-. html; James Anaya, Declaración del Relator Especial sobre los derechos de los pueblos indígenas al concluir su visita oficial a Panamá (July 26, 2013) http://unsr. jamesanaya. org/statements/declaracion-del-relator-especial-sobrelos-derechos-de-los-pueblos-indigenas-al-concluir-su-visita-oficial-a-panama.

[3] Press Release, SOMO Human Rights and Grievance Mechanism Programme, Panama Suspends Construction of FMO-funded Barro Blanco hydroelectric dam over environmental and human rights abuses (available at http://grievancemechanisms. org/news/panama-suspends-construction-offmo-funded-barro-blanco-hydroelectric-dam-over-environmental-and-human-rights-abuses). See also Panama National Environmental Authority (ANAM), Order to Suspend Dam Construction (available at http://miambiente. gob. pa/index. php/homepage/ultimas-noticias/otrasnoticias/959-anam-ordena-paralizacion-de-obras-del-proyecto-hidroelectrico-barro-blanco-porincumplimientos-de-eia).

In January 2014, FMO and DEG jointly established the ICM. ①

TEHE COMPLAINT: The dam, once completed, will flood 6.7 hectares of land belonging to the indigenous Ngöbe-Buglé territory (known as the comarca), created by law in 1997. The complaint was filed in May 2014 by the Cacica General of the Ngöbe-Buglé, the highest elected office representing the Ngöbe-Buglé people, and the Movimiento 10 de Abril (M-10), a grassroots organisation that represents the people who will be most directly affected by the dam. The complainants requested a compliance review. This was the first complaint handled by the ICM.

The complaint alleges a series of impacts to the environment and the rights of the Ngöbe-Buglé people. First and foremost, the complainants assert that they were not consulted about the project nor was the free, prior and informed consent of the Ngöbe-Buglé people obtained in a manner consistent with the procedures set forth in the law establishing the comarca. The area to be flooded is home to six large, extended families of up to 40 – 50 people each, all of whom will have to be relocated. However, that is likely to be an underestimate of the number of people affected by the loss of the land. The United Nations Development Programme (UNDP), which produced a series of studies on the dam's impact, found that because of the cohesion within Ngöbe-Buglé people, "the impact with respect to access and use of resources will affect not only the families that will suffer the flooding of their lands, but also those impacts will affect directly and indirectly all of the inhabitants of the three communities [Quebrada Caña, Kiad, and Nuevo Palomar]. " ②

Impacts affecting the Ngöbe-Buglé's natural resources and cultural heritage

---

① For more information on ICM, see DEG/FMO Independent Complaints Mechanism, Annual Report: First Panel Report January 2014 – 2015 (Aug. 6, 2015), https://www. fmo. nl/l/en/library/download/urn: uuid: a202083c-a943-47b3-ab16-8375dc68885c/icm + annual + report + 2014 + - + hy + 2015. pdf? format = save_ to_ disk&ext = . pdf. For a CSO perspective on its establishment, see Press Release, SOMO Human Rights and Grievance Mechanisms, Dutch development bank FMO now has a grievance mechanism, (available at http://grievancemechanisms. org/news/dutchdevelopment-bank-fmo-now-has-a-non-judicial-grievance-mechanism).

② United Nations Development Programme, Peritaje Al Proyecto Hidroelectrico Barro Blanco, at ¶ 15 (Sept. 2, 2013), available at http://www. pa. undp. org/content/dam/panama/docs/documentos/undp_ pa_ barro_ blanco_ aspectos_ ecologicos. pdf.

also require their consent. The location of the first and only school to teach the Ngöbe-Buglé language is located on the land to be flooded when the dam is completed. The gallery forest that will be inundated is an important source of wood, medicinal plants and other natural resources that the Ngöbe-Buglé use for traditional and artisanal products. The petroglyphs located in the river, which the Ngöbe-Buglé still use for religious and cultural ceremonies, will also be submerged.

THE RESULT: The ICM published its final compliance report in May 2015. The ICM only assessed compliance against the IFC's Performance Standards on Environmental and Social Sustainability (Performance Standards), although FMO also requires its clients to comply with the Organisation for Economic Co-operation and Development (OECD) Guidelines on Multinational Enterprises, among other policies. The ICM found that FMO and DEG were not in the position to assure themselves that the Barro Blanco project was fully compliant with Performance Standards 1 (on Social and Environmental Assessment and Management Systems), 5 (Land Acquisition and Involuntary Resettlement), 6 (Biodiversity Conservation and Sustainable Natural Resource Management), 7 (Indigenous Peoples) and 8 (Cultural Heritage).

More specifically, the ICM found that "while the [loan] agreement was reached prior to significant construction, significant issues related to social and environmental impact and, in particular, issues related to the rights of indigenous peoples were not completely assessed prior to the [loan] agreement". ① FMO/ DEG's failure to identify the potential impacts of the project led to a subsequent failure to require their client to take any action to mitigate those impacts. The environmental and social action plan appended to the loan agreement "contains no provision on land acquisition and resettlement and nothing on biodiversity and natural resources management. Neither does it contain any reference to issues

---

① Centre for Research on Multinational Corporations (SOMO) and Both ENDS, A summary of the Independent Complaints Mechanism's findings on Barro Blanco and FMO-DEG management response (Jun. 1, 2015) (available at http://somo. nl/news-en/indigenous-communities-and-civilsociety-shocked-by-fmos-inadequate-response-to-the-findings/at_ download/attachment).

related to cultural heritage. " ①

With regard to compliance with the Indigenous Peoples policy, the ICM found that "there are serious questions as to whether the lenders could be satisfied that the consultations with the affected communities have been conducted in a format and intensity (good faith negotiations) that is required by PS7, paragraph 13. The panel is of the opinion the lenders have not taken the resistance of the affected communities has not been taken [sic] seriously enough. This may be, to an extent, because a legal agreement was reached between [GENISA] and the regional council of the Comarca and this was considered by the lenders to be sufficient to deal with the issue. Nevertheless, the Indigenous Peoples report clearly documented that the directly affected communities challenged the legitimacy of such agreements. This should have triggered the further steps identified in the IP Report. "②

FMO and DEG's response to the ICM's report made very few concrete commitments to address the outstanding policy violations. ③ The response explains that many of the issues must be resolved by the Government of Panama, and that they and their client are "facing limitations in their influence" over government processes to come to a satisfactory agreement with all stakeholders involved. FMO and DEG also committed to "*strive for a more elaborate formal opinion from lawyers or other experts*, with defined expertise in indigenous peoples' rights and the local legal context" with regard to land, resettlement and displacement issues. It is unclear, however, whether that opinion, if obtained, will be shared with the complainants or if it will lead to any follow-up. Following the publication of the

---

① Centre for Research on Multinational Corporations (SOMO) and Both ENDS, A summary of the Independent Complaints Mechanism's findings on Barro Blanco and FMO-DEG management response (Jun. 1, 2015) (available at http://somo. nl/news-en/indigenous-communities-and-civilsociety-shocked-by-fmos-inadequate-response-to-the-findings/at_ download/attachment).

② ICM Barro Blanco Report, at ¶ 146.

③ DEG and FMO Management Response to the Independent Expert Panel's Compliance Review Report regarding the Complaint on the Investment in the Barro Blanco Hydroelectric Project (May 29, 2015), https://www. fmo. nl/l/en/library/download/urn: uuid: 3766a880 – 119e-44f6-9e8c-eae 30583194c/150529 + management + response. pdf? format = save_ to_ disk&ext = . pdf.

ICM's report and FMO/DEG's response, the complainants and their CSO allies sent a letter to the relevant Dutch and German ministers, expressing their dissatisfaction with FMO/DEG's response. [1]

As a result of the complainants' own initiative, a representative of the M-10 met with representatives from FMO, DEG and the ICM in The Hague, Netherlands at the end of June. FMO/DEG would not agree to request that their client should suspend construction on the dam to allow a dialogue to take place, but they did commit to hiring a mediator to work with the parties to come to an agreement on the conditions necessary for a dialogue to occur. In the meantime, the Government of Panama attempted to initiate a dialogue with the Ngöbe-Buglé. According to FMO/DEG, the Government of Panama did not accept their offer to provide a mediator for that process. Currently, the government is in talks with indigenous leaders, but the M-10 has not been invited to participate. FMO/DEG have not been in communication with the complainants for several months.

OUTCOME SATISFACTION[2]: According to Manolo Miranda, the M-10's contact point for this complaint, the M-10 was satisfied with the ICM's investigation report because it showed that there was no consent for the project. Miranda believes that the report, because it was written by independent experts, helped to make their concerns more credible and helped to ensure that the international community understands the conflict about the Barro Blanco dam.

Ultimately, however, the response from FMO/DEG was extremely disappointing. Miranda said, "nothing has changed ⋯ the banks and the company have done nothing to prevent the impacts on our culture, territory and religion". He would recommend using complaints mechanisms to other communities because it helps to

---

[1] Press Release, SOMO Human Rights and Grievance Mechanisms Programme, Movimiento 10 de Abril presents letter of concern to Dutch and German embassies in Panama (available at http://grievancemechanisms. org/news/movimiento-10-de-abril-presents-letter-of-concern-to-dutchand-german-embassies-in-panama).

[2] This case study draws on an interview with Manolo Miranda, the M-10's contact person for the complaints process, in addition to publicly available information and information from Both ENDS and the Centre for Research on Multinational Corporations (SOMO), international NGOs that supported the complainants in the case.

bring attention to the issues. However, in order for complaints to result in outcomes for communities, the human rights commitments of DFIs and international institutions should not be in paper only. He said: "rules are one thing, but their implementation is another". The efforts of the M-10 to defend their rights have not come without costs. The company has filed complaints against community leaders with the Public Ministry. There is a pending lawsuit against Miranda, allegedly for trespassing on the dam site, a charge that he vehemently denies. Defending these charges not only takes time, they also have an economic impact on the community.

PROCESS SATISFACTION: While Miranda expressed general satisfaction with their interaction with the ICM Panel members, noting that they "allowed us to tell the truth about what is happening", their trust in the process was significantly undermined because of a confidential, side agreement made between FMO/DEG, the ICM and the company in order to gain the client's cooperation in the complaints process.

The loan agreement with GENISA was signed before the ICM was established, and, as a result, there was no provision in the agreement that required the company's cooperation with the ICM. This situation is not unique to the ICM. Notwithstanding that every existing IAM was created well after the establishment of the DFI with which it is associated, there is no evidence that any other IAM/DFI has had to make a special accommodation in order to handle complaints regarding activities financed before the IAM was operational.

As complainants understand it, the company refused to cooperate in the process or to allow the ICM Panel members access to project documentation until the side agreement was reached. As a result, the Panel members were unable to have access to non-public information until five months after the complaint was submitted. Complainants were only informed about the reason for the delay after sending a letter to the ICM in October 2014, expressing concern about the progress of the complaint. The contents of the side agreement have never been shared with complainants.

The side agreement superseded the publicly available procedures of the ICM and allowed GENISA to review the draft and final investigation reports before they were shared with complainants. Complainants were informed that the purpose of the company review was to ensure that the ICM did not publish any business confidential information. In practice, the company review caused significant delays in the process, with the company and/or the DFIs refusing to allow the ICM to share the reports with complainants until the complainants threatened to go to the media. The draft compliance report shared with complainants already reflected the comments of FMO/DEG and their client, although complainants and their advisors interpreted the ICM's rules of procedures to mean that they would review the same draft as FMO/DEG. The company review combined with the sequencing of the disclosure undermined the complainants' confidence in the report's contents, despite reassurances from the ICM Panel members: "The banks and the company were the first to know about the report, and that was very worrying because it gave them the opportunity to change information that was not favourable to them".

FMO/DEG have said that it may have to conclude similar side agreements in future complaints regarding activities financed prior to the creation of the ICM. Doing so would seriously put in jeopardy the legitimacy, transparency and predictability of the ICM.

The M-10 attributes the accessibility of the mechanism to the support they received from CSO allies, including Chiriqui Natural, Both ENDS, and the Centre for Research on Multinational Enterprises (SOMO). M-10 had been in contact with FMO/DEG several years before it was possible to file a complaint. However, Miranda perceived that FMO/DEG did not trust them or recognise them as a directly affected stakeholder until Both ENDS became involved. The ICM Panel members also helped M-10 to understand FMO/DEG's policies and the role of the ICM. Although the ICM Panel members met with complainants during a site visit and organised several teleconferences, at times it was difficult to obtain information about the status of the case for the reasons described above. According to Miranda, not only was the outcome of the process not rights-compatible, due to the lack of an adequate response by FMO/DEG, the ICM's report did not fully analyse the human rights impacts of the projects, even though FMO/DEG's policies require compliance with national law and international human rights standards. At the time the project was approved, FMO required its clients to comply with the OECD Guidelines on Multinational Enterprises ("Guidelines"). The Guidelines contain a chapter on human rights that reflects the UN Guiding Principles on Business and Human Rights (UNGP), which state that corporations have a responsibility to respect all internationally recognized human rights, including those related to indigenous rights, when applicable. [1] The Panel, however, only assessed compliance against the IFC's Performance Standards, reasoning that, "lender's application of the Performance Standards was the appropriate way to seek to align project performance with both the UNGPs and the OECD guidelines". [2] As described in Annex 12, however, the IFC's Performance Standards do not require assessment of human rights impacts, as expected by the OECD Guidelines and the UNGPs, nor explicitly incorporate human rights standards.

Finally, the M-10 felt that FMO/DEG did not treat them equally. In Miranda's words: "It made us nervous to know that the banks thought the company was more important than we were. They never asked us information, they never talked to us, they never came to give us information. But the banks did give the company information. It made us feel that we were insignificant and the company was the priority."

Indeed, FMO/DEG were lobbying on behalf of the company during the complaints process. Following the suspension of the project by the Government of Panama in February 2015, FMO/DEG sent a letter to the Vice President of Panama, expressing their "great concern and consternation" about the suspension and requesting that the construction on the project be allowed to resume. [3] The lenders continued by saying that the government's decision "*may weigh upon future investment decisions, and harm the flow of long-term investments into Panama*". They discredit the basis for the Government's decision by asserting that their

---

[1] OECD, OECD GUIDELINES FOR MULTINATIONAL ENTERPRISES, chapter IV, °Π 1, Commentary ¶ 40 (2011), http://www. oecd. org/daf/inv/mne/48004323. pdf.

[2] ICM Barro Blanco Report, at ¶ 56.

[3] Press release, Both ENDS, Dutch FMO pushed Panama to continue construction Barro Blanco dam (May 18, 2015) (available at http://www. bothends. org/en/News/newsitem/413/Dutch-FMOpushed-Panama-to-continue-construction-Barro-Blanco-dam#_ga = 1. 75074836. 742010282. 1427962178). The letter sent by the FMO/DEG to the Vice President of Panama is on file with the authors.

consultants had not reported the same non-compliances of relevant standards. The government's decision to suspend the project cited, in part, the company's lack of agreement with the affected communities and absence of an approved management plan to address impacts to cultural heritage. ① At the time FMO/DEG sent the letter to the Vice President, they had already reviewed the ICM's draft compliance review, which raised these very issues.

4.2.6 CASE STUDY#6 IP: Promoting Basic Services Project, Ethiopia

BACKGROUND: World Bank designed the Protection of Basic Services (PBS) Project to support Ethiopia. ② Under PBS, block grants are transferred to sub-national government budgets for recurrent expenditures to expand access to and improve the quality of basic services in five sectors: education, health, agriculture, water and sanitation, and rural roads. Since 2006, PBS has been renewed twice, and in total, the World Bank has committed almost US $2 billion to the project. ③

THE COMPLAINT: In September 2012, representatives of Anuak indigenous people living in refugee camps in Kenya and South Sudan submitted a complaint to the World Bank Inspection Panel regarding the PBS project. The complainants allege that they were forcibly relocated from their fertile ancestral lands in Ethiopia's Gambella Region into centralized villages as a part of the regional government's Commune Development Programme, otherwise known as 'villagization'. According to the complaint, the official objective of villagization was to make it easier to improve access to basic services in the very same sectors targeted by PBS. ④

The complaint details mass forced displacement of the Anuak from their fertile

---

① Panama National Environmental Authority (ANAM), Order to Suspend Dam Construction.
② *Id.* at 3.
③ World Bank, Project Information Document Concept Stage Ethiopia PBS Program Phase III Project, (Apr. 4, 2012); World Bank, Ethiopia: PBS 3 Project, Summary of Discussion Meeting of Executive Directors (Sept. 25, 2012).
④ Request for Inspection by World Bank Inspection Panel, 1 (Sept. 24, 2012), http://ewebapps. worldbank. org/ apps/ip/PanelCases/82 – Request% 20for% 20Inspection% 20 (English). pdf.

ancestral land, and relocation to sites that were unsuitable for farming and lacked access to basic services such as schools, clinics and wells. ① According to the complaint, access to food was limited at the relocation sites. ②The complaint highlights the mutual objectives of PBS and the villagization programme in Gambella, and that, according to World Bank documents, PBS provides the main source of financing for the Gambellan Government, particularly for the salaries of public servants who were responsible for carrying out villagization. ③

THE RESULT: In the final investigation report, released in November 2014, the Inspection Panel did "not seek to verify allegations of specific human rights abuses linked to [villagization]."④ Having determined that the relocation of people under the villagization programme was not necessary to achieve PBS objectives, the Inspection Panel found the involuntary resettlement policy did not apply and that the Bank was therefore in compliance with OP/BP 4.12. However, the Inspection Panel found "an operational link" between PBS and the villagization programme, as they both "have the objective of providing improved basic services to the same populations, operate in the same geographical areas, and overlapped during a span of more than three years (2010 – 2013) when they were implemented concurrently". ⑤ As such, the Inspection Panel concluded that the Bank's design, appraisal, risk analysis, and project supervision were insufficient, in non-compliance with OMS 2.20, OP/BP 10.00, and OP/BP 10.02. ⑥ It determined that the weakness of internal controls supports the possibility that funds could have been diverted, and that Bank's assertion that it could fully track PBS expenditures

---

① Request for Inspection by World Bank Inspection Panel, 1 (Sept. 24, 2012), http://ewebapps. worldbank. org/ apps/ip/PanelCases/82 – Request% 20for% 20Inspection% 20 (English). pdf.

② *Id.*

③ *Id.*

④ World Bank Inspection Panel, Ethiopia: Promoting Basic Services Phase III Project Investigation Report, ¶ 311 (Nov. 24, 2014), http://ewebapps. worldbank. org/ apps/ip/PanelCases/82 – % 20Inspection% 20Panel% 20Investigation% 0Report% 20Ethiopia% 20PBS% 20Phase% 20III% 20Project. pdf.

⑤ *Id.* at ¶ 309.

⑥ *Id.* at ¶¶ 31 – 32.

"cannot be sustained" . ① The Panel also found the Bank in noncompliance with OP 4. 10 on Indigenous Peoples, as it failed to take the Anuak's livelihoods, well-being and access to basic services into account in designing PBS. ② Nonetheless, the Inspection Panel concluded that the Bank was not responsible for the harm suffered by the complainants. ③ Dissatisfied with the rigour of the investigation, Inclusive Development International prepared a detailed critique of the Inspection Panel's findings. ④

Bank management responded to the investigation's findings with an Action Plan in January 2015. ⑤ It noted that, since the complaint was filed, it had begun applying OP/BP 4. 10 on Indigenous Peoples to relevant projects in Ethiopia, something the government had previously refused. ⑥ It committed to various measures to improve accountability in development programmes in Ethiopia, including supporting the effectiveness of the Ethiopian Institution of the Ombudsman and district grievance redress officers, and building the capacity of district-level civil servants to implement the Bank's safeguard policies. ⑦ It also announced that it would replace PBS block grants with a Program for Results operation. ⑧ In a press release

---

① World Bank Inspection Panel, Ethiopia: Promoting Basic Services Phase III Project Investigation Report, ¶ 311 (Nov. 24, 2014), http://ewebapps. worldbank. org/ apps/ip/PanelCases/82 – % 20Inspection% 20Panel% 20Investigation% 0Report% 20Ethiopia% 20PBS% 20Phase% 20III% 20Project. pdf. at ¶¶ 30 – 31.

② *Id.* at ¶ 208.

③ *Id.* at ¶ 310.

④ Inclusive Development International, Ethiopia PBS Request for inspection: Analysis of World Bank Inspection Panel Investigation and Findings. (2015), http://www. inclusivedevelopment. net/ wpcontent/uploads/2015/06/IDI-Analysis-of-WBIP-Ethiopia-Investigation. pdf.

⑤ Ethiopia: Promoting Basic Services Project, Management Report and Recommendation in Response to the Inspection Panel Investigation Report (Jan. 31, 2015), http://ewebapps. worldbank. org/apps/ip/ PanelCases/82-Management% 20Report% 20and% 0Recommendation% 20 – % 20 Ethiopia% 20PBS% 20 – %20Phase%20III%20Project. pdf. [hereinafter Management's Response: Ethiopia Case].

⑥ *Id.* at ¶ 36.

⑦ Id. ; Press Release, World Bank, World Bank Board Discusses Inspection Panel Case in Ethiopia (Feb. 27, 2015) (available at http://ewebapps. worldbank. org/apps/ip/PanelCases/82-Press% 20Release% 20 – % 20World% 20Bank% 20Board% 20Discusses% 20Inspection% 20Panel% 20Case% 20in% 20Ethiopia. pdf) [hereinafter *Press Release: Ethiopia Case*].

⑧ Management's Response: Ethiopia Case, ¶ 53.

following the Board's approval of the Management Action Plan, the Bank further committed to supporting small-holder farmers in Gambella and ensuring that national programmes aimed at improving the quality of services and alleviating hunger reach people across Gambella. Importantly for the complainants, who have lived in refugee camps for several years, the Bank also said it would strengthen its work on improving the development prospects of refugees and other people living in borderland areas such as Gambella as part of its new Horn of Africa Initiative. ①

OUTCOME SATISFACTION②: Representatives of the complainants expressed dissatisfaction with the outcomes of the process, despite the Inspection Panel making several findings of non-compliance.

Complainants felt aggrieved that the Inspection Panel's final investigation report did not sufficiently document the most serious harms alleged in their complaint.

The complainants felt that their complaint to the Inspection Panel had some impact on the Government's actions and may have prevented further harm, but the process did not result in redress.

In an open letter to World Bank President Jim Yong Kim on 30 January 2015, the complainants appealed for support to "return to their ancestral land without fear of retribution" and demanded that their people should be consulted and have "ownership of our development" . ③ They did not feel that their appeals were listened to by the Bank or reflected in its Action Plan.

Asked whether they would advise others to use the Inspection Panel, the complainants responded that, even though they are not satisfied with the result, they had "*no other option*" for seeking justice.

PROCESS SATISFACTION: The complainants experienced many difficulties during the complaints process. The complainants said that, without the assistance

---

① Press Release: Ethiopia Case.
② This assessment is based on a focus group of six complainants. They were interviewed via Skype for this case study on June 21, 2015. The complainants' identities cannot be revealed for security reasons.
③ Open letter from Annual Ethiopian Refugees to Jim Yong Kim, President, World Bank (Jan. 31, 2015) (*available* at http://www. inclusivedevelopment. net/open-letter-from-anuak-ethiopian-refugeesto-the-president-of-the-world-bank-jim-yong-kim/).

of Inclusive Development International (IDI) and other organizations, the Inspection Panel would not have been accessible. They were only able to submit the complaint with the support of IDI, which explained to them the World Bank safeguard policies and the complaints process and helped them to prepare and submit their complaint.

The complainants did not think the Inspection Panel operated transparently. They told us: "from the time the Inspection Panel left the camp in South Sudan [after interviewing the complainants to assess the eligibility of the complaint], we never heard anything from them. They never updated or communicated with us; the only information we get is from IDI. "

Complainants also raised concerns relating to the legitimacy, predictability, and equitability of the process. Most importantly, although the Inspection Panel spoke to complainants during the eligibility site visit, they did not return to interview them during their investigation: "they never came back to us-they did their investigation in Gambella [but didn't come to the refugee camps], and then went back and did their own report. " As a result, the complainants did not feel as though their views were taken into consideration by Bank management. It was "not only on what they said to us, [but] their body language [as well]. We already knew that they came just to present their case-the action plan-but weren't expecting to listen to us or hear from us. " The complainants said after the World Bank " explained their action plan, we totally rejected it. They promised they would come back with a better action plan, but they never came back. "

The Inspection Panel process did not result in rights-compatible remedies for the complainants. Although the complainants believed that villagization in Gambella stopped because of the complaint to the Inspection Panel and the international attention that the advocacy garnered, they did not believe that they or others in Gambella received redress. They said, " we're still waiting for the impact" . The complainants remain in refugee camps that lack access to health clinics and schools, and they continue to fear for their safety. A complainant commented that, during the consultation meeting on the action plan, " [we] could even tell that they don't care about us and didn't do anything at all to protect us" .

In the Management Report and Recommendation, the Bank says regarding lessons learned that the "key lesson from implementation is the importance of improving citizen voice and accountability". [1] Management also comments that it learned "to identify constraints to achieving program goals", and "the continuous need for training and support to improve capacity at [the local government] level, whether it is with respect to fiduciary, safeguard, citizen voice or implementation issues". [2] World Bank President Jim Yong Kim also said in a press release, "We draw important lessons from this case to better anticipate ways to protect the poor and be more effective in fighting poverty". [3]

According to IDI's Legal Director Natalie Bugalski, "the Panel's decision not to consider allegations of human rights abuses and the forcible nature of the relocations, despite this being a central issue in the Request for Inspection, coupled with its finding that the Bank was not responsible for harms, despite a raft of policy violations, limited the potential for the Bank to learn lessons from the case". The result, Bugalski said, "was a missed opportunity for institutional reflection on the deficiency of the current system for environmental and social protections and accountability for direct budget support financing".

4.2.7 CASE STUDY#7 IP: Vishnugad Pipalkoti Hydro Electric Project, India

BACKGROUND: In June 2011, the World Bank approved a loan of US $648 million to a joint venture of the Government of India and the regional government of Uttarakhand, known as THDC. [4] It was used for the building of a hydroelectric

---

[1] Open letter from Annual Ethiopian Refugees to Jim Yong Kim, President, World Bank (Jan. 31, 2015) (*available* at http://www.inclusivedevelopment.net/open-letter-from-anuak-ethiopian-refugeesto-the-president-of-the-world-bank-jim-yong-kim/), at ¶ 49.

[2] *Id.*

[3] Press Release: Ethiopia Case.

[4] World Bank, Project and Operations, *Vishnugad Pipalkoti Hydro Electric Project*, http://www.worldbank.org/projects/P096124/vishnugad-pipalkoti-hydro-electric-project? lang = en (last visited June 11, 2015).

power plant in the Alaknanda River, a major tributary of the Ganga River.

THE COMPLAINT: For some members of the local communities, the building of the dam raised environmental, social and cultural concerns. They filed a complaint with the Inspection Panel in July 2012. [1] Their complaint describes many different aspects, including damage to houses, agricultural lands and forests, fear of loss of aquatic biodiversity, loss of benefits from the river such as sand, fish and drinking water, increased risk of landslides and earthquakes, and a fear for increased global warming through deforestation and methane gas emission. Also, the complainants were concerned about decreased freedom of local women, due to the large number of incoming construction workers. As the Alaknanda is a tributary to the religiously significant Ganga River, they worried about the loss of spiritual and cultural values of the river too. After the Inspection Panel had visited the project site, the complainants provided the Panel with supplementary information.

THE RESULT: The compliance investigation resulted in a final report, dated July 2014. The Panel concluded that the World Bank "for the most part is not only in compliance with its policies and procedures, but has also introduced best practice when possible, except for some gaps". [2] These gaps relate to two findings of noncompliance. The first concerns non-compliance with the Bank's policy on Environmental Assessment, finding that the Bank had not identified the necessary measures to take regarding whether the community's sources of drinking water were lost. The second related to the Bank's policy on Involuntary Resettlement, finding that the World Bank had not adequately assessed the situation of one local community. [3] This issue was not raised in the initial complaint, but was added after the eligibility visit of the Panel.

---

[1] Request for inspection, regarding the Loan to the THDC India Ltd. For the Vishnugad Pipalkoti Hydro Electric Project to the Executive Secretary, The Inspection Panel (July 23, 2012), http://ewebapps. worldbank. org/apps/ip/PanelCases/81-Request%20for%20Inspection%20%28English%29. pdf.

[2] Inspection Panel, Investigation Report: *India-Vishnugad Pipalkoti Hydro Electric Project* 93 (July 1, 2014), http://ewebapps. worldbank. org/apps/ip/PanelCases/81%20 -% 20Investigation%20Report%20 (English). pdf.

[3] *Id.* at 95.

In response to the Investigation Report, the management's action plan was published in September 2014. It addressed the first finding of non-compliance, loss of water sources, by committing to monitor the change in water sources. If a source dries up, the Bank will assess the replacement options THDC has suggested and will supervise the implementation. Regarding the involuntary resettlement, management committed to monitoring the resettlement after the community members have chosen one of the two options THDC has offered them. [1]

OUTCOME SATISFACTION: [2] Even though the Panel found two instances of noncompliance, the outcome of the complaint process is considered very disappointing by the complainants' representative, Dr. Bharat Jhunjhunwala.

This is mainly due to three factors. First, the final report does not address all the issues that were raised: "It is fair if you find my request not viable, but give me reasons for dismissing it. You cannot just keep quiet on the important parts of the request. " This feeling is exacerbated by the second factor, namely that there was no way to express that dissatisfaction to the Bank's leadership: "I have written to all Executive Directors of the Bank, I have written to the President of the Bank. And finally I got a reply from the Executive Director of the Netherlands. He forwarded my complaint to the Panel. But all I heard from them was that I could file a new complaint. So that was it. " The third factor contributing to the strong dissatisfaction about the outcome of the complaint is the belief that the Bank's management did not actively address the findings of non-compliance. Especially this latter factor has led to a general feeling that the whole complaints process was not worthwhile: " We have spent huge amounts of resources to file the complaint. Even the small violations that were recorded by the Panel have not been acted upon. It is a colossal waste of resources of poor people. We have been taken

---

[1] Inspection Panel, *India-Vishnugad Pipalkoti Hydro Electric Project*, *Summary of Management Actions* (2014), http://ewebapps. worldbank. org/apps/ip/PanelCases/81-Summary% 20of% 20Management% 20Actions (English). pdf (hereinafter Inspection Panel, VSummary of Management Actions: Vishnugad Project).

[2] Although this case study is based on an interview with the complainants' representative, Dr. Bharat Jhunjhunwala, who consented to the publication of his name, two additional, unnamed complainants reviewed and approved the final text.

for a ride. "

PROCESS SATISFACTION: Although the outcome was considered to be very unsatisfactory, Dr. Jhunjhunwala's opinion about the Panel's role in the complaints process is generally more positive: "I should put on record that the whole process, up to the Panel's visits, was quite satisfactory. I have no complaints about that. "

Dr. Jhunjhunwala considers the Panel to be accessible and predictable, although this seems mainly due to the help of an international NGO, the Bank Information Centre (BIC). BIC explained and advised Dr. Jhunjhunwala and the other complainants on the complaint process.

The legitimacy of the Panel is also positively assessed. Dr. Jhunjhunwala states he appreciated the measures the Panel took to maintain its independence during the site visits. For instance, he appreciated that the Panel made their own independent travel arrangements during their visit to the project site, and their willingness to communicate with everyone. However, he states that "insiders" told him that the final investigation report was not written by the people who visited the site. In his experience, this greatly damages the legitimacy of the report. His opinion of the conduct of the World Bank's staff during their visits is more negative. He felt that Bank staff members were not independent from THDC.

Transparency and equitability were also problematic in this complaint process. According to Dr. Jhunjhunwala, they waited 21 months between the visit and the final report. It was very unclear to the complainants what was happening in the meantime. This raised questions about the influence of the Bank management: "We only got one phone call from the Panel, asking whether the Management had contacted us. We told them they had not, and that was it. So why did it take 21 months? I think there was some politics, somewhere. "

Rights compatibility is a major concern in this case. First of all, according to the complainants, the situation has not improved in the areas where promises were made to do so. They feel that the commitments made by Bank management were simply ignored. Also, doubts exist regarding the solutions for the community's loss of water. Complainants are doubtful that the replacement options are actually feasible. For instance, providing water by trucks will be very challenging because of the difficult mountainous terrain. Finally, Dr. Jhunjhunwala states that the commitment to creating new packages regarding involuntary resettlement, which would comply with the Bank policies, has not been honoured.

Concerns regarding rights compatibility are not limited to only the outcomes of the compliance review. Even before the complaint was filed, community members experienced tremendous pressure from THDC. Since the Panel's visit, THDC seems to have increased its harassment. In some instances, the threats have escalated to physical violence. One community member witnessed her son being assaulted for protesting against the destruction of her shed and fruit trees by THDC in the middle of the night in order to clear the land to build a road. Even though the Panel was informed about harassment of the complainants and had even written about the intimidation by THDC in the eligibility report, the issue was not addressed in the investigation report, nor was it taken up in management's action plan.

There seem to be no learning processes related to this complaint. No lessons learned for future projects are taken up in management's action plan. ①

---

① Inspection Panel, *Summary of Management Actions: Vishnugad Project.*

5 Recommendations

Each complaint tells a story: a story about real people whose lives have been adversely affected by a development activity that was supposed to benefit them. At the same time, every complaint provides an opportunity, an opportunity for the DFIs to fulfil their missions and improve peoples' lives. They are a chance for the DFIs to learn and understand how to make development work for people. Thus while the aim of this report is to ensure that people who are harmed by development activities receive adequate remedy, the ultimate goal of the organisations that authored this report is that DFIs pursue a development model based on human rights that does not cause harm. [①] Until then, it is imperative that the accountability system is strengthened to ensure that anyone harmed by a development activity is provided with remedy.

The research undertaken for this report led to two types of recommendations to ensure those harmed by development activities receive remedy. One set of recommendations seeks to perfect the current system. The following section and the Table 2 below contain those general recommendations to the DFIs and IAMs. Annexes 5 – 15 (available at: www. glass-half-full. org) also include recommendations specific to each institution. Ultimately, though, the authors have concluded that the current system is inadequate to consistently provide remedy to those affected by DFI-financed activities. To do so requires the next evolution in DFI accountability. The second set of recommendations, then, seeks to inform that conversation.

---

① For a vision of what real development looks like, see IAP *Back to Development*.

5.1 Perfecting the System

The following recommendations will improve the current accountability system. They contain practices that are currently in use by one or more institutions or measures that can easily be incorporated into the current system. In many cases, these recommendations are the bare minimum to make the system work better.

Legitimacy

• The committee formed to select the IAM principals should include outside stakeholders, including representatives of civil society.

• IAM principals should be required to respect a cooling-off period before joining the mechanism if they have previously worked for the DFI. And the principals should be restricted from working for the DFI following their tenure on the IAM.

• IAMs should establish official external stakeholder advisory groups to provide them with feedback and guidance on their work.

Accessibility

• DFIs should require their clients to disclose the availability of the IAMs to project affected people at the same time as they are required to disclose the potential environmental and social impacts of the DFI-financed activity. Subsequently, the client's project-level grievance mechanism should be required to provide information about the IAMs to any interested stakeholder.

• IAMs should accept complaints requesting either compliance review or problem-solving from when the DFI has indicated it is considering financing. Complaints requesting problem-solving should be accepted as long as the loan is in repayment or the DFI maintains its investment. Complaints requesting compliance review should be accepted after the project is closed.

• DFIs should provide a highly visible link on their homepages to their IAMs' websites.

• IAMs should allow complaints in the language of the complainant and should provide information on their websites in multiple languages.

Predictability

- IAMs must consistently meet their deadlines in processing complaints.

- DFIs must provide IAMs with a sufficient budget to allow them the capacity to handle their caseloads.

- IAMs should provide regular status updates to complainants.

- DFIs should develop Management Action Plans that address every finding of non-compliance made in investigations undertaken by IAMs with a time-bound, implementation plan.

- All IAMs should be given the mandate to monitor commitments made through dispute resolution and instances of non-compliance found through compliance investigation. One important distinction to be made here is that the IAM should monitor whether the instances of non-compliance have been remedied, not whether the Management Action Plan has been implemented, as the Action Plan may not adequately address the instances of non-compliance. IAMs should publish monitoring reports at least once a year, which incorporate information provided by complainants on the implementation of the commitments made by the DFI or its client.

Equity

- Complainants should be given the same opportunity as the DFIs to review and comment on the IAMs' reports. The final report should be sent to the complainants at the same time it is sent to the board of directors, and it should contain the perspectives of the complainants.

- DFIs should develop and implement procedures for robust and participatory consultation with complainants prior to the development of Management Action Plans.

- IAMs should respect the role of complainants' advisor (s) and representative (s).

- DFIs should create an appeals process for those complainants who are unsatisfied with the results of the complaints process or the implementation of commitments by the DFI or its client.

- DFIs should provide sufficient resources to their IAMs to allow them to carry out their mandate and ensure complainants can meaningfully participate in the process.

Transparency

- IAMs should ensure their case registries contain all relevant information.

- DFIs should publish comprehensive information on the activities they finance, including environmental and social assessments, in a format and language that is accessible for those who will be affected by them. DFIs should publish information regarding the sub-projects supported by their financial intermediary clients.

Rights compatibility

- Make an explicit commitment not to fund projects that would cause, contribute to or exacerbate human rights abuses. To operationalize that commitment, DFIs should require clients to undertake assessments of human rights impacts. Assessments should include whether there are sufficient protections for people to voice objections about the activity being financed. DFIs should refrain from financing activities in contexts where it is not possible to comply with their policies, including provisions related to consultation and information disclosure.

- DFIs and IAMs should adopt protocols for protecting complainants from reprisals and responding to them should they occur.

- IAMs should be given the mandate to make recommendations to suspend financing or processing DFI-financed activities when they believe imminent harm could occur.

Lessons learned

- DFIs should develop a publicly available management tracking system that documents how they have responded to IAMs' findings and recommendations, what lessons they have learned from IAMs cases, and how they will apply those lessons to future investments.

- DFIs should refrain from providing additional financing for similar activities to clients who have been found to be in non-compliance with environmental and social standards until those clients have rectified the non-compliance. Prior to financing other clients for activities that pose similar risks, DFIs should ensure that they have applied the lessons of previous cases.

- IAMs should document lessons learned from their cases in order to facilitate improved DFI policy or practice.

• IAMs should have the primary responsibility of developing and reforming their own rules of procedure. Only reforms that would result in significant changes to an IAM's structure or mandate should require approval by the board of directors. Consultation processes for reviews of the IAMs' rules of procedure or the policies establishing them should be standardized and should include opportunity for comment from the DFIs and civil society and the disclosure of the final version to be considered for approval.

TABLE 2 contains the recommendations derived from the UNGP assessment of each IAM/DFI found in Annexes 5 – 15 (available at: www. glass-half-full. org). The recommendations describe the reforms needed to the policy and practice of each actor, the IAM and the DFI. It should be noted, however, that the power to implement some of these recommendations regarding the IAMs rests with the DFIs' boards of directors.

Table 2 Recommendations for Perfecting the System

		IRMA fDB	AMADB	CSRC GOC	PCM EBRD	CMEIB	ICMFM O/OEG	MICI IDB	CAOIF CMIGA	Exs. JIC A/JBIC	OAO PIC	IPWB
LEGITIMACY												
IAM	Observe pre-employment "cooling off" periods and post-employment bans for mechanism principals to prevent revolving door with DFI management	●	○	○	●	○	○	●	●	○	○	●
	Establish advisory group of external stakeholders, which meet regularly	○	○	○	●	○	○	○	●	●	○	○
DFI	Systematically include external stakeholders (e.g. CSOs) in selection committee for hiring new mechanism staff	○	○	○	●	○	○	○	●	●	○	○
ACCESSIBILITY												
IAM	Ensure communication with complainants and the public is available in multiple languages	○	●	○	●	○	○	○	●	○	○	●
	Remove barriers to filing complaints (from pre-approval to post-closure)	●	●	×	○	○	○	○	○	●	○	○
DFI	Require clients to disclose availability of the mechanism	○	●	○	○	○	○	○	○	○	○	○
	Improve the visibility of the mechanism on the DFI's homepage	○	●	○	●	●	○	●	○	○	●	●
PREDICTABILITY												
IAM	Adhere to deadlines	○	○	○	○	○	○	○	○	●	●	○
	Communicate better with complainants on process and status of complaints	◎	●	○	○	○	○	○	○	●	○	○

续表

		IRMA fDB	AMADB	CSRC GOC	PCM EBRD	CMEIB	ICMFM O/OEG	MICI IDB	CAOIF CMIGA	Exs. JIC A/JBIC	OAO PIC	IPWB
IAM	Monitor commitments made through dispute resolution and instances of non-compliance found through compliance inverstigation	○	○	○	○	○	○	○	●	○	○	○
DFI	Develop and implement effective Management Action Plans anytime there are findings of non-compliance	○	○	×	○	○	○	○	○	○	○	○
EQUITABILITY	Allow complainants to comment on draft reports and include their perspective in final reports to the DFI's Board/Management	○		○		○	○	○	○	○	○	○
IAM	Share final reports with complainants and DFI Board simutaneously	●	○	●	○	○	○	○	○	●	○	○
	Respect role of advisors/representatives chosen by complainants	○	○	○	●	●	●	●	○	●	○	●
	Meaningfully consult with complainants on the development of Management Action Plans	○	○	×	○	○	○	○	○	○	○	
DFI	Provide mechanism with sufficient resources	●	◎	○	○	◎	○	○	○	◎	○	
	Create a process to appleal the decision of the DFI/IAM to an external body	○	○	○	○	●	○	●	○	○	○	○
TRANSPARENCY IAM	Update and publish complete and specific information on website (inal. case registries, budget, complaints that are ineligible)	○	○	○	○	○	○	○	○	○	○	○

续表

		IRMA fDB	AMADB	CSRC GOC	PCM EBRD	CMEIB	ICMFM O/OEG	MICI IDB	CAOIF CMIGA	Exs. JIC A/JBIC	OAO PIC	IPWB
DFI	Disclose more information on financed activities (incl. client names, impact assessments, loan agreements, sub-projects of financial intermediaries) in a systematic and accessible way and in the language of project-affected communities	○		○	○	○	○	○	○	○	○	○
IAM	**RIGHTS COMPATIBILITY** Adopt additional measures to protect complainants from retaliation	○	○	○	○	○	○	○	○	○	○	○
	Assume the authority to make recommen-dations to suspent projects in case of imminent harm	●	○	×	●	●	○	●	○	○	○	○
DFI	Commit not to fund activities that would cause, contribute to or exacerbate human rights violations (and operationalize through assessment of human rights impacts)	○	○	○	○	○	○	○	○	○	○	○
	Take measures to address retaliation against complainants	○	○	○	○	○	○	○	○	○	○	○
IAM	**LESSONS LEARNED** Standardize the consultation process for plicy/procedure reviews	○	○	○	●	○	○	○	○	○	○	○
	Analyse and document lessons learned from cases for the institution and the mechanism	●	●	○	○	○	○	○	●	○	○	●

续表

		IRMA fDB	AMADB	CSRC GOC	PCM EBRD	CMEIB	ICMFM O/OEG	MICI IDB	CAOIF CMIGA	Exs. JIC A/JBIC	OAO PIC	IPWB
DFI	Develop and publish a monitoring and tracking tool to report on implementation of commitments and changes in policy/procedure	○	○	○	○	○	○	○	○	○	○	○
	Refrain from providing additional financing for similar activities to clients who have been found to be in non-compliance with environmental and social standards until those clients have rectified the non-compliance	○	○	○	○	○	○	○	○	○	○	○

HEV: ○ = means that this specific recommendation applies to this actor ● = means the actor has implemented this recommentdation × = not applicable ◎ = not sufficient information to determine

5.2 Accountability in the 21st Century

The following recommendations chart a bold new course for accountability. They are ambitious and, as such, the authors do not expect them to be adopted immediately. Nor are they exhaustive. They are intended to contribute to a wider and much-needed dialogue regarding what real development looks like and to whom it is accountable.

- IAMs must be given the mandate to compel action. The accountability system for DFIs, as it was developed more than 20 years ago, depends on the DFI board and management assuming responsibility for the harm that occurred to project-affected people as a result of activities it financed. However, as this report demonstrates, DFIs have proven unable or unwilling to discharge that responsibility. The result is that the findings and/or recommendations made by the IAMs go unheeded and the complainants are left without remedy for their harms. IAMs should have the mandate to direct DFI staff and clients to take action to address non-compliance and remedy harm.

- All development financing should fall under the jurisdiction of an IAM. This recommendation applies to both existing and new DFIs. The financial instruments offered by DFIs are becoming increasingly complex, while the environmental and social standards applied to them have become more limited and flexible, if they exist at all. For IAMs to fulfil their accountability mandates, they must be able to assess compliance against rules-based standards regardless of the activity that is financed. The DFI landscape is changing rapidly as well, with new or different actors financing development activities. IAMs must not be seen as an impediment to development, but as a crucial element to achieving development outcomes. New DFIs, such as the Asian Infrastructure Investment Bank and the New Development Bank, must establish state-of-the-art IAMs in order to fulfil their development missions. Existing bilateral DFIs without an IAM could consider sharing an IAM with another DFI, like FMO and DEG have done.

- DFIs should create a remedy fund for complainants. Complainants must be made whole if they have experienced harm as a result of DFI-financed activities. Bringing the activity back into compliance with the DFI's environmental and social standards may result in the cessation of the harm but may fail to compensate complainants for the harm that occurred. Similarly, even successful mediation with DFI clients may leave complainants with unmet needs. In those cases, as part of meeting their own responsibility in causing or contributing to the harm, the DFI must be prepared to use their own funds to make the complainants whole again.

• DFIs should abandon their claims to immunity for environmental and social harms. The UN Office of the High Commissioner on Human Rights and the OECD have made it clear that financial institutions, including state-owned enterprises and minority shareholders, can cause or contribute to human rights abuses. [1] There is no argument, development or otherwise, that DFIs should be immune from liability for those harms. Development outcomes are undermined when rights are denied and people are harmed. While IAMs will always have an important role to play, project-affected communities should have the option of bringing a lawsuit to court or arbitration tribunal. One way for DFIs to implement this recommendation is to grant project-affected people third party rights under the agreement with their clients. Project-affected people would then have access to contractual remedies should the client violate the environmental and social provisions of the agreement.

• Complainants should participate in DFI board meetings when cases are discussed. Currently, the board only has the benefit of the perspectives of the IAM, which is supposed to be neutral, and management, but no one is present to represent the views of the complainants. Complainants should be invited to participate in board meetings to express their views on the findings and/or recommendations of the IAMs and the adequacy of the Management Action Plan. Those board meetings should also be live-steamed online so that project-affected people have access to the decisions that affect them.

---

[1] OECD, Expert letters and statements on the application of the OECD Guidelines for Multinational Enterprises and UN Guiding Principles on Business and Human Rights in the context of the financial sector (June 2014), available at http://mneguidelines.oecd.org/globalforumonresponsiblebus-inessconduct/GFRBC–2014-financial-sectordocument-3.pdf.

图书在版编目(CIP)数据

开发性金融机构问责机制研究报告：汉、英／（美）
克里斯汀·吉诺维斯（Kristen Genovese）等编；陈渝
译. -- 北京：社会科学文献出版社，2020.12
　ISBN 978 - 7 - 5201 - 5269 - 3

　Ⅰ.①开… 　Ⅱ.①克… ②陈… 　Ⅲ.①金融机构 - 责
任制 - 研究报告 - 汉、英 　Ⅳ.①F830.3

　中国版本图书馆 CIP 数据核字（2019）第 263251 号

开发性金融机构问责机制研究报告

编　　者／〔美〕克里斯汀·吉诺维斯（Kristen Genovese）等
译　　者／陈渝

出 版 人／王利民
责任编辑／刘同辉

出　　版／社会科学文献出版社（010）59366556
　　　　　　地址：北京市北三环中路甲 29 号院华龙大厦　邮编：100029
　　　　　　网址：www.ssap.com.cn
发　　行／市场营销中心（010）59367081　59367083
印　　装／三河市尚艺印装有限公司

规　　格／开　本：787mm × 1092mm　1/16
　　　　　　印　张：14.5　字　数：243 千字
版　　次／2020 年 12 月第 1 版　2020 年 12 月第 1 次印刷
书　　号／ISBN 978 - 7 - 5201 - 5269 - 3
定　　价／79.00 元

本书如有印装质量问题，请与读者服务中心（010 - 59367028）联系